Temples,
Tombs and
Hieroglyphs

Temples, Tombs and Hieroglyphs

A POPULAR HISTORY OF ANCIENT EGYPT

REVISED EDITION

Barbara Mertz

Illustrated with maps, photographs and drawings

Brockhampton Press

To John A. Wilson
1899-1976
Scholar, teacher, humanist

This edition published 1999 by Brockhampton Press,
a member of Hodder Headline PLC Group

ISBN 1 86019 910 0

Michael O'Mara Books Limited
9 Lion Yard, Tremadoc Road,
London SW4 7NQ

Published by agreement with Peter Bedrick Books, New York

A CIP catalogue record for this book is available from the British Library

Printed and bound in Great Britain by
Creative Print and Design (Wales), Ebbw Vale.

Contents

FOREWORD   xi

GLOSSARY   xv

I The Two Lands   1

Geb the Hunter / 1
The Wagon or the Mountain / 15
Wearer of the Double Crown / 21
Troubles with Time / 30
The Wars of Religion / 39

II Houses of Eternity   45

King Djoser's Magician / 45
The Stone Mountains / 54
Children of Re / 77
The Doors of the South / 88

III The Good Shepherd   99

Despair and Deliverance / 99
Binder of the Two Lands / 112

IV The Fight for Freedom   133

Invasion / 133
Liberation / 138

V The Woman Who Was King   148

The Hatshepsut Problem / 173

VI The Conqueror   178

VII The Power and the Glory   202

VIII The Great Heresy   211

IX The Phoenix Enfeebled   249

Birds, Bees, and Flowers / 249
Look on My Works! / 260
Peoples of the Sea / 276
The Last of the Ramessids / 281

X The Long Dying   288

Adventures of a Man of No Consequence / 288
The Quick and the Dead / 292
Miscellaneous Dynasties / 300

Horsemen from the Holy Mountain / 301
Back to the Drawing Board / 310
The Final Humiliation / 314

CHRONOLOGY   323

ADDITIONAL READING   325

INDEX   331

MAPS

ANCIENT EGYPT   13
NUBIA   91
THE NEAR EAST DURING
    THE NEW KINGDOM PERIOD   180
THREE ROADS TO MEGIDDO   182
SETTING OF THE BATTLE OF KADESH   267

Foreword

My *affaire de coeur* with ancient Egypt began in remote childhood, when I first encountered James Henry Breasted's *History of
Egypt* at the local library; it is still flourishing, although many
years and many distractions have intervened. It is necessary to
make this highly subjective statement, I think, both to explain the
reason for this book and to justify some of the statements which
appear herein. There are occasions, in the following pages, when
serious Egyptologists may be offended by what strikes them as a
frivolous or fantastical tone. Frivolity there may be; but it should
not be taken for disparagement of the field of Egyptology in general or of particular scholars and their pet theories. Few academic
subjects are improved by being approached in a spirit of deadly
seriousness. I suspect, in fact, that most of them can profit by a bit
of kindly mockery, particularly if it is self-administered. That I
venture to smile at a field to which I personally adhere above all
others should be proof that I act from a general principle, and not
from particular malice. "They do but jest, poison in jest; no of-
fence i' the world."

It is only fair to warn the reader that this is not a history book; it is, rather, an informal study of Egyptology—a study of all things Egyptian. My criterion for selection of material has been very simple; I have included anything I found interesting. Hence you will encounter straight archaeological reporting, gossip, and historical theorizing in uneven quantities. You will also encounter—I hope—people. The individual has been rather out of fashion in serious history, although the trend is swinging back in his favor of late. I follow the fairly conventional viewpoint which holds that events are the product both of The Man and The Background, but I do believe that the shape of events is fashioned by the particular man who holds the reins of destiny at a particular moment in time. Therefore I have frankly and unashamedly talked about people when I was able to do so; about kings and queens for the most part, but also about artists, magicians, and even civil servants.

Any attempt to evaluate, or even describe, the character of a historical personage is difficult and highly subjective; often the biographer inadvertently tells more about himself than about the subject of his biography. In the case of ancient Egyptian individuals it is virtually impossible—in fact, you can leave out "virtually"—to do more than speculate. Our knowledge even of events is scanty and incomplete; insight into motives and influences is completely lacking. I have tried to indicate the points at which I leave solid ground and sail off into happy flights of fancy, but undoubtedly I have forgotten to label all the pertinent cases. My consolation is that the same error has been, and is being, committed by professional historians.

I have often speculated as to why so many people are attracted to the study of archaeology. Certain appeals, such as the lure of buried treasure, are fairly obvious; it is to this imaginative human urge that most popular books on archaeology cater. But there is another type of problem involved in archaeology, and in history in general, which also appeals to a wide audience—the people who like puzzles, riddles, and exercises in simple logic. When we, as students, read a history textbook, we are presented with a series of statements which we accept, with more or less indifference, as true. We do not see the skillful patchwork, the blending together of data from dozens of different sources, which creates a coherent picture of events; and we miss the fascination of following the mental processes by which the patches are matched and hooked together. To follow out these processes in detail is not only entertaining but profitable, for in the end we find ourselves questioning the sources of certain statements, and even disagreeing with the conclusions which are drawn from them. Here is a consummation devoutly to be wished; the questioning mind should be developed by any person who reads a daily newspaper. I have tried to indicate some of the sources and some of the methods which we apply in order to derive what we call Egyptian history. Many of them transcend Egyptology, but are seen just as clearly in this context as in others.

Any book of this kind, abridged and simplified for a nontechnical reader, involves certain problems of omission. Most of these will be painfully evident to the specialist. None of the translations are literal; they have been abridged, smoothed out, and otherwise altered, in order to render them more easily readable. I have tried to preserve the original *esprit*. The translations inevitably owe much of whatever value they may contain to the professors who endeavored to drum into my head the knowledge of the Egyptian language, and I have not hesitated to lean heavily upon the translations of such authorities as Breasted, Gardiner, and Wilson. Any egregious errors may be attributed to my stubborn refusal to accept the superior renderings of the above-mentioned experts. In one case, I have copied verbatim the translation of a well-known scholar: Sir Alan H. Gardiner's version of the second Harper's Song seems to me one of the most beautiful renderings into English of any ancient text. I could not improve on it, so I borrowed it; and I would like to thank Sir Alan for his permission to use it. Translations of non-Egyptian texts were taken from the work of Goetze in Pritchard's excellent book, *Ancient Near Eastern Texts Relating to the Old Testament*. The Amarna letters come from Breasted; I have used his versions, which are derived from the translations of a German scholar named Winckler, in preference to later editions, because the language of the translations was so beautifully literary. The Biblical quotes come from the King James version, for a similar reason.

I owe so many people so much gratitude that I may not be able to work them all in here: to Sir Alan, again, my thanks for permission to quote his letter from Rudyard Kipling, and for the guidance and inspiration his long years in Egyptology provided to many students, myself among them; to Drs. Caroline Peck and Jürgen von Beckerath for articles and reprints; to Dr. Siegfried Horn for help on all levels, including the reading of the manuscript—friendship hath no truer test; to Dr. John A. Wilson of the Oriental Institute for answering specific questions, particularly on the problem of the Aswan Dam, and for the still-enduring stimulus of his superb lectures on Egyptian history. M. Jacques Vandier of the Louvre and Dr. Henry Fischer and his staff at the Met labored mightily to get copies of photographs for me. Other institutions and museums have allowed me to use photographs from their collections; credit for these appears with the pictures. Lastly, my thanks to my suffering friends and relations, who listened to me talk until they were sick of the whole subject of archaeology; to my agent, Mr. Theron Raines, who encouraged what had been only a dimly envisioned possibility; to neighbors and friends, particularly Mrs. Lucy Rathjens, whose voluntary kindness gave me free hours in which to perpetrate this work; and to my poor family, who submitted to the inconvenience of a working wife and mother with exemplary patience.

BARBARA MERTZ

Glossary

ba   One of the forms of manifestations of the dead; a human-headed bird which hovered near the tomb.

cartouche   The oval figure enclosing the name of a king or (in later periods) a queen.

faience   Not "glazed pottery," as Egyptologists use the word; rather, a substance made of powdered quartz and formed into a paste by means of natron or some other binder; molded into small objects such as rings, statuettes, amulets, etc., and glazed, usually bright blue or green.

ka   An aspect of the human personality, created with a man and in his own image; it survived the living man and offerings were made to it.

mastaba   The tomb of the earlier period; low, rectangular, with sloping sides.

nome   One of the 42 provinces into which Egypt was divided; governed by a prince or "nomarch."

obelisk   A tall, square pillar coming to a pyramid-shaped point on top; the same shape as the Washington Monument, but Egyptian obelisks were inscribed.

pectoral An ornament worn on the breast, usually suspended from a necklace of beads or wire.

portcullis A heavy monolithic stone lowered after the burial to block a passageway in a tomb or pyramid.

pylon A ceremonial gateway with two flanking towers in the shape of massive truncated pyramids.

stela A slab of stone carved and inscribed to commemorate an event or a man; Egyptian stelae usually had straight sides and a rounded top.

The Two Lands

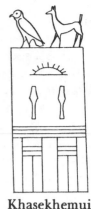

Khasekhemui

Geb the Hunter

ONE bright summer afternoon in the year 5263 B.C., a man stood on the cliffs high above the Nile valley. He was slightly built, and only five and a half feet tall; his brown body was naked except for a kilt of tanned hide. But he held himself proudly, for he was a tall man among his people, and a leader of men. The people he led clustered about him—women peering timidly out from a tangle of black hair, hushing the children in their arms; men bearing their weapons, bow and arrow and stone ax. The wind blew hot behind them; they had turned their backs on the desert. Once it had not been desert. Once, in the time of their ancestors, there had been water, and green growing things, and animals to kill for food. Now the god had withdrawn his hand from their homeland. And so they looked with bright apprehensive eyes into the new land below, a green slash of life cutting through the growing desolation all around. The leader's keen vision saw the gleam of water and the flicker of birds' wings; his hunter's ears caught the far-off bellow of a hippopotamus. There was food below, and water; yet still the leader of the tribe hesitated. He knew the old life, with all its perils. Could he face the

1

more chilling peril of the unknown, and, unaware of destiny, take the first step toward the Pyramids?

It is a pity that this picturesque episode must belong to fiction rather than history. Some of the details may be true. The first prehistoric settlements in Egypt are dated to around 5000 B.C., but not even the miracle of carbon 14 could give a date so specific as the one mentioned above. At some point in the remote past, man came down off the plateau, which was becoming uninhabitable desert, into the valley of the Nile; he may have looked something like the leader of the tribe who, in a historical novel, would be christened Geb, or Ab, or something equally monosyllabic and prehistoric. But it is unlikely that Geb had a sense of destiny. He was looking for a better place in which to live, and he had no idea that the change of habitat would dramatically alter his people's way of life.

Admittedly, the signs of the great change are not dramatic when they are seen in dusty museum cases—flint knife blades and arrowheads, not very different from the crude tools of all primivite peoples; tattered scraps of a woven basket which once held grain; the bones of a dog, appearing, to an untrained eye, like the bones of any wild beast. Yet the transition, from nomadic hunters to village farmers, is more important than the pyramids and more exciting, in its implications, than the golden treasure of a Tutankhamon. We find ourselves here at the beginning of a long and momentous chapter in the great book of man. As the pages turn, we will meet kings and conquerors, poets and inventors. We will conjure up visions of treasure unsurpassed by the most luxuriant forms of imaginative fiction; we will encounter the darker aspects of the human spirit as well as its bright triumphs. Yet never again, perhaps, will we see the human animal take a step so gigantic as this first one, little known and poorly recorded as it is.

Scholars usually place the first "revolution" in man's way of life between the Palaeolithic and Neolithic eras. These terms, which mean "Old Stone Age" and "New Stone Age," were coined to describe a change in the techniques of working stone implements: the men of the Neolithic era polished their tools and weapons. But the new method of polishing stone is the least significant of the differences between the two periods. The wandering hunters of the Old Stone Age became the farmers and shepherds of the Neolithic; the permanent settlement of a tribe means agriculture, and domesticated animals. Naturally, these tremendous changes did not take place overnight. There are long centuries of transition between the hunter and the first farming community. In Egypt, unlike other parts of the Near East, the transitional period is lacking altogether. Except for some flint tools scattered on the desert fringe—the refuse of the ancient hunters—our evidence from Egypt begins with village life already developed. Our data for the oldest known predynastic culture of Egypt comes from "kitchen middens"—an archaeological euphemism for garbage dumps. The prehistoric equivalents of beer cans and melon rinds are fish and animal bones, worn-out flint tools, and scraps of broken pottery. There must have been settlements of some sort near these ancient garbage dumps, though we would not dignify them by the name of villages; the "houses" might have been merely crude shelters of reeds and sticks. Later—not much later, in archaeological time—the villages got fancier.

The imagination must indeed be well-developed to see anything very "fancy" about the first village cultures. Life was not exactly luxurious. The houses were dismal places, built of mud and sticks and consisting of a single dark room, unfloored and unventilated except for a smoke hole in the roof. The bodies of the dead were laid in shallow holes scooped in the sand, with no covering except straw mats or skins. But in the goods buried with them we may see the groping of the human spirit toward immortality. They could only postulate a continuance of the life they knew; so the hunter has his spear, the woman her beads (*vanitas vanitatum*, against the fleshless skull), and the pitiful child bones sometimes huddle against the dust of a once-cherished toy.

The bones and their belongings can speak to us, sometimes with poignant clarity. And the mute stone and baked clay can speak as well, to those who know how to listen. So meager are the remains from this distant time, before the dawn of history, that archaeologists have developed ingenious techniques for wringing the greatest possible amount of information from each tiny scrap. They rely upon the skills of many specialists—biologists, who can identify the species of the gnawed bones in the kitchen middens;

paleobotanists, who ponder the withered grains left in the bottom of the granary basket by a thriftless ancient housewife. (Contrary to popular report, none of the "mummy seeds" found in Egypt has ever produced a living plant; there is a limit to the preservative qualities of even Egyptian soil.)

Most of the archaeological evidence from prehistoric Egypt comes from graves. There are also the kitchen middens, and a few town sites. From these admittedly scanty remains archaeologists have defined a number of predynastic cultures, interrelated, but having each its own typical assemblage (the collection of objects produced and used by the men of a given culture). In this period, such an assemblage might include flint weapons, beads and amulets, baskets, and pottery made of clay or stone.

I have never been able to decide which is duller, flints or pottery; but I distinctly remember the appalling blankness that used to seize my mind when I was asked to identify bits of pottery during an examination. Probably this attests to my underdeveloped imagination, for pottery has been one of the most useful tools of the archaeologist. It has no intrinsic value, so people throw it away when it breaks and tomb robbers sneer at it. For this reason pottery is an invaluable clue to chronology, since it is seldom removed from the spot in which it was originally dumped. Though a pot can be smashed, its fragments are virtually indestructible. But it is fair to say that no one ever dreamed of the far-reaching implications of potsherds until Sir William Flinders Petrie started thinking about them.

It is fitting that Petrie's should be the first name we mention, for he was truly *the* formidable figure in Egyptology. Some scholars call him the father of "scientific" archaeology (for certain dark reasons of my own, I prefer the adjective "critical"). To list his accomplishments in the methods of excavation alone would take pages, but even his pioneering work in technique was less important than his approach, rigorously logical and painfully exact. The new approach came from Petrie himself, not from his training; as he plaintively remarks, there was nobody around to train him. He arrived in Egypt at a time when Maspero, the dedicated French director of the Egyptian Antiquities Department, was beginning to insist upon rules and regulations in excavation, thus destroying all the fun of what had been a joyous free-for-all of plunder and wanton destruction. But Petrie, who carried on a loud private war with both native and foreign thieves, did not even think much of Maspero. Petrie had a marvelous gift of invective; his blasphemous comments upon inefficiency and crooked dealing were uttered in an elegant scholarly style which gave them even greater force. In his autobiography, Petrie inveighs against other archaeologists, the Department of Antiquities, Maspero, the British Museum, the French in general, and a good many Egyptians in particular. This may suggest that it was Petrie, and not the rest of the world, who was out of step. He was; but only because he was leading the parade, and his contemporaries had not yet learned the precise and intricate measure of the movements he set. Very little of Petrie's passion is personal; the people he damns to the lowest pits are those who, through stupidity or venality, allowed his precious antiquities to suffer. He liked most of the Egyptians he worked with, and won their affection and loyalty so completely that the men he trained in excavation, inhabitants of a village called Quft, supplied archaeological expeditions with headmen and diggers for many years.

The aspect of Petrie's character that astounds us even more than his fanatical insistence on detail is his fantastic energy. He ranged over Egypt, from the Delta to the cataracts of Nubia, like a mythological dragon, gulping in raw material and ejecting it in the form of neat volumes which catalogued bones, stones, beads and pots. The real proof of his genius is that stories are beginning to collect about him, as is the case with the absent-minded scholars in other fields whose passion for their work leaves them little time for the unimportant amenities of everyday life. Petrie himself describes, with characteristic gusto, how he used to work naked in the stifling corridors of the pyramids like "the Japanese carpenter who had nothing on but a pair of spectacles, except that I do not need the spectacles." He thought nothing of walking ten or twenty miles across the desert to collect the weekly payroll for his crew; and on one dig in Palestine he and his assistants had to get their drinking water from a well whose contents, in color and consistency, resembled thick split-pea soup. This was all to the good, Petrie comments blandly; in one dish they were getting not only water, but vegetables and meat as well.

Working for Petrie must have been rather a strain. His eating habits, which he expected his students to emulate, were particularly difficult. A row of tin cans and a can opener were set out on a slab in the tomb which served as the expedition dining room, and when Petrie had finished he left what remained in the can for the next diner. It is rumored that two of his students fell in love while nursing one another through simultaneous bouts of food poisoning.

I have no qualms about repeating these tales, because in my opinion they add to, rather than detract from, the stature of a great scholar. Most of the major contributions to the sum of learning have been made by men who had something else on their minds besides the amount of salt in the soup.

Among Petrie's many accomplishments was the classification of the prehistoric Egyptian cultures. He had no written material, and even the most basic chronological tool of the archaeologist, a stratified site, was lacking to him. Such sites are rare in Egypt, but common in other parts of the Near East, where they have provided the best source of relative chronology. The best examples occur in the area between the Tigris and Euphrates, once the kingdom of Babylonia. Here the flat land is broken by steep-sided mounds, or tells, which were long regarded as man-made even before archaeologists started digging into them. The tells are city sites, representing centuries of continuous occupation. The earliest settlement was built on ground level. When it was destroyed, by armed conflict or by the natural processes of decay, the succeeding inhabitants leveled the ruined walls and built on top of them. Over the centuries the town grew higher and higher, perching placidly upon the ruins of its ancestors. When an archaeologist digs such a site he can therefore assume that the town on the top of the heap is the latest in time, and the remains on the lowest level are the earliest. He can thus derive a "floating" chronology which gives the sequence of the different cultures, but not their absolute dates. He may number the cultures in order, or give them letters of the alphabet, working from the top down or the bottom up; and I, for one, wish he would get together with his associates and decide on a consistent method. The third level from the top of a mound called Tell Asmar may be referred to as Asmar III, or Asmar C—or Asmar VI, if the mound has nine levels. In order to pin down his floating chronology in terms of absolute time, the archaeologist must have at least one object which can be dated, either by an inscription upon it or by cross-reference with another culture whose absolute chronology has been fixed.

Petrie had no such site, and no reference books for cross-checking. A pioneer has to write his own books. All he had were graves—hundreds of them, scattered, and lacking any obvious relationship to each other or to anything else. The graves were only pits scooped out of the sand. They contained a variety of objects, though most of them had two things in common: bones and pottery. Yet Petrie dared to ask himself whether these holes in the ground could be arranged into a time sequence. That he ventured to ask the question at all is proof of his talent; that he could answer it, comes very close to genius.

The bones did not look promising, so Petrie turned to the pots. There were a lot of them, and—more important—they were not all alike. Pottery has another handy quality, in addition to the ones we have mentioned. It is subject to the dictates of fashion; it changes.

Taking a group of some seven hundred graves, Petrie, who had begun life as a statistician, made an index slip for each grave. The slip was ruled in columns, one for each type of pot found in the grave. These had already been divided into a number of general categories by their appearance—red-polished ware, black-topped ware, rough ware, and so on. As his starting point Petrie chose a type called "Wavy-handled" (because it has wavy

Petrie's wavy-handled pots

From left to right: earliest to latest forms, showing degeneration of the handles

handles). These pots are derived from foreign types; we can trace their development from primitive prototypes in Palestine, but they appear fully formed in Egypt. The waves are ridges pressed into the ledge handle by the fingers of the potter; they enabled the carrier to get a better grip on the vessel.

In the earliest stage, these pots are globular, with pronounced handles and well-defined ridges. Later they become slimmer, with less prominent handles. In the last stage, the Wavy-handled pot is a tall cylinder with a simple waved pattern—the remains of the original handle—around its upper section.

In defining these stages, Petrie made an assumption: that, as time went on, the features of a pottery type "degenerated" from functional to purely decorative. This assumption was supported by the change in the contents of the jars. At first they contained an aromatic ointment covered by a thin layer of clay. Then the ointment was replaced by scented clay. Last of all were the jars containing only solid clay. Here the notion of degeneration is more obvious, and it does not speak well for the predynastic Egyptians. As the relatives of the dead became more sophisticated, they decided that, while they could certainly use the precious ointment themselves, its utility to the dead was only problematical. The poor corpse was not really cheated. His needs could be served by magic, and the proper incantation could turn the clay into ghostly ointment. In later periods, this process of magical substitution reached its logical culmination; the dead were equipped for the hereafter by means of models, or even pictures, of the objects they would need.

Having established the earlier and later types of this particular pottery class, which he called "W," Petrie had the beginning of a chronological sequence. Now he could begin to tie in the other pottery classes which were found in company with the Wavy-handled examples. Some of the graves which contained Wavy-handled pots also had pottery of a class which Petrie designated "L," for "Late," because it continued in use up to historic times. This gave him a terminal point, since the examples of the "L" type which occurred in First Dynasty graves could be dated. In all, Petrie worked with nine classes of prehistoric pottery. Besides the "L" and "W" classes he had a Black-topped red group (B), a Red-polished (P), a Rough (R), and others. Not all the graves contained all nine classes of pottery, but each grave contained at least two; if a grave did not have more than one class, it was useless for a comparative methodology, and Petrie did not include it within his corpus of examples.

Through correlation with the Wavy-handled types, Petrie was able to work out sequence patterns for the other classes of pottery. Of course, the chronological developments of various classes had to be consistent. For example, let us assume that subtypes 9–12 of Wavy-handled pottery are consistently found with subtypes 1–3 of the Red-polished ware. Then subtypes 4–6 of the Red-polished ware cannot occur with the Wavy-handled subtypes of an earlier date—subtypes 1–9. If they do, then something is wrong with the internal arrangement of one class or the other—or both. This is a very simplified example of the sort of cross-check Petrie had to make with nine different classes of pottery and 700 graves. The logical processes involved are not especially profound, but the scope of the material is so broad that one's imagination reels in considering it.

However, this was precisely the sort of problem at which Petrie excelled; as a recorder of multitudinous details, he was probably without a peer among archaeologists. He gave numbers to all the subtypes within his nine classes, and wrote the numbers on his index slips, one slip for each grave. Having transformed his pots into mathematical symbols, he could juggle bits of paper rather than objects; and we can picture him hovering over a big table spread with an intellectual feast of seven hundred index slips, rushing from one side of the table to the other in order to find the right spot for a particular slip, and feasting his eyes on a particularly consistent arrangement like a gourmet at a seven (or seven-hundred) course dinner.

In the end, Petrie had a series of grave groups whose pottery formed a consistent and logical pattern. The pottery classes overlapped in time, naturally; one category might be in its last stages of development before another category came on the scene, and the oldest class might have vanished altogether before the latest one appeared. Yet the overlapping of classes was continuous, and there was never a point at which a comparative method, involving at least two types, could not be applied. Petrie had forced his scattered graves into a sequence; and the numbers he assigned to the grave groups were called "sequence dates," for they had no connection with years B.C. There were fifty numbers in all, running from thirty to eighty; it was typical of Petrie that he left a range open for future discoveries which might antedate his earliest graves.

Petrie had developed a framework into which newly discovered graves could be fitted by a simple comparison of pottery types. There was still no way of dating prehistoric objects in terms of absolute time, nor would there be until the carbon-14 technique was developed. However, the framework did provide a comparative chronology, and it was capable of being broken down into broader subdivisions than single-sequence dates. Certain groups of graves, and hence of sequence dates, formed distinctive assemblages, which had enough in common to be labeled as separate "cultures." The criteria used to distinguish cultures involve materials other than pottery—stone tools and weapons, ornaments, bones, and so on. In addition to the graves, we have the remains of a number of prehistoric villages; the objects found at these sites form coherent asemblages and may be extremely useful in the definition of cultures. There are many such prehistoric sites in Egypt, the ruins of villages so old that the builders of the Giza Pyramids, 4,500 years before our time, had forgotten their very existence. At one of these sites, a discovery made in 1925 took Petrie's work out of the realm of theory. Miss Gertrude Caton-Thompson, working at Hememieh, found a stratified site, and there were Petrie's prehistoric cultures in the sequence he had postulated. Below the earliest he had known she found a still earlier culture, which was assigned sequence dates from the numbers the great pioneer had left open for just such an eventuality.

Thanks to the work of many such dedicated scholars as Petrie and Caton-Thompson, we now have a general picture of prehistoric life in ancient Egypt, but the picture is still very patchy and incomplete. Even at this early period we must distinguish between the two major geographical subdivisions of the country—Upper Egypt and Lower Egypt. In order to comprehend this terminology, the reader must adjust to what may seem a piece of striking illogic: Upper Egypt is the valley of the Nile, from the Cairo region south, and Lower Egypt is the Delta. The illogic is only illusory; it arises from the fact that the Nile flows from south to north, and the region nearest the source is properly "upper" in relation to the mouth of the river. Since the Delta is at the top of modern maps, with the river hanging down like a tail, most people find the Upper-Egypt–Lower-Egypt concept hard to keep in mind. I don't blame them. It was years before I could read "Upper Egypt" without making a conscious mental effort to remember where it was. All I can do, however, is sympathize, because the names are often used by archaeologists and there is no changing them now. To confuse the issue still more, some scholars believe that in ancient times Upper Egypt ended near Assiut, with Lower Egypt being everything north of that city.

The two regions differ from one another in many ways, the most obvious being that of physical topography. Upper Egypt is a fantastic country—five hundred miles long by perhaps five miles wide. On either side of the river is a narrow strip of fertile black soil, bounded by sand and by the steep cliffs of the desert plateau through which the river has, through immemorial ages, carved and deepened its channel. The line between living and dead land is sharply defined; one may stand today with one foot on the sand and the other on the green-growing fields. The ancient Egyptians were keenly conscious of the difference between the "Black Land" and the barren "Red Land," and these two terms occur frequently in their literature. The black land was precious, and cherished. Temples, palaces, and towns were built whenever possible on the wasteland of sand which lay between the fertile strip and the barrier of cliffs, so that not an inch of cultivable soil would be wasted. The two narrow ribbons of black land, one on either side of the river, have always supported a disproportionately large population, when one considers the actual acreage under cultivation. This situation is possible because of the unfailing fertility of the soil, which is the result of a unique phenomenon—the annual refertilization of the soil by the flooding of the river. Other rivers perform this obliging service, but never with the regularity of the Nile; so predictable is the Nile rise that the ancient Egyptians called one of their seasons "Inundation," for during those months the land was always under water, soaking up the life-giving minerals which the river had taken up in its northward flow.

The idea of automated irrigation may sound paradisaical to a farmer, but it was not so easy as one might suppose. The height of the river varied from year to year, and a difference of inches might mean the difference between famine or prosperity. Further, the water had to be directed to the proper place during the dry months, which are very dry indeed.

When the Nile nears the Mediterranean, it breaks up into several branches whose beds form the large river delta. In ancient times this land was swamp, thick with reed and papyrus and teeming with bird and animal life. There was no need for irrigation or inundation here; the problem was that of too much water.

There was a contrast between the Delta and the river valley in psychological, as well as physical, terms. The Delta bordered on the sea, which was the ancient highway of commerce and conquest; the valley was isolated on both sides by wild deserts and wilder people. The contacts of the Delta were with the young civilizations of the Fertile Crescent; the valley knew only the barbaric Nubians of the south and the wandering desert tribes.

It would seem logical, then, that the Delta region developed earlier, and more quickly, than did the south. Perhaps it did, but we can't prove the point. Material which survived in the hot, dry air of Upper Egypt rotted away in the Delta swamps. This fact affects archaeological knowledge in two ways; not only is there less material to be found in Lower Egypt, but less work has been done there. It is frustrating to excavate in a region where you have to work in water up to your knees, and infuriating to get only indistinguishable lumps of rotted material for your pains. It is no wonder that archaeologists prefer to breathe the salubrious desert air of the south, which has preserved even such fragile objects as textiles and painted reliefs.

As the situation now stands, we can only vex one another with inconclusive theories. The sea—the "Great Green," as the Egyptians called it—may be a highroad for contacts between peoples, but it may also be a barrier. An island is hard to invade, and in one sense all of Egypt was an "island" society. The sea protected it on the north, and inhospitable deserts barred invasion on both

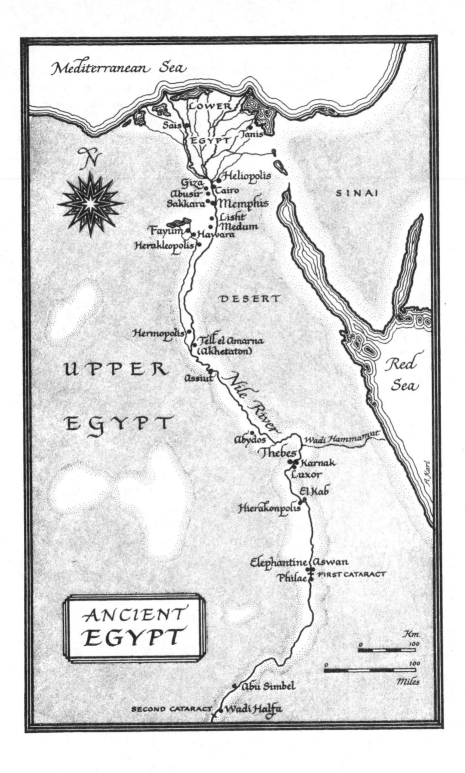

sides. Conquest from the south was equally unlikely because of the nature of the river upstream from Egypt. From Aswan north to the Mediterranean the Nile is easily navigable, but just south of Aswan there is a cataract region, a stretch of river filled with rocks and waterfalls, which renders the passage of ships difficult and peril-filled. As we continue southward along the river we find five more cataracts, the sixth near Khartoum, and some of them are even more dangerous than the first. Yet even this first cataract was, for many years, the southern boundary of ancient Egypt.

Barriers, of water or desert, keep out other things besides invading armies—trade, and new ideas, for instance. One theory of the beginning of history in Egypt maintains that the valley was the first part of Egypt to develop. If Egyptian civilization owes something to external stimulation, the stimuli could have been transmitted via the Red Sea route and brought overland across a well-known caravan route which leads from the sea to the region around Thebes. So far, excavation in the area has not turned up any physical proof of such contact. This may be an accident of excavation, or it may be significant; negative evidence is a double-edged sword, which can be turned against either side of an argument.

When I was a graduate student—back in antedeluvian times—we were given neat lists of prehistoric cultures, one succeeding the other like steps on a ladder: Tasian, Badarian, Amratian, Gerzean, Semainean in the south; Fayuum A, Merimde and Maadi in the north. Each culture had a few more amenities than the one that preceded it, and the latest, Gerzean-Semainean, had achieved a fairly high standard of living for a prehistoric culture, with painted pottery, beautifully worked flint tools, stone vessels, metal, and neat houses.

All these cultures were named after the type site, the place where that particular culture was first unearthed. This is a time-honored and hideously confusing device, as anyone who has encountered the Aurignacians and Levalloisians of European prehistory knows to his sorrow. It becomes even more confusing when archaeologists change their minds about the names—as they almost always do. Semainean was always a suspect culture; it is now generally believed to be a variant of the Gerzean. Tasian may not exist either, except as a form of the Badarian, and Fayuum A also rates a question mark. Merimde and Maadi may be examples of Gerzean, which is called Naqāda II by some scholars, while Amratian is Naqāda I. You will be happy to hear that so far Badarian is still Badarian. It is the one Miss Caton-Thompson found at Hememieh, underneath Petrie's two major cultures—Amratian and Gerzean, or Naqāda I and II.

Perhaps the most useful remark we can make about the predynastic cultures is that they are related to one another, not only chronologically, but causally; each has certain things in common with the one which followed it. In general, the nearer in time to the First Dynasty, the more complex is the society—the more "civilized," in our terms. Yet conventionally the beginning of civilization in Egypt does not occur until historic times, with the beginning of the First Dynasty. We are cautiously tiptoeing around the edges of a problem which is, in part, one of terminology; scholars are not as precise as they might be in defining words like "culture" and "civilization." The two words are sometimes used interchangeably, but not all cultures are civilizations. Civilization itself may be used specifically, as in the phrases "Egyptian civilization" and "Chinese civilization," or it may be used as an abstraction, to describe a state of affairs which is contrasted with barbarism. The lack of precision is regrettable; however, we may avoid a certain amount of confusion by restricting ourselves, at this point, to the second of the two meanings. We have been talking about prehistoric, or predynastic, cultures. Gerzean, Amratian, and the rest are not civilizations, nor are they "civilization." At what point, then, does a culture acquire the traits which enable it to be considered a civilization? More significantly, perhaps—*from* what point does it acquire such traits?

The Wagon or the Mountain

After the phenomenal leap from nomadism to settled village life, prehistoric culture shuffled along rather placidly for a few thousand years. Then something peculiar happened.

Scholars who concern themselves with the broader problems of history often anthropomorphize the cultures they are comparing. The man-shaped figures that represent civilizations may be pictured as climbing a ladder or a mountain slope, progressing ever higher on their way to—what? The ultimate goal is admittedly hard to define. But if we are determined to have an analogy, we might say that the process of civilization more closely resembles the acceleration of a wheeled vehicle on a downward slope; slow at first, then ponderously gaining speed until it rushes headlong across the level plain beneath. Momentum carries it on for some distance, initially at a speed so great that it may seem as if acceleration were still taking place. But eventually the heavy vehicle slows . . . and slows . . . and stops. And there it remains, in a state of rest, until some unknown force returns to push it toward another slope.

We cannot really compare a culture to a wagon any more than to a human being climbing a mountain. But analogies are a lot of fun, and this one gives a mental picture which may be useful to us. For something did give the Egyptian prehistoric culture a shove, during the late period we call Gerzean. The picture of society we see then is noticeably different from that of the earlier cultures. People lived in houses with windows and doors, and wore clothing woven out of flax. The flint tools are elegant, even to an anti-flint observer; and copper is increasingly used for artifacts which had been made of stone. Graves are deeper and more carefully built, sometimes lined with wooden planks. The struggle for existence was less agonizing, and men had time for nonproductive activities; they played games and they painted pictures on their pots. The old brown and red pottery continues, but a new type enters, made of a new kind of clay and decorated with quaint little stick figures of men and animals and boats. The boats carry insignias, which may be the standards or devices of small political units; we assume that in this period the land of Egypt consisted of many communities, each governed by a local chief. These changes are striking; but they are not so striking as the further changes which are about to occur. We are very close to the First Dynasty now—to the beginning of history and of civilization, properly speaking. We are curious, not only about what happened, but about why it happened.

Let us go back to the wagon on the slope. We might carry the analogy one step further and ask: Does the wagon creep along (we will grandly ignore the fact that neither a culture nor a wagon can be said to "creep") until it reaches the point at which the ground drops away from beneath its wheels; or does someone come up behind it and give it a shove? More pedantically: Does civilization arise naturally out of a primitive culture because that culture has, by slow accretion, reached a critical stage of development; or does an external stimulus serve as the catalytic agent?

We may argue about exactly what distinguishes a civilization from a primitive culture, or even about whether such a clear-cut distinction can be made. Let's not argue about it. Let us merely suggest that certain new elements are found in most of the groups we call civilizations: monumental architecture, writing, centralized government, and a division of labor resulting in social classes. If we think about these elements, we see that each of them implies more than it says about the society in question. Monumental architecture, for instance, requires advanced techniques in the preparation of materials, and some understanding of basic architectural and mechanical principles; it also suggests that the state can spare some of its members from the basic labor of food production to work on labor gangs; further, it implies that there is an elite group within the state which has the power to order and supervise such labor.

Unless we believe in visitors from Mars or supermen from lost Atlantis, we must conclude that some society, somewhere, was the first to discover the various components of civilization. Did the idea spread outward from the original center to other societies, or did it occur independently in all civilizations? If it did occur only once, where was the cradle of civilization?

The problem of Diffusion versus Independent Creation is still being debated by scholars, but for a long time Egypt looked like the best answer to the second question. Recently, Egyptologists have had to relinquish their proud position, for it appears that the ancient Sumerians beat the Egyptians to it. Not only is Sumerian civilization older, but the Egyptians may have stolen the whole idea from their neighbors.

At first glance this may seem unreasonable. The two cultures appear so dissimilar—the mud-brick ziggurats of Mesopotamia and

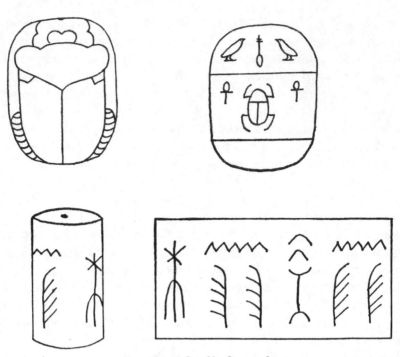

Scarab and cylinder seals
Left, the seals themselves; right, the impressions

the stone pyramids, the pretty picture writing of Egypt and the bird-track cuneiform. Yet the signs of Mesopotamian influence in Egypt at the very end of the predynastic period are indisputable. They appear in the Nile valley suddenly and fully formed, whereas in Mesopotamia we can trace their development through various stages. This is always a sure sign of cultural borrowing, and the borrowed elements themselves are definitely non-Egyptian. Cylinder seals are typical of Mesopotamia and atypical of Egypt, but there are cylinder seals in late predynastic graves. Building stone is scarce in the flat plains of the Land of the Two Rivers, so the natives of that region built in brick; the earliest large-scale architecture of Egypt is in the same brick, and it imitates a well-known Mesopotamian style, recessed brick niching. Even when the Egyptians began to quarry their numerous fine sources of stone, they cut it up into brick-sized pieces.

Why do we fail to think of these things as "Egyptian"? Because all of them (there were others besides the ones we have mentioned) died out early in Egypt and were replaced by "Egyptian" ways of doing things. Stone architecture began to employ the monolithic blocks we can see in the Giza pyramids; seal impressions were made with stamp seals—scarabs—instead of with the cylinder type. And the writing, of course, is completely dissimilar. The pictures of objects which became the hieroglyphic symbols of Egyptian writing were all Egyptian objects.

Obviously what we have in Egypt is not simple copying; but it is not independent creation, either. The American anthropologist A. L. Kroeber has suggested the term "stimulus diffusion" to cover this type of borrowing. A people may borrow the idea of doing something from another culture, but the way in which it is done may be their own way. The Egyptians did not copy Sumerian writing; all they needed was the great idea that the spoken word could be recorded. Obviously the borrowing culture—the Egyptians here—must have reached a stage of development in which the new concept is understood and desired. In terms of our analogy, both a change in terrain and a push are needed to get the wagon going; the stimulus would not be felt if the circumstances were adverse.

Not all scholars accept "stimulus diffusion" as the explanation for how civilization arose in Egypt. Some of them believe in a "dynastic race" who entered Egypt at the end of the prehistoric period, bringing with them the gifts of civilization. They unified the land and, like the Normans in England, ruled the conquered indigenes as a racially distinct noble class, before interbreeding and contact produced a single people. The dynastic race came from Asia—a large place, but one cannot summarize the conflicting theories of origin more precisely than that. They spoke a Semitic language, which mingled with the Hamitic (African) tongue of the natives to produce the Egyptian speech.

We are bound to have a certain prejudice against the word "race." Anthropologists use it to delimit certain groups of human beings in terms of "nonessential" differences—skin color, hair texture, shape of skull, and so on. Physical anthropologists may not agree on the exact groupings which result from the use of these criteria, but I doubt if any of them would call the various predynastic skeletal types different "races." The new products, the new inventions, may or may not be the gifts of a new *ethnic* group—but not of a new "race." The word has as little validity when applied to linguistic as to cultural groups; to talk of a Semitic "race" is not even accepted *popular* usage (see Webster's *Unabridged*).

Even if we knock out the offending term "race," we still have some serious questions about the dynastic supermen. Study of predynastic skeletons suggest that they may belong to several different physical subtypes, but we can't be sure who these people were, where they came from, or what they actually did. All sorts of people came into Egypt, from prehistoric times onward— merchants, traders, invading armies, immigrants, envoys. We will see them coming—and sometimes going—as we follow the long centuries of Egyptian history, and once we get well into history proper we can document foreign influences more accurately. But in preliterate cultures we don't have written records, or even much material. Often the evidence for a "race of invaders" consists of cultural changes—which, in prehistoric societies, means primarily new kinds of pots. I have a prejudice against this sort of argument. I get idiotic mental images of invading armies brandishing pots, which they thrust threateningly into the trembling hands of the conquered indigenes. Undoubtedly I am being unreasonable. However, I suspect that cultural change, even in pottery, can result from trade rather than conquest.

This has been an unsatisfactory sort of discussion; instead of answering questions, it raises new ones. But this is the subject matter of prehistoric archaeology, when it goes beyond the simple cataloguing of bones and pottery. The questions raised are important questions. If they are ever answered, we will learn much, not only about Egypt, but about the human animal in general. The scope of the problem is universal, and the answers deal with man himself.

Wearer of the Double Crown

We have now reached the edge of historic times in Egypt, and are about to deal with more concrete facts than the illiterate and generally undated cultures of the predynastic period could provide. The beginning of civilization in Egypt is signalized by a noteworthy event—the unification of the country into a single nation, whose boundaries ran from the sea in the north to the First Cataract of Aswan. We know very little about political organization before this consolidation. We assume that the small tribal units of the early predynastic gradually amalgamated and formed larger social and political groupings. At one time Egypt may have been made up of several dozen little states, each ruled by a prince or count or chief. Through conquest, and marriage, and the other techniques of imperialism, the smaller units were eventually joined into two sizable kingdoms, one in the north and one in the south. Each kingdom had its own set of symbols and insignias and its own protective gods and goddesses. The king of Upper Egypt wore a distinctive White Crown and the king of Lower Egypt a Red Crown.

This brief description of the two great predynastic kingdoms is based on very scanty evidence. On the basis of the archaeological remains, we might suppose that a complex, united state sprang suddenly into existence out of a hodge-podge of hundreds of little villages, all of which were organized like an anarchist's dream of the ideal socialist paradise. I suspect that this is one of the many gaps which face us in our survey of Egyptian history—a gap so wide, in this case, that it looks like a canyon.

We know that there were kings of the southland, for one of them was the Unifier, who conquered the north and became the first king of the Two Lands of Egypt. We know his name, the first name of an individual in ancient Egypt. The name is Menes.

For a long time historians were inclined to place Menes among the shadowy heroes of legend, in the company of Roland and King Arthur. Tradition, to be sure, named him as the Unifier; but Tradition, scholars feel, is a tricky wench, to be handled with caution. Archaeological evidence confirmed the assumption hat a conquest did take place, and that it was initiated by a king of the south, but the name of the Conqueror was long in doubt. There was even a question as to whether a single king might claim that distinction.

We know of the Conquest, and of conquering kings, from a series of carved stone objects dated to the end of the predynastic— mace heads, knife handles, and slate palettes. The most useful of all is the Narmer Palette, now in the Cairo Museum. Stone palettes are common in predynastic graves; they were used for grinding cosmetics. As time went on they got bigger and their surface became a ground for bas-relief. The palette of Narmer shows a quaint little king, dressed in a kilt and in the White Crown of the south, coolly preparing to bash a kneeling captive on the head. Above the prisoner is a curious symbol depicting a hawk (which signified the king) in triumph over the Delta region. Behind the predatory king is the diminutive figure of his

The Narmer Palette
Recto of the slate palette, now in the Cairo Museum

sandal-bearer (sizes in Egyptian relief indicated relative importance rather than actual stature). At the top, between two heads
of the goddess Hathor, are the signs which spell the king's name—
Narmer. On the back of the palette, Narmer, with his faithful
sandal-bearer still in attendance, wears the Red Crown of the
north.

It does not require too much imagination to interpret the
reliefs on this palette as scenes of conquest—conquest of north by
south. King Narmer, then, is a likely candidate for the title of
Unifier.

What about Menes, Tradition's candidate? Some scholars
would like to identify him with King Narmer. The Menes-
Narmer equation is a fetching bit of logic. It goes like this: 1. On
the palette, Narmer is shown conquering people from the Delta
and wearing the two crowns; 2. Therefore, Narmer unified the
country; 3. Menes unified the country; 4. Menes = Narmer.
Q.E.D.

There is nothing wrong with this argument, so far as it goes.
Egyptian kings had more than one name, and Menes could have
called himself Narmer if he had wanted to. However, there is
another equation which makes better sense. It would identify
Menes with a king named Aha, whose tomb has been found.

Among the objects dated by archaeologists to the First Dynasty
are small tags of ivory or wood, insignificant in appearance but all-
important in that they bear some of the earliest Egyptian writing.
Unfortunately, we cannot read all the signs; they are extremely
primitive and not all can be identified with hieroglyphic symbols
of later periods. Scholars are making progress with the decipherment of these tags, however, and we can make some deductions
about the names and titles of the period in question.

The full "titulary" of the Egyptian king was not developed
until much later. In its final form it consisted of five titles and five
names; two of the names were surrounded by the oval figures
called "cartouches," which were only used by kings and queens.
The complete fivefold titulary took up a lot of space in an inscription, and kings normally used only one or two of their names and
titles. During the first two dynasties the titulary had merely three
elements; the most popular was the one called the "Horus name,"

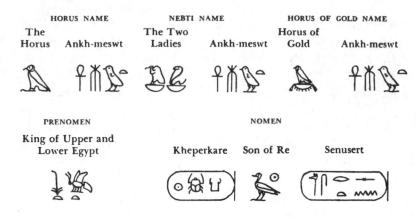

HORUS NAME		NEBTI NAME		HORUS OF GOLD NAME	
The Horus	Ankh-meswt	The Two Ladies	Ankh-meswt	Horus of Gold	Ankh-meswt

PRENOMEN		NOMEN	
King of Upper and Lower Egypt	Kheperkare	Son of Re	Senusert

The fivefold titulary of Senusert I
from the Twelfth Dynasty

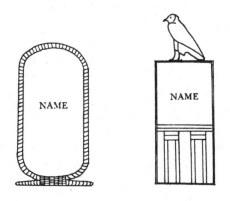

A cartouche and serekh

written not in a cartouche but in an oblong box called a "serekh," which is a simplified representation of the façade of the royal palace. On the "roof" stands the hawk-god Horus, who was identified with the king, and his figure is read as a title: the Horus So-and-So.

Aha is the Horus name of a First Dynasty king; it has been found on many labels, or tags. In the course of the excavation of the tomb of Aha's mother, the queen Merneith, at the site of Naqāda, a piece of an ivory label turned up which bore the king's

The Nebti name of Menes

Horus name and beside it another name—Men. The Men name was written under the so-called Nebti title, just as Aha was written under the Horus title. The word Nebti means "the Two Ladies," and refers to the two great goddesses of north and south; logically it could only be claimed by a king of both areas. But, more important, Men and Aha may be names of the same king.

The excavator of the tomb, John Garstang, was so excited about the broken label that he redug the entire tomb looking for the missing pieces. (Imagine running across a stone with a carved ARTHURUS REX in the ruins of a Cornwall castle!) The usual frustration of the archaeologist searching for one particular needle in a haystack was not Garstang's; he found the pieces, and the two names and titles are certainly there.

Most scholars think that the two names belong to one individual, and believe that the Naqāda label actually does bear the only contemporary mention of the name of fabled Menes. I think so too, for what that is worth. We do not need to worry about a missing "s" here or there; the name "Menes" is a Greek form. However, another label has the name of Narmer alternating with the "men" sign; so it is possible that Narmer is Menes, and Aha is his successor. Take your choice.

Having verified the claims of Tradition for consideration in one respect at least, we may return to that source for further

information about Menes the Conqueror. He is supposed to have
built a new capital at Memphis, not far from modern Cairo. This
was the boundary between the Delta and the valley, and the location was shrewdly selected. Menes may have been a skillful politician as well as a great warrior; instead of suppressing the
conquered North he assumed its insignia, its gods, and its customs
—not to mention its women, for there is reason to believe that his
mother or his wife was a princess of the Delta. From Menes on,
the parallelism based on the notion of the Two Lands is a funda-
mental aspect of Egyptian thought. The king wears the Two
Crowns (whose combined appearance makes it evident that they
were not joined for aesthetic reasons). He calls himself King of
Upper and Lower Egypt, and Lord of the Two Lands, and he is
protected by the Two Ladies. If Menes deliberately adopted this
procedure, we may see why he succeeded where others, perhaps,
had failed; for there are tales of a predynastic union of the two

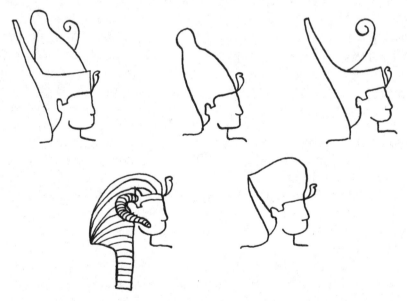

Crowns of the King of Egypt

Left to right, top row: Double Crown, White Crown, Red
Crown; bottom row: *Nemes* Headdress, Blue or Battle
Crown

areas which was impermanent. As a technique it has proved useful to many a succeeding conqueror.

An oft-repeated complaint in archaeological circles is "Not enough material!" We don't know a lot about Menes, but actually it is more than we might expect to know about a legendary character. Indeed, as we proceed we will find ourselves saddled with that archaeological rarity, an *embarras de richesses*. In Holmesian terms, it might be called "The Perplexing Problem of the Duplicate Tombs."

Two hundred miles north of Luxor lies the very ancient holy city of Osiris, god of the dead. It is called Abydos, and it was a place all the kings of Egypt delighted to honor. Before Osiris came to dwell there, it was the sanctuary of another, even older, mortuary god, and pilgrims from all over Egypt laid their bones in that sanctified ground in order to win greater glory in the world to come. The tomb of Osiris himself was there; its exact location was well known to the devout Egyptians.

When archaeologists began to excavate at Abydos, they were not expecting to find Osiris, nor did they. What they did uncover was almost equally unexpected—tombs of the kings and queens of the First Dynasty, including the tomb of King Aha. The excavators must have felt almost as much awe as they would have felt at finding Osiris himself. These monarchs were from a time so far in the past that even their names had been forgotten.

One of the first people to excavate at Abydos was—correct. William Flinders Petrie. He won permission to dig at the site only after some difficulty, for the concession had been given by the Department of Antiquities to another archaeologist, a Frenchman named Amélineau. It is considered courteous these days to give the early excavators a polite tip of the hat, in tribute to their intentions if not their methods; but it is hard to say anything very complimentary about Amélineau. He drove Petrie to distraction. Indeed, most people drove Petrie to distraction, for few of them could live up to his high standards and he did not brook fools lightly. In the case of Amélineau we can sympathize with Petrie, for after the French excavator had dismembered the site of Abydos, Petrie was given the pieces. Amélineau had, of course, removed all the interesting items he found, without—to Petrie's fury—keeping records of how and where they were found. He had also ruthlessly destroyed much of the material he could not carry away. Yet Abydos was to show Petrie's ability in all its glory. His publication is still a standard reference work.

Petrie's thoroughness led him to one spectacular discovery which Amélineau had missed—the mummified arm of a long-dead king or queen which still wore a set of exquisite bracelets made of gold, amethyst, turquoise and lapis lazuli. Tomb robbers had rifled the coffin in remote antiquity and ripped off the jewels, arm and all. But something disturbed them in the midst of their job, and they had to run for their lives. In so doing, one of them stuck the mummified arm into a crack in the rock, planning to come back for it later when the heat was off. We may reasonably hope that the ancient gendarmes caught up with this particular member of the third or fourth oldest profession, for he never came back for his loot. It is surprisingly attractive, this jewelry, and surprisingly well made. It gave Petrie an impression, which is borne out by other excavations, that the First Dynasty, so near in time to the primitive, was much more complex and sophisticated than one might expect.

This same Abydos tomb, which belonged to a king called Djer, provided a clue to a darker part of Egypt's past. Most readers know of Sir Leonard Woolley's discoveries at Ur, in Mesopotamia —the great royal tombs with their treasures of gold and the slaughtered bodies of hundreds of courtiers and slaves, who went to serve their masters in death as they had in life. Egyptologists have been mildly smug about the more civilized habits of *their* people, who supplied dead kings with wooden servant figures and painted pictures of slaves instead of the real article. Unfortunately for these assumptions of superiority, the Abydos excavations turned up a large tomb with surrounding rows of smaller graves which appeared to have been occupied at the same time as the principal burial. Most of the victims were women.

This is not the only royal tomb to have rows of subsidiary burials. One of them, which belonged to a queen, had not only the bodies of her servants but the implements with which they had rendered service—vases with the potter, paints with the artist, needles with the court ladies. In all fairness to the Egyptians it must be said that the First Dynasty tombs are the only ones which have these sacrificial burials, and it has not been proved to everyone's satisfaction that the bodies of the servants were really buried at the same time as the royal interment. If such a custom did exist we would expect to find signs of it in predynastic burials, since such extravagance with human life is more typical of barbaric periods (at least we civilized folk like to think so). More sophisticated cultures tend to develop magical substitutes.

When the Abydos royal tombs were discovered, everyone shook hands all around and checked one point off the list: First Dynasty royal tombs, O.K. Then somebody began digging at Sakkara.

Every tourist to Egypt knows Sakkara. It is one of the ancient cemeteries of Memphis, conveniently close to modern Cairo. The said tourist is dragged to Sakkara by his guide in order to see the Step Pyramid of the Third Dynasty, the private tombs of the Fifth and Sixth Dynasties, and the Serapeum of the late Empire. He rides a morose little donkey to these places, and is plagued and harassed by the drivers of the donkeys, who have no trouble running as fast as their burdened beasts. He spends a morning, or a day, and comes away with a mild antipathy toward donkey drivers and the correct impression that there is a lot to see at Sakkara.

Since Memphis was founded by Menes, we would have every reason to expect that he and his successors would choose to be buried near the new capital. If the First Dynasty tombs had not been discovered at Abydos, it would have been a safe bet to look for them at Sakkara.

So, when someone looked, there they were—more First Dynasty royal tombs, some of which belonged to the same kings whose names had already been found at Abydos. Even a divine king has only one body; why should he require two tombs?

The answer is pretty obvious: one was a real tomb, and one a cenotaph. Cenotaphs are erected when the body of the man to be memorialized is missing, as in the case of sailors lost at sea. The great sarcophagus of Dante in the church of Santa Croce in Florence is a cenotaph; the Florentines tried to add Dante to their collection of great men by every means up to and including body snatching, but the authorities of Ravenna, where the poet chose to be buried, and where his bones still lie, foiled the attempts. The Egyptian kings of the early period might have built two tombs in order to be represented, funereally speaking, in both sections of the country which they called the Two Lands.

Since both sets of monuments were thoroughly plundered, we may never know which are the true tombs and which the cenotaphs. The argument still rages—if one may use such a violent expression about the courteous discussions of scholars. It is based upon such inconclusive evidence as relative size, kinds of objects found, and resemblances to other types of tombs, both royal and commoner.

If Menes was Aha, we have tombs at Abydos and also at Sakkara which probably belonged to him. There is not much left of them now; only pits in the sand, with the crumbling remains of what was the superstructure. In their time they must have been impressive structures, fitting memorials for a famous conqueror. Through the Unification, Menes laid the foundations of a great state, whose intellectual and material accomplishments were of a high order. The event is dated to 3400 B.C.; or 3110 B.C.; or maybe 2850 B.C.

A relative chronology like Petrie's presents problems of one order; absolute dating has its own difficulties, and they are not minor ones. The adjective "absolute" may sound misleading. How can a system be absolute when we can give three alternative dates for an event like the beginning of the First Dynasty? We would expect one date, or none at all. Let us now consider some of the techniques used in Egyptian chronology. It is a complicated subject and deserves a section all to itself.

Troubles with Time

If the reader is up-to-date on archaeological matters, he may expect a short, snappy answer to all the problems of chronology: carbon 14. He would be mistaken, on two counts: there is nothing short or simple about the radiocarbon process, or its applicability to historical problems; and, in fact, it did not solve any of the chronological questions of dynastic Egypt. The process is certainly fantastically useful in other parts of the past, particularly in those very remote eras which are the province of the archaeologist-anthropologist rather than the archaeologist-historian. But in the case of Egypt, the previously established dating system helped to establish the validity of the carbon-14 process rather than the reverse.

The savage reader (to plagiarize Mark Twain) may reasonably ask at this point, "Why talk about it, then?" There are several good, logical answers to the question. One is that the radiocarbon process is very useful in dealing with Egyptian prehistory; another is that carbon 14 is only one of a number of related methods, the great gift of the physical sciences to history, which deserve a more than cursory treatment. But the real reason I want to discuss carbon 14 is because it delights me by its inherent improbability. Fifty years ago, the suggestion that a physicist could tell an archaeologist the age of a piece of wood by purely physical, laboratory techniques would have struck the said archaeologist as completely preposterous. This is the real excitement of archaeology—and of life in general: that the horizon of what may be known is not bounded by what is known. And, of course, the development of the radiocarbon process is a fascinating intellectual adventure in itself.

In 1945, Dr. Willard F. Libby of the University of Chicago was studying the effect of cosmic ray neutrons upon the nitrogen of the atmosphere. The result of the meeting was a genuine, if tiny, nuclear reaction; the product was radioactive carbon. Libby argued that since its *chemical* behavior is the same as that of ordinary carbon, this carbon 14, or radiocarbon, should form carbon dioxide molecules and mix in with the ordinary carbon dioxide of the atmosphere. Every high school student of biology knows that carbon dioxide is taken in by plants in the process of photosynthesis. Since animals live off plants, the conclusion was logical, though rather startling: all living matter should be weakly radioactive, from the tiny proportion of carbon 14 which it absorbs.

The first verification of Dr. Libby's theory came from a decidedly inglorious source—the methane gas given off by the city of Baltimore's sewage. Not only did this decaying organic material give off radioactivity, but it contained exactly the proportion of carbon 14 that Libby had predicted. Subsequent tests were performed on samples of wood, oil and other material from all over the world. The proportions were as predicted.

This was a good confirmation of the theory, but it was more than that. Dr. Libby immediately saw the possible application of the process to dating. Among his samples had been wood from the tombs of Snefru and Djoser, kings of the Third and Fourth Dynasties. The dates given by radiocarbon checked out with the calculations Egyptologists had made independently.

How does it work? Obviously the laboratory apparatus did not contain a neon coil that lit up and read *4,500 years*. Before the laboratory results could be translated into years of time, a lot of work had to be done.

Let's take a specific organic object as an example—an oak tree, perhaps. When the tree died, it of course stopped taking in carbon 14. As it lay in the earth, or in the walls of a building in the form of planks, the radiocarbon it contained at its demise, being unstable, began to disintegrate. Dr. Libby calculates that the rate is about one percent each 80 years. The process of decay is exponential; that is, in the first 80 years one percent of the total decays, in the next 80 years one percent of the *remaining* total, and so on. Scientists talk about decay rate in terms of its "half-life"—the length of time it takes for half the original radioactive content to decay. At the latest measurement, the half-life of carbon 14 is 5,568 years.

Thus, by measuring the amount of carbon 14 remaining in our oak tree, or any piece of it, we can calculate (and if that sounds simple, it is not) how many years have passed since the tree stopped living. Truly, the process is brilliantly conceived. But it has certain limitations.

These limitations arise from various causes. One is the problem of the increase of error. You may have seen radiocarbon dates given in various publications; they look something like this: 3,325 years ± 150. The "plus or minus" indicates the range of possible error. The older the date given, the greater the range. Why the lack of precision? Well, for one thing, it is very difficult to get an uncontaminated sample, free of modern organic substances. If the sample we are working with is fairly recent in age, it still contains a large part of the original radiocarbon; hence, the intrusion of a chunk of modern carbon 14 represents only a small proportion of the total, and does not affect the results too much. But if our object is 30,000 years old, it has lost all but a tiny amount of the carbon 14 it contained at its demise; the amount is so small that it is hard to detect even with precise laboratory instruments, and any intrusion, however minute, affects the results enormously. The problem of contamination was a serious one at first, when the process was new and unfamiliar; field workers packed samples in straw or allowed bits of root from living trees to get into the container. Another source of contamination is the atmosphere itself; laboratory instruments must be carefully shielded against cosmic rays and must themselves be completely free from radioactive contamination. The composition of the atmosphere has been changed in the past century, not so much by atomic explosions as by the "old" carbon released by the combustion of coal and oil since the industrial revolution.

All these factors affect the accuracy of radiocarbon dates. Then there is the pleasingly mysterious "systematic uncertainty," the causes of which seem to be unknown, which gives errors of one hundred to two hundred years. Further limitations come from the fact that only certain materials are suitable for processing. Charcoal and well-preserved wood are best; bone, for various reasons, has given unsatisfactory results. The sample must be burned to be tested, which means that choice specimens are not readily relinquished. And, because of the rapid (in geologic terms) decay rate of carbon 14, the process cannot be used with any material that is over 70,000 years old. This is plenty long enough, from our point of view, but it frustrates archaeologists who work with fossil man and his immediate ancestors.

Amazing, this technique—we might even say, unlikely! We can only wonder what the next leap across improbability will bring forth as a new tool for historians. Time travel, perhaps, or at the very least a television apparatus which can be tuned in to the Battle of Marathon.

The reason why the radiocarbon method has not been widely used in Egyptian dynastic periods is simply that the chronology was already fixed before the technique was discovered, and fixed so accurately that the margin of error in the carbon-14 process is greater than the area of uncertainty remaining in the known dates. The methods used in establishing Egyptian chronology were not complex in themselves, but the total process of comparison and induction represents an impressive example of historical scholarship.

One of the people who worked on chronology back at the beginning of the present century was James Henry Breasted, who is the United States' most famous Egyptologist. Born in the small midwest town of Rockford, Illinois, Breasted had a long way to go to get to Egypt. In his day it was essential for an Egyptologist to study in Berlin, where the monumental figure of Adolf Erman was placing the Egyptian language on a sound philological basis for the first time. Breasted's family was not wealthy, but he got to Berlin, and later to Egypt. Like Petrie, the American Egyptologist was a man of tremendous energy; but his talents lay in philology and administration rather than in excavation. His *History of Egypt* is still a classic work, though more than half a century has elapsed since it was published; it is an exciting, elegantly written book which gives the lie to the old accusation that scholars cannot write well. Breasted's *magnum opus* was the translation of every known historical text from Egypt; the result fills five thick volumes, and required the personal inspection and copying by Breasted of almost every text included—most of the pre-Breasted copies of inscriptions look as if they were made at twilight by a myopic scholar who had lost his glasses.

The book, *Ancient Records of Egypt*, is Breasted's great work in terms of published material, but many would say that his true monument is an institution, not a book. This is the renowned Oriental Institute of the University of Chicago, the first department for the study of Egyptology on American soil. I believe—though I've never made an official check—that the Institute offers more courses in Egyptian history, languages, and archaeology than does any other institution in America; its expeditions have worked for many years in other parts of the Near East as well as in Egypt, and its publications number in the hundreds.

How did the impecunious young man from Rockford, Illinois, accomplish this feat? He enlisted the interest and financial support of John D. Rockefeller, whose name should be somewhat familiar.

We will encounter the name of Breasted again; in fact, it should be borne in mind every time we quote from ancient Egyptian records, for in nine cases out of ten Breasted translated the text and did such a good job of it that his renditions have been corrected only in minor details. The first volume of the *Ancient Records* also contains a lucid summary of basic methods of Egyptian chronology. These methods have been refined since Breasted's time, but the essential sources remain relatively unchanged.

The nearest thing to a contemporary history of Egypt we possess is the work of an Egyptian priest named Manetho, who wrote and lived under Ptolemy II Philadelphus, in the middle of the third century B.C. "Possess" is a misleading term, for we do not have the text of Manetho's history. What we have are quotations and synopses made by later historians of Roman times. The quotations come mainly from Josephus, a Jewish historian who was trying to make out a case for the antiquity of his people; the superior attitude of his Greek fellow scholars had riled him. Josephus is a biased source; he had an ax to grind, and even if he was too honest to misquote consciously, his bias would probably affect his choice of material.

The other sources merely summarize Manetho, giving lists of kings and sometimes a sentence of description. The copies do not always agree with one another, and they garble names and dates most horribly. How much of the error is due to the copyist, and how much to Manetho himself—who was, after all, a long way in time from the beginnings of Egyptian history—we do not know. But we know that Manetho is not to be trusted blindly, at least not in the copies we have. We use his dynastic breakdowns, and other information, only when there is nothing to contradict it.

Painstaking archaeological spadework, and the study of hieroglyphic inscriptions, have enabled scholars to check Manetho's list of kings against contemporary records, and to construct lists of their own that sometimes differ drastically from the Greek's. By the time of the Middle Kingdom the Egyptians were dating events by the years of a king's reign. If a mass of dated objects gives year 23 as the latest year for a particular monarch, we can assume that he probably ruled no longer than twenty-three years. The records are fairly complete for the later period of Egyptian history; so, counting back from 525 B.C., when the Persians invaded Egypt, we can estimate the length of the later dynasties with fair accuracy.

Records from the earlier dynasties are still fragmentary. The Old Kingdom, which includes Dynasties One through Six, was followed by a period of confusion, when the country broke apart into smaller units ruled by local princes, some of whom continued to claim the titles of pharaoh. This First Intermediate Period, as it is called, causes chronological problems because the Dynasties Seven through Eleven which comprise the period were, in some cases, contemporaneous. By the end of the Eleventh Dynasty the kingdom was again united under kings who kept good records. This is the Middle Kingdom, which includes Dynasties Eleven and Twelve. Another period of disunion followed the Twelfth Dynasty, and again there is disagreement about the length of Dynasties Thirteen through Seventeen. The Eighteenth Dynasty marks the beginning of the Late Kingdom, or Empire, as it used to be called; documentary evidence from this period is good, but here the chronological problem is confused by possible coregencies, which have provided Egyptologists with some of their most exciting and inspiring sources of argument. There are other chronological confusions between the end of the Eighteenth Dynasty and the end of Egyptian history proper; so we cannot simply add up the known years of various kings' reigns to find out when the First Dynasty began. Fortunately, there are other methods.

Everybody knows that the Egyptians discovered the calendar. However, this is one of the pleasant oversimplifications which appear in high school history books; the Egyptians had, not one calendar, but several. Probably the earliest was a lunar calendar whose months ran from one new moon to the next. A number of primitive peoples have lunar calendars, but in Egypt the rhythmical activity of the river soon suggested another method of dividing the year—a division into seasons. One of these seasons was called "Inundation," and the rise of the Nile at the beginning of the annual flood was an event eagerly awaited and anxiously noted. During the Fourth Millennium B.C. an event of quite a different character occurred at about the same time as the beginning of Inundation—the reappearance of the brightest star in the heavens after a period of invisibility. Sirius, the Dog Star, which the Greeks called "Sothis," came to be regarded as the harbinger of the Inundation, and its heliacal rising was named *wp rnpt*, the "Opening of the Year."

The primitive lunar calendar worked admirably for a simple agricultural people; but as society became more complex, it was seen to have disadvantages. Every new month had to be established by observation, and no one knew in advance whether it would have thirty days or twenty-nine. At the end of the lunar year there would be a space of days, even weeks, before the opening of the new year, which was signalized by the rising of Sirius. So some busy bureaucrat decided, with royal approval, to set up another year whose exact length would be known in advance. This is called the "civil calendar," and it is the distant ancestor of the one we use. It had twelve months of thirty days each, with five "intercalary" days at the end of the year. We don't know how this unknown genius arrived at the number 365; he might have counted the days between successive risings of Sirius or he might have averaged out the number of days which elapsed between Inundations over a period of years.

Even this admirable solution to the problem of time has a difficulty which the reader has probably noticed. The true solar year does not have 365 days, but 365 and a quarter and then some. Hence, if the "Opening of the Year" occurred on day one, month one, when the civil calendar was first set up, four years later it would fall on day two, month one. A period of 1,460 years (four times 365) constituted what we call a "Sothic cycle" and brought the rising of Sirius back to "day one, month one" of the civil calendar once again.

One would think that the Egyptians, nonchalant as they were about consistency, would have noticed that something peculiar was going on after a century or so. Professor Richard Parker, of

Brown University, to whom I owe many of the details of the preceding description, thought so too. Disagreeing with many Egyptologists who wanted to tie the Sothic rising to the establishment of the civil calendar, Parker maintained that the civil calendar was really connected with the old lunar year and not the astronomical year. In time, a discrepancy would be noted; but because the lunar year was irregular anyhow, it would take a long time before the difference became really important. When this happened, the Egyptians constructed a second, or later, lunar calendar to coincide with the civil year, and the old lunar calendar simply continued side by side with the new arrangement.

The reader who is interested in Egyptian calendars had better turn to Professor Parker's book, which is mentioned in the Bibliography; it explains his ingenious deductions much better than I can.

What really matters for our purpose is the Sothic cycle. From time to time the Egyptians saw fit to mention the rising of the Dog Star in connection with a date of their civil calendar. Now we know, from Roman sources, that a Sothic cycle—the coincidence of the rising of the star and the first day of the civil calendar—began in A.D. 139. By a simple process of arithmetic we can calculate that the previous cycle started in 1322 B.C., and the one before that in 2782 B.C.* We have a mention of a Sothic rising, with date, in the Twelfth Dynasty, and another in the Eighteenth. Hence we can establish these events in terms of our own time scheme with as much accuracy as we can hope to obtain (until the time-travel machine materializes), and we find that the dates given by dead reckoning check out with the astronomical data. Knowing the dates of the Twelfth and Eighteenth Dynasties enables us to fix the approximate length of the confused period between these two stable periods.

We do not have, as yet, any astronomical reference from the Old Kingdom. As one might expect, given the perversity of things in general, the inscriptional material is scantiest just when we need it most; when, in other words, we must depend on dead reckoning rather than on astronomical methods. There are two document which attempt to give a king list, with dates, for the

---

* In performing these calculations, bear in mind that there is no year 0.

Old Kingdom. One of them is in pieces and the other is in fragments. The fate of the Turin Papyrus is told in a story which is probably apocryphal, but whose general spirit is unhappily too typical of the early days of archaeology. It was complete when it was discovered in 1823 by a gentleman named Drovetti, who stuck it into a jar which he tied around his waist. He then rode off to town on his donkey. The gait of a donkey being what it is, Egyptologists have been pushing the pieces of the papyrus around ever since, and cursing Drovetti as they do so. The other document, the Palermo Stone, is equally fragmented, though its material would seem so much more durable. Several bits of it have been found and the absence of the remainder is all the more frustrating because it gives year-by-year accounts of events for every king of the first five dynasties.

If the reader finds the foregoing discussion confusing, let me assure him that I have simplified the various problems to a degree most Egyptologists would consider unscholarly in the extreme. There are many other criteria involved in Egyptian chronology, including references to Egypt in various foreign chronologies, each one of which has its own internal problems! At least you can see why, although most authorities agree that the Twelfth Dynasty began around 1990 B.C., they differ by as much as four hundred years when it comes to the beginning of the First Dynasty. However, the evidence seems more and more to confirm the date of approximately 3110 B.C. as the start of history in Egypt; and unless something drastically unexpected happens to contradict it, it is unlikely that there will be much change in the date.

The Wars of Religion

Contrary to the general rule—that our knowledge increases as we move forward in time—we know less of the Second Dynasty than we do of the First. We lack a basic source, the tombs of the kings. There are only two Second Dynasty tombs at Abydos, and they date from the very end of the period. The excavations at Sakkara have produced two tombs which may belong to the Second Dynasty—but not to the two kings who have tombs at Abydos.

Speaking of dynasties, we should note that they are derived from Manetho, who was trying to distinguish separate royal houses or families. In view of the fact that Manetho is damned with such faint praise, one might ask why we rely on him for this breakdown. The answer, as most Egyptologists sourly admit, is because Manetho's concept has been used for so long that it would be inconvenient to discard it. In some cases we cannot see any evidence that a particular royal line really ended where Manetho says it did. We don't know why he started a new dynasty with the Second, but the oddity of the missing tombs does suggest that there was something going on which prevented the new (?) royal family from following the burial habits of its predecessors. There are definite signs of dissension, and they take an unexpected form. The country had only been unified for a few generations, and we might expect that the conquered had not completely given up their dreams of independent power. But the rebellion against the central authority was not solely a matter of political conflict. It was tied in with religion.

Of all the gods and goddesses of Egypt, the best known are probably Isis and Osiris. Osiris was regarded as the earliest king of Egypt, who had brought the Egyptians out of savagery, giving them laws and teaching them how to cultivate the land. He married his sister, Isis, and their wise and benevolent rule was praised by gods and men alike. But Osiris's jealous brother Set murdered the king and usurped his throne. The body of Osiris was recovered by his devoted wife, whose laments so moved the gods that they restored Osiris and gave him kingship over the land of the dead. The posthumous son of the royal pair, Horus, finally defeated his wicked uncle, Set, in a bloody hand-to-hand combat, and regained the throne. Hence the king of Egypt was called "the Horus." When he died he became Osiris, and was buried by his son, the new Horus, with the same pious devotion that the god Horus had shown his father.

This myth has been interpreted in a number of ways. The followers of the "Dynastic Race" idea regard Horus as the patron deity of the conquerors and Set as the god of the indigenous population. The events were narrated by the winners, so their god became the avenging son and Set became the manifestation of evil; as someone has pointed out, the Devil has never had the story told from his point of view either.

Another theory views Set as the god of the south (he was originally the local god of a town called Ombos in Upper Egypt) and Horus (Set's opposite number) as the god of the north. If we are determined to make political hay out of the story, this identification leaves us stuck with an unrecorded conquest of the south by the north, the exact opposite of Menes' conquest.

If this pre-Conquest conquest is history, it is very ancient history indeed, and is not verified by any archaeological remains. There is a third interpretation, which is that the story is theological in import, representing a rather naïve version of the conflict between good and evil, light and darkness. The protagonists in the battle are not Osiris and his brother, but Horus and Set. The "Contendings" of this belligerent pair were a favorite motif in folklore and literature. Horus' symbol is the hawk; the little picture of the bird is the hieroglyph used to write the god's name. The symbolic animal of the Antagonist, Set, is a more mysterious beast. We still do not know what creature was portrayed by the squatting or standing quadruped with the long and pointed ears, so we just call it the "Set-animal."

The Egyptian duality of Good and Evil is not so clear-cut as are other versions. Unlike Lucifer and Ahriman, Set did not become a devil after he fell. He was a good god *and* a bad god, and he could turn from one to the other with a speed that makes Dr. Jekyll look like a tyro. When Set was defeated by Horus he was not cast into outer darkness. Even Isis pleaded for him, and he was given the desert and foreign lands as his domain. As the murderer of Osiris, Set was evil, and the pilgrims to Abydos used to watch his defeat, which was reenacted in a great annual mystery play, with happy cries of "Go it, Horus!"—or something like that. But in his other manifestation, Set was a perfectly good god, and was worshiped like any other. Other cosmologies knew a similar dichotomy; the Aztec Tezcatlipoca was both a sun-god and the sun-god's diabolic opponent; the slim huntress Diana could also be the frightful triform Hecate, goddess of witches and black magic.

Horus the falcon is so thoroughly identified with the king that it comes as something of a shock to see a heretical monarch reject-

Serekhs of Sekhemib-Peribsen

Left, the serekh with the king's earlier name of Sekhemib, topped by the conventional Horus; right, the later name Peribsen, topped by the Set-animal

ing Horus in favor of his *bête noire* Set. This Second Dynasty iconoclast was named, originally, the Horus Sekhemib. We mentioned, while discussing the kings of the First Dynasty, that the Horus name was written in a serekh with a falcon on top. When King Sekhemib changed his Horus name he changed the whole structure. His name became Peribsen, and his serekh was topped by the Set-animal instead of the Horus falcon.

This change of ritual, which looks so small on a stone seal or stela, must have signified far-reaching and dramatic events. Many of the First Dynasty royal monuments, both at Sakkara and at Abydos, were set afire in ancient times, perhaps during this very period. The next king, Khasekhem, is noted for his military exploits, and several campaigns were fought in the north. There is certainly a suggestion of a battle for the crown, if not outright civil war. The last king of the dynasty, Khasekhemui, has a name that means "Appearance of the Two Powers." The two powers, in

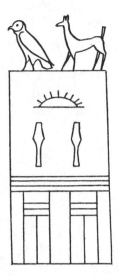

Serekh of Khasekhemui
Note the unique appearance of both Horus and Set-animal
on top of the serekh.

this case, may well have been the old enemies Horus and Set; the king's name is, uniquely, surmounted by both gods standing in amity upon the serekh. Possibly Khasekhem and Khasekhemui are the same king, with the change of name signalizing a reconciliation—forcible or diplomatic—between the two factions which had been in opposition. The fact that no tomb has been found for Khasekhem at Abydos, although the tombs of Peribsen and Khasekhemui are there, supports this theory.

The Wars of Religion of our own era are adequate proof that men may take up weapons over an idea, but it is rather startling to find the easygoing, tolerant Egyptians fighting about their gods when they could, and did, accept new additions to the pantheon without a murmur of complaint or confusion. Was the Set Rebellion, like Akhenaton's later heresy, an attempt at exclusiveness— an attempt, in short, at monotheism? Well—no. There is no evidence for such a conclusion. We may never know the details of, or the reasons for, the religious upheaval of the Second Dynasty; inscriptional material from this period is so sparse as to be almost nonexistent. Still, archaeology may have surprises in store for us. Purely physical remains may throw a new light on this fascinating period, or some new and unexpected tool of history may be discovered. Fifty years ago the technique of carbon dating would have seemed as fantastic to the archaeologist as time travel.

II

Houses
of Eternity

Khufu

King Djoser's Magician

ONE of the advantages of armchair travel is that we can spare ourselves the physical discomforts attendant upon the real thing. Let us, then, avoid the unhappy donkeys of Sakkara and imagine that we are already at that site looking up—and I do mean up—at a fantastic construction called the Step Pyramid.

It comes at the very beginning of the Third Dynasty, this large architectural jewel; and at first glance it seems unbelievable that the people who were playing around with mud bricks and holes in the ground during the Second Dynasty could have leaped so swiftly out of the hole and into the sky, with cut stone as their ladder. Less than fifty years elapsed between the stone-lined pits of the late Second Dynasty and the Step Pyramid; less than a century between the fumbling amateurs and the building of the Great Pyramid at Giza. There is a lot of sand in Egypt which has never been shifted. But even if we moved all of it we would still be left with the wonder of the accomplishment in so short a time; and we might find, even then, that the greater part of the credit must be given to the genius of one man.

The Step Pyramid of King Djoser. *Photo by the author.*

Tradition, that much maligned handmaiden of history, had long credited the construction of the Step Pyramid to one Imhotep, the vizier and architect of Djoser, first or second king of the Third Dynasty. His name has been found in the Step Pyramid area, and there is little doubt but that Tradition was correct. Imhotep was one of those talented people who captured the popular imagination; by Greek times he had become a godling, and was credited with astounding accomplishments in medicine, magic, and scribal lore as well as in architecture.

When his lord and master asked Imhotep what sort of tomb he ought to build, the architect's first notion was to construct a huge mastaba—the type of tomb which was built by kings and nobles alike during the First and Second Dynasties. It continued to be used by commoners after their rulers had soared in ambition to the splendor of the pyramid. In shape, a mastaba is a low, flat-topped rectangle, something like a shoe box with sloping sides.

It would be fascinating to have the tomb autobiography of Imhotep, as we have the autobiographies of later architects and officials; to know when and how the idea first came to him to

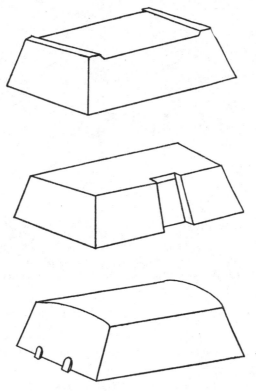

Types of Old Kingdom mastabas

superimpose another smaller mastaba on top of the first and a third on top of the second, and so on, forming a four-step pyramid. Later the design was enlarged to a six-step pyramid, by broadening the base and building on along one of the extant faces of the structure. In essence, this is how most later pyramids were constructed, in layers. The Step Pyramid differs from later pyramids in that it was never faced with stone to give a smooth, uninterrupted slope. But it served as an inspiration for a thousand years, and we are happy to be able to give the architect his due instead of crediting Anonymous, as we must do so often in ancient Egypt.

The first pyramid did not stand alone. The Egyptian Antiquities Department has restored some of the buildings which sur-

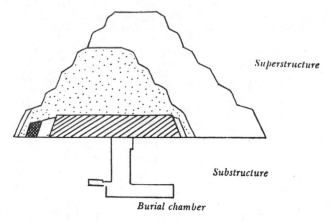

Superstructure

Substructure

Burial chamber

Building stages of the Step Pyramid

The original mastaba can be seen at the bottom of the structure. It was succeeded by a four-step pyramid, which was in turn succeeded by the final six-step construction.

rounded it, so we can visualize, with only a moderate straining of the imagination, what the immense tomb complex of King Djoser looked like in the days of its pristine glory.

All the buildings, including the pyramid, were enclosed by a wall built of small white limestone blocks. The size of the stones was a survival of the older brick construction; the Egyptians had yet to learn how to exploit the new building material properly. Inside the wall lay courts and buildings and tombs of various types; so complicated is the structure that archaeologists are still finding things within the Step Pyramid enclosure, though work has been carried on there for many years. The broken remains of the buildings are important for the study of domestic architecture, since some of them reproduce the actual living quarters of the king which were built of less durable materials than stone.

The pyramid itself is solid (we think); the burial corridors and chambers were underground, entered through a passage from the funerary temple next to the pyramid. This is not typical of later pyramids, and the Step Pyramid substructure is more elaborate than the other Old Kingdom examples. Some of the walls had reliefs, done in a subtle and skilled style; others were covered with

small blue-green glazed tile in imitation of matting. A badly battered, but once magnificent statue of Djoser was found near the
pyramid, but the body of the king has long since disappeared. A
few bones, flung irreverently on the floor of the burial chamber,
may be all that remains of him.

Of the master architect Imhotep even less has survived. A few
years ago, the world of Egyptology was more or less electrified by
the discovery of what may have been the tomb of Imhotep. Unfortunately we can't be more specific than that even now, after several seasons of excavation. The tomb is—or isn't—at Sakkara, one
of a group of large Third Dynasty mastabas—those of important
people, to judge by their size. Not only were all these tombs
thoroughly plundered in antiquity, but they were virtually destroyed by later builders. Professor Emery, who first excavated in
the area, believed that Imhotep's tomb was there, somewhere, and
that it served as the cult center for a Ptolemaic temple dedicated
to the deified vizier. Ensuing excavations uncovered a fantastic
labyrinth of underground galleries containing the mummies of
hundreds of thousands of ibises and baboons. These animals were
sacred to Thoth, god of learning, who was regarded as the divine
father of Imhotep. Perhaps one of the desecrated tombs was his,
but thanks to the wholesale destruction of the cemetery it is unlikely that we will ever be able to prove it.

A statue base in the Step Pyramid area bearing his name con-
firms Imhotep's connection with that masterpiece, which is in
itself a sizeable substantiation of one of Imhotep's reputed talents;
and we are entitled to wonder whether Tradition may not have
been equally accurate about his other abilities. Imhotep's age, the
Third Dynasty, was a formative period. An efflorescence of creativity took place, paving the way for the massive accomplishments
of Egyptian culture which we will see fully developed during the
next dynasty. Djoser's statue shows that the fumbling attempts of
earlier sculptors had been replaced by a technique which was to
become the traditional method of carving stone. In the realm of
abstract ideas, equally significant discoveries were being made. I
want to talk about one of these discoveries now.

Those of us who have reached the years of wisdom and dignity
are perhaps fortunate enough to remember the farm kitchen of a

grandparent or uncle: the black wood-burning stove; the basin and ewer where the men washed up when they came in from the fields; the long table covered with oilcloth; the heavy sideboard which held souvenir cups from the World's Fair and the family library—a Bible, the Sears Roebuck catalogue, an almanac and a leech book.

The leech book I own is not my grandmother's; I bought it for fifty cents at a secondhand book store, in a fit of nostalgia. When I hold it in my hands I can tell myself, if I am feeling sentimental, that I am holding the direct descendant of an ancient Egyptian book of medical science. We can trace the lineage of these works, through the Greeks to the Romans to Medieval Europe, and then across the seas to America. They are not what we would call scientific books. Mixed in with practical remedies for rheumatism and spavins and "fits" are many incantations of a purely magical character. The distinction between science and magic is a relatively modern one. The Egyptians, like many of their descendants all over the world, saw only the effect. When the effect was an obvious one—a hole in the head following a blow with a mace—no people were more pragmatic about explaining the cause and dealing with the results. But when the cause of the trouble was less clear they did not hesitate to ascribe it to demons and devils.

There are half a dozen major papyri from Pharaonic Egypt which are basically medical in purpose. One contains diagnoses of diseases of the stomach, another deals with gynecology and a third with ailments of the anus and rectum. Perhaps the most famous of the medical books is the Edwin Smith Papyrus, which was found in 1862. Its subject is the surgical treatment of wounds and fractures.

Most of our copies of the medical papyri were written during the New Kingdom. But it is in cases like this that the painstaking, plodding labors of the philologist contribute to historical study. So thorough is modern knowledge of the Egyptian language that we can tell the probable date of a manuscript by internal evidence alone—by stylistic, grammatical, and epigraphical details—just as a student of English literature can distinguish a work of the fourteenth century from one of the seventeenth. The Edwin Smith Papyrus is very old; it was probably composed during the Fourth Dynasty, or even earlier.

Like the leech books, Egyptian "medical" texts contain two distinct types of material. The great majority is medical in *intent*; the purpose is to cure, but the methods are those of magic. Normally these methods involved two elements: an incantation, calling upon the demon to give up its hold upon the body of the sufferer; and a ritual act. Often the ritual was as painful for the patient as for the hypothetical demon; the afflicted member might be burned with hot irons or jabbed with needles. We know of these techniques from many lands and many ages; indeed, so widespread and so consistent is the belief in demoniac possession that if unanimity of belief were a valid criterion of truth we would be forced to give it more credence than we do. However, we have learned—and it took us time to learn it—that hot irons are not as effective as penicillin, nor incantations as curative as quinine.

What makes us catch our breath is a hint—only a hint—that some Egyptian leech of the third millennium B.C. may have learned the same thing. In the Edwin Smith Papyrus there are forty-eight long sections which differ drastically both in format and in approach from the magical spells which fill the rest of this papyrus and most of the others. Each section has five subheadings: 1. title; 2. symptoms; 3. diagnosis; 4. opinion; and 5. treatment. The opinion consists of the doctor's judgment on the severity of the case, and is stated in one of three ways: "This is an affliction with which I will contend," or "with which I will not contend," or "which I will cure." The approach is rigorously matter-of-fact; there is no mention of supernatural causes.

To be sure, the cases in Edwin Smith deal with wounds and fractures in which the cause of the injury is apparent even to a superstitious eye. But there is one case of partial paralysis resulting from injury to a section of the brain which surely involves analysis one step removed from the simple observation of a broken bone. The ancient observer here makes a revolutionary statement. This is not, he says, a question of something entering from outside of a man; it is something which his own flesh has produced. In other words—no demons.

Some scholars believe that other medical papyri contain excerpts from the same ancient surgical treatise which was the source of the forty-eight sections in the Edwin Smith Papyrus. The Edwin Smith Papyrus is a hodge-podge, a collection of material from various sources; if it was put together during the Old Kingdom, the surgical source book must be even older. We will not be stretching probability too far if we assign it to the Third Dynasty.

But the spirit of inquiry did not flourish. All down the centuries the magical formulae persist and multiply, and if any leech did get the eccentric notion that all illnesses, like the paralysis resulting from the brain injury, were caused by physical agents rather than diabolic ones, he never, to the best of our knowledge, voiced such heresy. Medicine and magic, sorcerer and leech— except for rare periods in the history of the human mind, they have been identical. It is indeed odd that we should be able to see a suggestion of scientific inquiry at so early a period in Egypt— odder still that it should occur at about the same time as the lifespan of the legendary wise man Imhotep. To the Greeks, Imhotep was not only the builder of the Step Pyramid and the patron saint of scribes; above all he was a master physician, and was identified with Aesculapius. So great was Imhotep's renown as a doctor that in Ptolemaic times a young wife would say:

"With my husband I prayed to the Lord God Imhotep, son of Ptah, the giver of favors, who grants sons to those who have none, and he answered our prayer, as he does for those who pray unto him. . . ."

Perhaps her prayers had a sounder basis than she knew.

If Imhotep's scientific insights fell on sterile soil, his architectural innovation was accorded the most sincere form of flattery— imitation. Djoser was not the only Third Dynasty king to begin a pyramid. Air photographs, a useful modern aid to archaeological mapping, had shown that there was some sort of construction on the desert sands close to the Step Pyramid complex; it was rectangular in shape, but there did not appear to be anything inside it. In 1953–4 this strange structure was excavated by an Egyptian archaeologist who found unmistakable evidence that another step pyramid had been begun. It was meant to be as big as Djoser's, but it never got beyond the second level of building, perhaps because the ambitious king died too soon. The aerial photo had brought out the shape of the enclosure wall. There was also a substructure with many galleries where the excavators found vases and jar stoppers and, more thrilling, a number of gold bracelets. Generations of conscientious tomb robbers had somehow missed the gold, though they had removed the other contents of the tomb, which must have been fabulous—there were over 120 storerooms in the subterranean galleries. But the most momentous find was a sarcophagus in the burial chamber. Unlike the usual sarcophagus, whose top lifts like the lid of a box, this one had a sliding panel at one end. And, wonder of wonders, the panel was still sealed with plaster; on top of the sarcophagus lay the withered remains of a funeral wreath.

A Third Dynasty royal burial would have been a unique find indeed. The small world of Egyptology waited with some excitement until May of 1954, when the sealed panel was raised. The sarcophagus was bare; it still remains one of the unexplained mysteries of Egyptology, and has led some archaeologists to suspect that this pyramid has surprises in store even yet. If the empty sarcophagus was a trick to fool thieves, the real burial may still lie hidden.

This pyramid is attributed to one of Djoser's successors, a king named Sekhemkhet. Then we have two peculiar tombs at the site of Zawaiyet el Aryan, near Giza, which are also ascribed to the Third Dynasty. Neither was finished, but from the little that remains archaeologists have deduced that they were meant to be step pyramids of considerable size. One of these structures, called the Layer Pyramid, was never used for a burial; perhaps its royal builder died before it was finished, but one still wonders what alternative arrangements were made for the body. The second Zawaiyet el Aryan pyramid, appropriately named the Unfinished, is even more mystifying; work on its superstructure never even began, but the substructure contained an oval sarcophagus, sealed shut—and empty.

These vanished pyramids, monuments to the failure of human vanity, are not spectacular in themselves; but they fill in the historical gap between the Step Pyramid, at the very beginning of the Third Dynasty, and the series of *true* pyramids which were built during the Fourth Dynasty. The Fourth Dynasty pyramids culminate in the three great monuments of Giza. Beside the great-est of the three lies another house of Eternity, a tomb which is not a pyramid, but which deserves a visit because it is the source of one of the most romantic stories in all the annals of Egyptology.

The Stone Mountains

The great vizier, Hemiun—overseer of all the king's works, favored of the Horus Khufu, whom the Greeks called Cheops—Hemiun was slumbering peacefully one morning when a rude interruption ended his repose. An agitated messenger, pale with alarm and stammering in his haste and terror, dared to intrude himself into the presence of the vizier, greatest in the land under the king. But Hemiun's outrage was forgotten when he heard the news; it was news to make the bravest cower. The sacred tomb of the queen Hetepheres, mother of the King of Upper and Lower Egypt himself, had been entered by thieves and robbed of all its treasures. Hemiun omitted the usual morning ceremonies. Within an hour he was in his litter, on his way to the scene of the crime.

The two mighty pyramids of Dahshur soared above the golden sand like young mountains, their slopes of white limestone glor-ious in the sun. Hemiun had no eye for their splendor, or for the gallant show of the painted temples before them His proud face remained impassive (a nobleman does not bare his mind before slaves and other low persons) but his heart must have sunk down to the soles of his sandaled patrician feet. This was worse than he had feared; this was catastrophe. Not only had the queen's fab-ulous jewels been stolen, but the queen herself was gone. A frenzied search of the surrounding sand produced no royal mummy—not even bones, which at this point Hemiun would have accepted for want of anything better.

The vizier had descended from his litter by this time. He was an imposing figure of a man even without the jeweled collar which half covered his broad chest. The years had added a roll of fat to his middle, but his aquiline features held pride so great and so habitual that it was as much a part of his face as were the bones of his skull. It was pride alone that held him erect; dignity alone that kept him from flinging himself down on the hot sand and howling like a beaten slave. His distress was not solely due to piety. It was caused chiefly by reflections on what was going to happen to him, Hemiun, when the Lord of the Two Lands found out that his mother's holy remains had provided entertainment, if not much nourishment, for the jackals of the desert. As vizier, Hemiun was responsible for the royal tombs, among a hundred other matters. It was no use telling Khufu that he couldn't keep track of everything; if a vizier couldn't keep track of everything, he had no business being vizier. It would have been dangerous enough to face the god-king with the fact that the tomb had been robbed. When Khufu found out that his mother's bones were missing, he would see to it that Hemiun the vizier went to make his peace with the royal lady's spirit.

Hemiun did not feel the hot sun scorching his bare head; he was too busy thinking. He came of an illustrious family, one which was related to the royal house itself, but he had not held the highest appointed post in the land for so many years by virture of birth alone. He was a shrewd, capable man, and it did not take him long to see the only way out of his peril. Absently he brushed a few grains of sand from the spotless white linen of his kilt, and ordered his litter to be fetched. More or less in passing he also ordered the execution of the guards whose negligence had led to the disaster.

As vizier, Hemiun had immediate access to the king. He made no attempt to conceal his agitation when he was admitted to the royal presence; who would not be distressed at discovering that thieves had tried to enter the tomb of the king's mother? It was lucky for Khufu, his vizier insinuated, that his officials were so alert to their duties; not only had the thieves been foiled, but he, Hemiun, had conceived a clever plan to prevent future danger. With his Majesty's concurrence, he would arrange for the queen's reburial in a new and hidden spot, a spot so secret that no one would ever find it (in this he was not far wrong). Naturally, the move must be made at once; the longer the delay, the greater the danger of a repetition of the "attempt." Yes, he knew the king had a hard day ahead of him—reports on a new canal in the Delta, visits from the treasurers, a rebellion in Nubia—he would take care of the whole thing. When the new tomb was ready to be sealed (he recommended that this take place at night, for reasons of security) he would himself notify the king, that he might pay his filial respects. On his way out of the presence chamber Hemiun paused to answer a question. The thieves? Oh, naturally, they were already on their way to the West. He had known that the king would not wish to defile his eyes with the sight of such vileness. . . .

A number of sweating workmen had cause to curse the tomb robbers as they hauled the queen's funerary equipment—only the heaviest and most unwieldy pieces were left—to the new tomb. Hemiun had chosen a good spot, right beside the passage leading from the king's funerary temple to the still unfinished pyramid at Giza. In months to come the hidden entrance would be trampled over by hundreds of feet.

So, late one night, the king was summoned to approve the vigilance and wisdom of his vizier. Borne high in a gold-inlaid litter upon the brawny arms of four slaves, Khufu was carried along the road from Memphis up to the plateau on which his pyramid was being built. By the flickering light of torches he saw the shaft going down into the heart of the rock. If he had entertained any pious hopes of laying a funeral wreath on the maternal bier, he dismissed them at that moment. "How far down does this go?" he demanded. Hemiun did not conceal his pride. A hundred feet below the surface lay the tomb chamber—infinitely more secure than the old tomb, and all accomplished in so short a time!

Khufu nodded gravely. Darkness welled up in the shaft only a few feet below the surface. He could not see the glitter of the golden hieroglyphs upon the stately chair and bed, the gift of his father Snefru to Hetepheres, nor could he catch so much as a glimmer of the white sarcophagus. But he knew they were there; it never entered his head that they were not. Again he nodded, pleased and impressed. He must plan a suitable reward for his enterprising vizier.

The king watched as the shaft was filled with stone, and plaster tinted to match the rock of the plateau was spread over the opening. When all was done the king went home to bed; a group of slaves went to the mines of Sinai, or to a farther place; and the vizier probably betook himself to a quiet corner of his villa where he could collapse and get drunk.

The Egyptians did get drunk. They brewed more kinds of beer than anyone up to, if not including, the Bavarians, and when time and finances permitted the excess they drank more of it than was good for them. It is, of course, a flight of fancy to imply that Hemiun celebrated the success of his colossal trick in this fashion, though we would not blame him if he did. However, Hemiun's fine portrait statue is not that of a man who yielded to weakness very often; gazing at the imperious, rather ugly face, we find ourselves thinking that if any man could have carried off such a risk, this one could. The stately vizier succeeded beyond his fondest hopes, for the tomb of Queen Hetepheres survived the centuries in safety. Not until A.D. 1925 did any living man dream that such a tomb existed.

The Giza expedition of Harvard University had been working at that site for some years when the leg of a photographer's tripod chipped the plaster covering the tomb and told the excavators that the seemingly solid rock was not what it looked to be. When the shaft was uncovered and the big stone blocks which filled it were seen to be undisturbed, the hopes of the staff of the expedition began to rise. At last the shaft was cleared and the men could descend, rather perilously, to the burial chamber. The sarcophagus was there, its massive lid still in place. This was a significant point, for when tomb robbers went to the trouble of removing one of these lids, whose weight is calculated in tons, they did not bother to put it back when they were through.

At this high moment of anticipation the shaft had to be refilled, for Reisner, the head of the expedition, was in the United States. George Reisner was one of America's finest archaeologists. The accuracy and detail of his excavation reports have seldom been equaled; his work at Giza and in the Sudan produced definitive information on large areas of Egyptian history and archaeology. Much of Reisner's later work was carried on under the threat of eventual blindness. Several operations for cataracts proved unsuccessful, but Reisner never stopped working on his *magnum opus*, a study of the architectural development of the Egyptian tomb, which is now a basic reference book. With limited sight and increasingly feeble health he continued digging throughout the Second World War, diving into a tomb when an enemy plane appeared over the pyramids. He died during the war, still in harness; neither blindness nor worldwide conflict kept him from his work.

But in 1926 the shadow of tragedy was still in the future, and Reisner was at the height of his powers. He needed them; for when he hurried back to Giza after receiving a rapturous cablegram from his staff, he found a really meaty problem of excavation awaiting him. The tantalizing, closed sarcophagus was the *pièce de résistance*, but it was not the only thing in the chamber. The tomb was filled with the tattered remnants of what had once been an elaborate set of mortuary equipment.

Seeing a photograph of the original condition of the tomb

The burial chamber of Queen Hetepheres, as it first appeared. *The Museum of Fine Arts, Boston.*

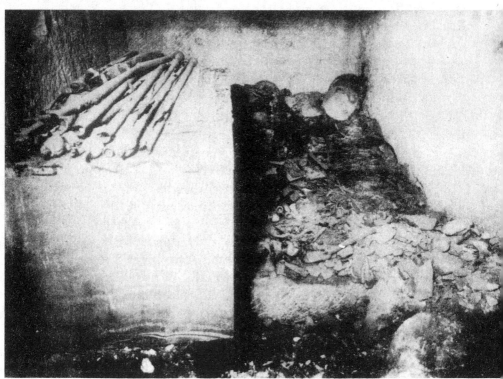

chamber, one wonders why the excavators did not simply remove the debris with a shovel. This emergency burial chamber was too small to begin with. A bed canopy, in pieces, and the box which held its curtains, had been laid atop the sarcophagus for lack of floor space. Next to it was a chest filled with objects, and a carrying chair on top of a low bed. There were also two large armchairs, boxes, baskets, jars, and so on.

The furniture had been made of wood covered with thin sheets of gold or inlaid with ebony. The wood decayed with the years, crumbling quite literally into dust and allowing the inlay and the gold leaf to collapse to the floor. A number of stone jars, heavy things made of alabaster, had been placed on wooden shelves; when the shelves collapsed, the jars fell into the piles of broken inlay, making confusion complete.

Today the bed, carrying chair, and other furniture of the queen adorn the Cairo Museum, looking just as they looked in the days when the royal lady stood among them. They are often ignored by the modern visitor because of their proximity to the showier and more costly tomb furnishings of Tutankhamon, but

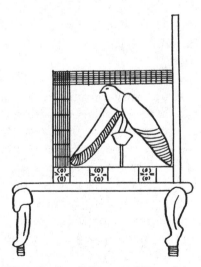

The chair of Queen Hetepheres
The author's sketch gives only a rough idea of the beauty of proportions and decorative elements.

they are probably more beautiful than anything that notorious king ever owned. The designs, in their austere simplicity, are striking in themselves, and the details are exquisite. The titles of the queen and her husband were inlaid in gold hieroglyphs upon an ebony background. Each hieroglyph is less than an inch high, and is carved in low relief so fine that every feather of the tiny birds and every scale of the little serpents is clearly distinct. They are the most beautiful hieroglyphs ever carved or painted, whether you look at them individually or study the over-all decorative effect. The reconstruction of this furniture is a brilliant example of archaeological skill and patience at its best.

The work of clearing the tomb chamber took months. The position of every tiny fragment had to be recorded, since the way in which it had fallen might provide a clue to the original design. At last the slow, agonizing task was completed and the chamber was empty of everything except the sarcophagus. Two years after Reisner got back from the United States, distinguished visitors and high government officials were lowered down the shaft in basket chairs and crammed themselves into the little room. The great moment had arrived. The heavy sarcophagus lid was prized up. In a hush of anticipation Reisner stooped to peer inside.

Then he straightened and faced the distinguished audience.

"Gentlemen," he said wryly, "I regret Queen Hetepheres is not receiving."

Egyptologists become philosophical about such disappointments; Tutankhamon was only too unique. What puzzled Reisner was why the elaborate care and secrecy had been expended on the burial of an empty sarcophagus. It had been used for a burial; certain discolorations on the bottom proved that much, to Reisner's satisfaction. After much cogitation he came up with the story I have related as being the only one that fits the facts. Certainly no one has been able to suggest a plausible alternative. However, this theory bothers me, although I appreciate it for its dramatic qualities as much as for its ingenuity. Late at night I worry about Hetepheres—after I have finished worrying about burglars, and why the cat hasn't come in. What disturbs me is the fact that there have been other sarcophagi found in place, unopened—and empty.

The Unfinished Pyramid of Zawaiyet el Aryan contained an uninhabited sarcophagus whose polished lid was firmly cemented in place. The pyramid of Sekhemkhet at Sakkara had an alabaster sarcophagus which was not only sealed, but which still had on its top the withered scraps of the funeral wreaths. Both these tombs come from the Third Dynasty, not so distant in time from the heyday of Hetepheres. The cases are not exactly parallel, but yet there remains the incontestable and bewildering common feature of the empty sarcophagi.

Understand, I have absolutely no useful suggestion to make as to why such care was lavished on empty stone. If the reader has any sensible ideas on the subject, I and a few other people would be interested in hearing them. But I wonder whether there may not be an unknown magical or cult practice involved; whether, in short, the true story of the death and subsequent adventures of the lady Hetepheres has yet been told. Certainly no one would regret more than I the discovery that Reisner's brilliant and picturesque reconstruction is not the correct one, and until something better comes along, it will do.

Besides being the mother of Khufu, Hetepheres was the wife of Snefru, the first king of the Fourth Dynasty. Once again we are mildly baffled by Manetho's reasons for starting a new dynasty here. Snefru was probably the son of Huni, last king of Dynasty Three; he was certainly on good terms with his predecessor. Huni had started a pyramid for himself at Medum, not far from Giza. It is a conspicuous landmark today, though it does not look much like a pyramid, owing to the fact that its outer casing has been stripped away and the lower courses are buried in sand. Huni died before his tomb was completed, so Snefru piously finished it for him—with such success that it was attributed to the younger king by succeeding generations, and caused archaeologists a number of headaches. They knew that Snefru had two tombs, because of an ancient inscription which mentioned that king's "North" and "South" pyramids. They also knew that the Medum pyramid was believed by the Egyptians to be one of Snefru's tombs.

Admiring students of ancient Egypt have credited the Egyptians with the invention of many interesting and useful pursuits, but no one has ever given them their due as the originators of the pernicious habit of scribbling on tourist attractions. It is a habit which must arise from some basic human urge, for it has continued unabated till the present day. When the Egyptians of the Eighteenth Dynasty—a thousand years after Snefru—came to visit Medum, they carved their names on the temple walls and added comments. Age, which sanctifies many things, has legitimized even tourist scribbles, and the ancient scribbles are dignified by the name of graffiti. It is from the graffiti at Medum that we learn that Snefru was believed to be the builder of the pyramid there; and this naïve belief led to a lot of trouble.

You see, there are also two pyramids at Dahshur, another of the burial grounds of ancient Memphis. The Dahshur pyramids are not usually visited by modern tourists, but they can be seen from Sakkara as little geometric shapes against the flat horizon. One of them is a very strange shape indeed. It is known as the Bent or Rhomboidal Pyramid, since it changes the angle of its slope about halfway up. The other Dahshur tomb is a true pyramid.

Formerly the Bent Pyramid was attributed to King Huni, and the Medum Pyramid, whose attribution seemed so sure, was considered to be Snefru's southern tomb, with the true pyramid of Dahshur as his northern. Why the confusion? Because, with all the thousands of square yards of stone surface used in such a pyramid, in no place was the name of the man who built it to be found. This is one of the most astonishing facts in archaeological research —the scanty, almost negative, evidence upon which the ownership

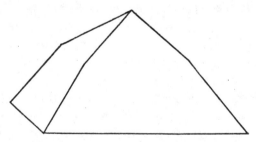

The Bent Pyramid
An outline sketch showing the change of angle of the slope

of the great stone tombs is based. In some cases the decision is
made on the basis of the surrounding tombs, for it was customary
that a king's servants and courtiers be buried near him. In recent
years, careful excavation at the pyramid sites has turned up conclusive evidence, but one can understand why the free and easy
"hurrah-for-the-dynamite" methods of the early archaeologists
failed to find kings' names in the pyramids. In the Bent Pyramid,
Snefru's name appears in the quarry marks hastily scrawled in
red crayon on the undersides of certain blocks for the convenience
of the workmen. This discovery was made in 1947, and it settled
the ownership of the Bent Pyramid. Similar marks on the stones
of the true pyramid at Dahshur make it certain that this is
Snefru's northern tomb. Thus we have discovered the two tombs
mentioned in the ancient text, and can safely leave the Medum
Pyramid to Huni, basing the misconceptions of the Egyptian tourists on the fact that Snefru finished the tomb for his predecessor.
He was a more impressive king anyway, and it is always a temptation to attribute even greater accomplishments to the man who
has accomplished much.

The majority of Snefru's accomplishments were in areas which
we would consider proper for a talented Egyptian ruler of this
period. He sent fleets to the Lebanon for cedar, some of which was
used in his pyramid; he fought in Nubia and worked the turquoise mines of Sinai with such success that he became the patron
deity of that region, and later kings boasted of their expeditions
that "nothing like it was seen since the days of Snefru." But in
one respect Snefru differs from his fellows. In Greek times he was
regarded as the kindest and most benevolent of all the ancient
kings; he was the only one who was honored by the epithet "benefi-
cent." Professor Battiscombe Gunn, a well-known British scholar,
suggested that these attractive character traits are depicted in an
ancient text which claims to have been composed in the time of
Snefru. In the story, the king is shown as a jolly good fellow; when
he calls in a prophet to entertain him with tales, he himself takes
pen in hand to record the words, calling the commoner prophet
"my friend" and addressing his courtiers with the word "comrades," which was used by laborers and artisans as a mode of address to one another. "Make thy name to endure through the love

of thee," advises one Egyptian sage, and Snefru evidently succeeded. The names that most often survive the centuries are those
of warriors and conquerors; it is pleasant to be able to honor one
man for a virtue less conspicuous and more attractive than brutality. A tip of the hat, then, to "good King Snefru."

It may seem extraordinary to the lay reader that Snefru, however virtuous, needed two tombs. It seems extraordinary to an
archaeologist, too, especially since the explanation given for the
double tombs of the First Dynasty—one in each of the "Two
Lands"—will not fit here, as both pyramids are in the same
cemetery. We don't even know in which of his two tombs Snefru
decided to be buried.

Of the two Dahshur pyramids, the Bent is the more intriguing.
When Perring and Vyse, the first Europeans to work systematic-
ally around ancient Memphis, cleared this pyramid in 1839, they
reported a strange and suggestive incident. Conditions within the
deep passages of the pyramid were very bad, and the workmen
suffered intensely from heat and bad air. On October 15, 1839,
when the perspiring laborers were gasping for lack of oxygen,
suddenly a strong cold wind began to blow through the choked
passages. It blew for two days, so fiercely that it was difficult for
the men to keep their lamps lit; then, just as abruptly, it stopped.
Ahmed Fakhry, one of Egypt's most distinguished archaeologists,
heard odd noises in one of the passages when he worked there in
1951. In view of these occurrences, it is distinctly possible that
there are passages and chambers within or under the Bent Pyramid which have never been found. Perhaps the real burial
chamber of Snefru is still hidden. The interior of the pyramid,
though not so complex as those of later periods, is complicated
enough, with heavy portcullis stones blocking the passages, hidden
corridors opening from a wall entrance, and other devices intended to confuse and distract.

Yes, there is still work to be done, even in areas which have
been searched and re-searched. We know, for instance, that every
pyramid from this time on had several other buildings connected
with it. So standardized are the various elements of the "pyramid
complex" that we can look for one structure or another with confidence, even when no traces of its walls show above the ever-

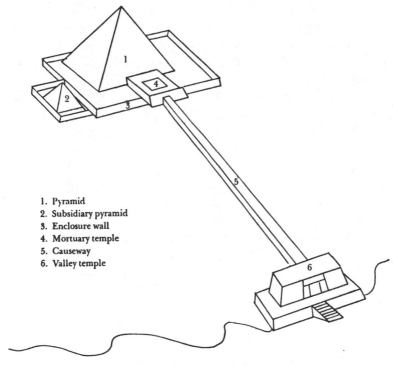

1. Pyramid
2. Subsidiary pyramid
3. Enclosure wall
4. Mortuary temple
5. Causeway
6. Valley temple

The pyramid complex

drifting sands. The pyramid was usually enclosed by a wall, and had a chapel near the northern entrance to the burial chamber. A smaller, subsidiary pyramid within the enclosure walls is also a standard feature, though its precise function is still unknown. The wooden "solar boats" found near the Great Pyramid apparently represent another standard part of the complex, since boat-shaped pits have been found at other places. Against the east side of the pyramid was the mortuary temple. In this building the soul of the dead king was tended by priests, who presented offerings and recited prayers for his well-being in the Land of the West, the abode of spirits. From the entrance to the mortuary temple a long causeway led down to the edge of the cultivated land. Here it joined the Valley Temple, whence the body of the king was brought by boat when the river had overflowed the fields in the annual inundation; here he was mummified and here the priests performed the important ceremony of the Opening of the Mouth, which enabled the dead to speak and to take food.

This is the Pyramid Age—more properly called the Old Kingdom—and we are about to discuss the biggest pyramid of them all, which was built by Khufu, or Cheops, the son and successor of good King Snefru. Khufu is remembered for only one accomplishment of magnitude; yet the size of the one is so gigantic that it overshadows all his father's military and trading exploits, and has brought Khufu's name and fame down undiminished through four thousand years. So much has been written about the Great Pyramid of Giza that it is impossible to add any new facts or even approach it from a fresh viewpoint. Everybody wrote about it—poets, statesmen, tourists, archaeologists, novelists, engineers, fortunetellers. Even Mark Twain's carefully cultivated contempt for the Old World deserted him when he stood under the Great Pyramid's immensity of stone.

The pyramid form has a certain austere beauty, and the tawny gold of the stone is capable of bewitching and subtle variations in color as the sunlight changes. But it is not the aesthetic qualities of the Great Pyramid which have hypnotized so many people. Partly, it is the size—two and one-half *million* blocks of stone, averaging two and a half tons each, comprising a structure which covers an area equal to the combined base areas of the cathedrals of Florence, Milan, St. Peter's, St. Paul's *and* Westminster Abbey. In part the attention lies in the atmosphere of mystery and mysticism which has surrounded the pyramids from the beginning. They were Houses of Eternity even to the Egyptians, dwelling in a land which was beyond mortal comprehension. "No one has returned from there to tell us how they fare." When Greeks supplanted Egyptians, and Romans conquered Greeks, and the ancient heritage of Egypt was shadowed by ignorance, the imaginative visitors of classical and later times added their inventions to swell the mystery. Even in modern times when people, one would think, should know better, the Great Pyramid of Giza has proved a fertile field for fantasy.

The people who do not know better are the Pyramid mystics,

who believe that the Great Pyramid is a gigantic prophecy in stone, built by a group of ancient adepts in magic. Egyptologists sometimes uncharitably refer to this group as "Pyramidiots," but the school continues to flourish despite scholarly anathemas. I cannot refrain from quoting a few of the more entertaining blunders of the mystics, which appear in one of the books they publish with such alarming frequency.

"The Egyptian word Pir-em-us meant to them something of great vertical height." (No such word; the Egyptian name for pyramid is *mer*.) "In *The Book of the Dead* the Great Pyramid is called 'The Temple of Amen.'" (Sorry, but no.) "The subterranean temple which is mentioned in the ancient mystical writings, and whose existence as an initiatory center scholars long denied, has recently been discovered." (I guess the temple is the Valley Temple of the Second Pyramid, whose function had to do with the mummification of the dead; it was not built underground but was buried by sand and silt.) "The great stone in front of the breast of the Sphinx with its symbolic writings and laws for the initiate has been discovered." (This must be the stela of Thutmose IV, which explains how he acquired the throne, and which is about as mystical as a campaign speech.) "This stone . . . would open to the commands of candidates upon the pronunciation of the proper word." (No comment.) "In adopting the mystical pyramid inch as a unit of measurement, the Egyptians realized that the Anglo-Saxon races (*sic*) would be the first to recognize the unit of measurement and look upon the messages concealed in the Great Pyramid as intended for them principally."

The last statement is beyond criticism, surely. I have not mentioned the specific prophecies of the Pyramid, in which significant dates in world history are marked by bumps or lumps or cracks along the walls of the passages. Petrie wrote, with fine contempt, that he once caught one of the mystics surreptitiously filing down a stone boss in order to make its measurements conform to his theory. Sir William Flinders can hardly be called a biased witness; indeed, he is sometimes hailed by the Pyramidiots as one of their own because his first year's work at Giza was undertaken at the request of a friend of his father's, one of the leading Pyramid mystics of his day. I think Petrie's conclusions, arrived at after a long season of measuring and comparison, are worth quoting:

> The theories as to the size of the pyramid are thus proved entirely impossible. . . . The fantastic theories, however, are still poured out, and the theorists still assert that the facts correspond to their requirements. It is useless to state the real truth of the matter, as it has no effect on those who are subject to this type of hallucination.

There is no way out; the Great Pyramid of Giza was a royal tomb, and nothing else. There is no "lost mystery" about the methods of its construction, which required only unlimited manpower and the simplest of tools. We know how this pyramid and others were built, and we could build another one just like it, using the same methods, if we had any desire to do so—and if we could conscript enough workers. Most of the stone was quarried near Cairo and was floated across the river on barges at the time of inundation, when the water extends to the edge of the desert. From that point the blocks were dragged, possibly on rollers, up the slope to the plateau. The first course of stones was laid in a square, on a site already surveyed and leveled. There is no doubt that the Egyptians knew enough about astronomy and geometry to get their angles straight. They did a beautiful job of laying out the ground plan of the Great Pyramid; the errors of orientation are astoundingly small. But they could have done it with very simple tools and equally basic mathematics.

When the first layer was in place, the second level was added by hauling the stones up a ramp of sand and brickwork. When the third layer was added, the ramp was raised, its angle remaining constant, so that by the time the structure was finished, it was hidden on all four sides by sand ramps, sloping out for hundreds of yards from the pyramid. Most of the interior rooms and passages were built while the exterior was in process of construction; the huge stone sarcophagus in Khufu's pyramid was lowered into the burial chamber before the roofing blocks were put on. Then the facing of fine white limestone was added as the ramps were moved downward, so that when all was done the slopes of the

Cartouche of King Khufu

An elaborate example of the cartouche and enclosed hieroglyphs

pyramid presented a smooth, unbroken surface, glistening in the
sun and looking from a distance as if they had been neatly frosted.
This fine casing material is gone today, which is why the Great
Pyramid looks like a giant four-sided staircase; the blocks were a
handy source of buildiing stone for later kings and conquerors.

Khufu's Valley Temple lies under a modern village whose
inhabitants are naturally resistant to the idea of allowing it to be
excavated. His pyramid temple has been cleared, but it is in bad
shape. The pyramid and its temple are the only monuments of
Khufu's we possess, and we actually know very little about the
monarch who constructed the largest single monument ever raised
to the glory of one individual. Khufu had a bad reputation among
the Greeks. Like modern visitors to Giza, they took one look at all
that stone and immediately started calculating in terms of man-
hours. Their calculations were supported by the ancient dragomen, who told Herodotus that it took 100,000 men twenty years
to build the Great Pyramid. The figure may not be too far wrong,
but it would be unfair to picture Khufu as the maniacal whip-
wielding tyrant the Greeks envisioned. Most of the work was
carried on during the season of Inundation, when the big blocks
of stone could be floated close to the building area. At this time
the fields were under water and the peasants were perforce idle.

They were fed while they were working on the pyramid, and if the crops had been bad they were probably glad to get the work.

The Second and Third Pyramids of Giza were built by Khufu's successors, though not in unbroken sequence. The kings who came between Khufu and Khafre (Chephren) and Khafre and Menkaure (Mycerinus) built pyramids at other sites, but these tombs, when they can be identified at all, are in sad condition. Khafre's tomb is the Second Pyramid; it suffers only by comparison to its larger neighbor, and still possesses, at its very tip, several courses of the original white casing stone. Menkaure, who built pyramid number three, died before it was finished; an eloquent, if mute, witness to his premature demise may be seen today on the lower courses of casing stones around the base of his pyramid. These blocks were of red Aswan granite instead of the usual white limestone. The outer faces of the stones were not smoothed off until after they were put in place, and we can still see the exact point at which the ancient workers laid down their tools when word came that the god had joined his fathers. This pyramid is the last of the big Fourth Dynasty tombs, and Menkaure is the last of the big Fourth Dynasty kings. This pyramid is also of interest because it is the only one of the Giza group to have its owner's name inscribed in or upon it. The hieroglyphic text says that Menkaure died on the twenty-third day of the fourth month; it was discovered in 1968 when workmen cleared some of the rubble from the north face, near the entrance.

The other great tourist attraction at Giza is the Sphinx. There are a lot of other sphinxes in Egypt, but this is the biggest. I personally am unmoved by this large and maltreated monster, but the remains of the Valley Temple of the Second Pyramid, near the Sphinx, are decidedly worth attention. The dark granite which lines the walls was brought down the river, five hundred miles, from Aswan, and it is laid with such precision that one can hardly see the lines where the enormous blocks fit together. The stark simplicity of the building's design is almost forbidding in its dignity.

The three great pyramids are not the only tombs at Giza, by a long way. There are seven smaller queens' pyramids near the big ones, and there are private tombs all over the plateau. Khufu, the

The Valley Temple of the Second Pyramid of Giza. View of one end of the long vestibule, with the original walls. The roof has disappeared. *Photo by the author.*

first king to build a pyramid at Giza, also began the private cemeteries. Wishing to ensure his numerous progeny and friends a good life in the next world, he laid out a real City of the Dead, close to his pyramid so that his relatives might profit from his superior presence. The houses of the City were huge stone mastabas laid out in neat rows like city blocks. They must have looked attractive when first built, with their glistening sugar-white walls and painted offering tablets. Later hoi polloi, ambitious for eternity, spoiled the symmetry by building smaller brick tombs around and between and atop the older mastabas. There were sixty-four tombs near Khufu's pyramid to begin with; one of the largest was built for our old friend, the vizier Hemiun, whose shenanigans with the royal mother's sarcophagus had obviously gone undetected.

One can wander for hours among these tombs, reflecting with gentle melancholy upon the various philosophical considerations which cemeteries should induce. The impression we get of Giza today is not one of neatness but of a bewildering honeycomb of holes and pits and tomb entrances. We can walk into one of these tombs, stand where the family of the dead man stood to pay him the last rites, and see his face and figure on the funeral stela. Here we may sense how other people in other times sought immortality —not the common people, for their lot was a hole in the sand of the desert, where they had, indeed, a better chance of bodily survival than did their wealthier contemporaries. The greatest enemy of the dead in Egypt was not time, nor the natural processes of decay, but the tomb robber, who would not bother with a peasant's grave. Almost all the mastaba tombs were robbed in antiquity, some within a few months of the funeral service and by the very stoneworkers who had built the tomb. The massive pyramids fared no better; the devices used to foil prospective thieves posed no problem to the ingenuity of the ancient crooks. Even the heavy stone portcullises, which were lowered after the burial to block the entrance passages, were not serious obstacles; disdaining subterfuge, the tomb robbers cut straight through them. It was toilsome work, but it paid better than any other profession the robbers could have taken up.

Despite a thousand generations of tomb robbers, some precious objects from the Old Kingdom have survived—because they were not precious to the robbers. These are the works of art with which the tombs were furnished: offering tablets and statues and, in later tombs, painted wall reliefs. To the Egyptian, beauty was not its own excuse for being; his art had a very practical purpose, for it served the vital business of survival. Painted and carved reliefs supplied the dead man, magically, with all the objects he might require in the future life, and pictured the activities he hoped to enjoy. The full-length statues and busts were emergency equipment, in case the carefully preserved body did not survive.

Still, an artist may serve a pragmatic aim without losing sight of the beautiful. The Egyptian style of painting looks strange to someone who is accustomed to our notions of perspective; the human form, for instance, is always shown with the head in profile, eyes and shoulders in front view, and the rest of the body in profile again. The Egyptians did not work in this way because they could not draw a face in front view; behind their technique was a concept of the universe which made visual impressions unimportant. They did not care what something *looked* like, but what it *was* like, and they worked out a way of expressing the essential qualities of objects that satisfied them so thoroughly that they continued to use it for three thousand years. The rules governing painting and sculpture were set early in the game, probably by the end of the Third Dynasty, and are so strict that archaeologists refer to them as the Canon. They were never written out, but they were exemplified in every major work of art the Egyptian artist produced, as the Greek Polyclitus exemplified his own canon in the magnificent male figure called "The Doryphorus."

For a non-specialist, Egyptian sculpture is easier to enjoy than is Egyptian painting, since it was subjected to none of the radical distortions of two-dimensional art. The sculpture of the Old Kingdom is often quite stunning. Like the architecture, it is dignified, austere, and stately; like the architecture, it creates an unforgettable impression. It was equaled in later periods, but never really surpassed; in fact, it was never surpassed in any time or any nation until Phidias of Athens took chisel in hand and showed his pupils how to make the white marble move and breathe.

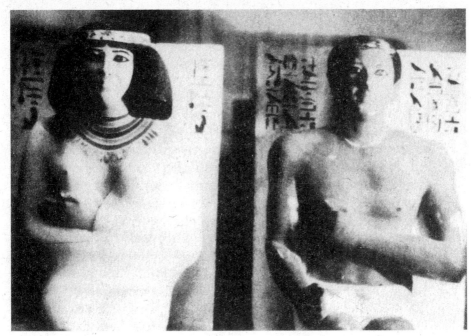

Rahotep and his wife Nefret. *The Cairo Mus*

It is hard to photograph statuary properly, and few of the photographs of Egyptian sculptures do them justice. One must see them to appreciate them fully, and unfortunately one must visit Egypt to see the best, which are in the Cairo Museum. Here sits Khafre, enthroned, with the protective wings of the divine falcon enfolding his head, facing eternity with inhuman calm and confidence; nowhere else, perhaps, has the notion of divine kingship been expressed so concisely in a human face. Here too are such lesser folks as the noble Rahotep, with his neat little Clark Gable mustache, and his buxom wife Nefret. These last two statues are life-sized and vividly painted; the eyes are inlaid with obsidian and rock crystal, and are so alive that the fellahin who first discovered them ran shrieking from the tomb when sunlight first illuminated the interested stare of the vizier and his lady.

I had studied Egyptian art for many years before I got to Cairo; I knew each of the famous statues at once, without the aid

King Khafre, builder of the Second Pyramid. Head of a statue in the Cairo Museum. *Photo from The Metropolitan Museum of Art.*

of identifying labels. Yet I had the feeling that I was seeing them for the first time, so superior is the actuality to the photograph.

Egyptologists sometimes play a game called "Pick Your Period." Of the three broadly defined major periods of Egyptian history, some prefer the Empire for its luxury, cosmopolitanism, and sophistication. Others vote for the Middle Kingdom because of its social advances; Egypt then showed the nearest approach to our favorite ideals of democracy and social welfare. But a good-sized school of thought vaunts the triumphs of the Old Kingdom. At this time, they say, the real bases of Egyptian culture were laid. Later periods used them, altering them only slightly and not always for the better. Old Kingdom sculpture appeals to the classicist and the purist; and in architecture, what form could be more simple and more satisfying than the pyramid? We have already considered the achievements of medical science, and medicine was not the only profession which had been developed at this early time. Here is an excerpt from a mortuary document of a Fourth Dynasty official who was establishing the endowment of his tomb in the proper legal form:

> Whatsoever mortuary priest of the endowment shall institute legal proceedings against his fellow, and he shall make a writ of his claim against the mortuary priest, by which he forfeits the portion in his possession; the lands, people and everything shall be taken from him which I gave to him for making mortuary offerings to me therewith. It shall be conveyed back to him because of not instituting proceedings before the officials concerning the lands, people and everything which I conveyed to the mortuary priests. . . .

I don't know what a lawyer might think of this document, but to me it has all the sophistication and legalistic detail which we could expect to find in a modern will. In its way, it testifies to the complexity of the society of which it was a product just as vividly—if less beautifully—than does the wonderful Fourth Dynasty sculpture.

Children of Re

Sun-gods are popular in polytheistic cultures, for the solar orb is one of the most conspicuous natural objects. Its effects are equally conspicuous and very important to primitive peoples; before the discovery of fire the sun furnished the sole source of both heat and light, and its dawning banished the dangers and demons of darkness. The Egyptian sun-god, most commonly known as Re, was always an important deity. But during the Fifth Dynasty something happened to give him even greater preeminence, so that for a time he was Top God of Egypt.

This religious *coup d'état* may have been accomplished through the clever machinations of a group of scheming priests. Unfortunately we have only the scantiest scraps of evidence on which to base our assumption that a *coup d'état* did take place, and almost no knowledge of how it came about. We know that at this time the title "Son of Re" became a standard part of the royal titulary, and that the kings of the Fifth Dynasty erected huge sun temples far more impressive than their tombs. And we have a popular tale which gives an allegorical version of the triumphs of Re. So let us consider the story of King Khufu and the Magicians.

Once upon a time it happened that the great king Khufu found himself suffering from a painful royal disease: boredom. So he summoned his sons and commanded that they entertain him, each with a tale of wonder or of magic. The first tale is lost; it dealt with events during the reign of Djoser of the early Third Dynasty.

The second story was told by Prince Khafre, who informed his father that the events he would narrate took place under Nebka, another Third Dynasty king. Khafre's was a moral tale about an adulterous wife who was married to a magician—not the easiest type to deceive. When he found out about his wife's duplicity, the magician fashioned a crocodile out of wax and threw it into the river as his wife's lover came to bathe. Immediately it became a real crocodile and seized the lover. The magician went to the king and invited him to come down to the river to behold a marvel. He summoned the crocodile, which terrified king and courtiers with its ferocity. But when the magician took it in his hand, it turned back into a waxen image. Then the magician told the king the whole story and the monarch ordered that the unfaithful wife be slain.

The next son related a wonder which had occurred under Snefru, Khufu's father. One day Snefru too became bored with life; he wandered through all the palace in search of amusement and found none. So he sent for the priest and magician Zazaem-ankh, and asked him to make a suggestion. Said the sage: "Let your Majesty go to the royal lake: equip a boat with all the beautiful girls of the palace. The heart of your Majesty will be entertained watching them row up and down." The king liked the idea, and refined it further by ordering that the young ladies be attired only in nets of mesh.

For a space the heart of his Majesty was happy as the maidens rowed up and down. But then the leader of the damsels dropped a pretty ornament into the water, and in her distress she stopped rowing. The king demanded the reason and the girl told him. "Give her another one," said Snefru impatiently; but the girl refused, with a proverb—*I want my pot down to its bottom*—which meant, "I want my own ornament, not another like it."

Faced with feminine stubbornness, the king threw up his hands and again summoned the magician. Zazaemankh pronounced an incantation which folded the lake back like a sandwich, half the water upon the other half. Upon the exposed bottom lay the ornament, which the magician returned to its owner. He then put the water back in its place and the rowing continued, to the pleasure of the king.

When it came to the turn of Prince Dedefhor to tell a story, he said: "We have been hearing tales of past times, in which it is hard to tell truth from fiction; but, sire, I must tell you that you have in your own kingdom a great magician who is the equal of all those you have heard about."

In great excitement the king sent his son to fetch the venerable sage, whose name was Djedi. The meeting of prince and wise man is charmingly told; the sage greeted the royal youth with courteous words of praise, and the prince helped him to his feet and gave him his arm to assist him to the waiting boat, for Djedi was very old.

When Djedi arrived at the palace, the king asked him to perform his famous trick of putting back a head that had been cut off. The sage was willing, but when the king ordered a prisoner to be brought out, Djedi protested: "No, not a man, O sovereign, my lord; for this is forbidden." So the guards decapitated a goose and Djedi repaired it, to the admiration of all beholders.

After these magical divertissements, the tale gets down to essentials. The king asked about a particular magical secret and Djedi informed him that it would be brought to him by the eldest of three children who were not yet born. The secret is only a device to introduce the children; for, Djedi tells the astounded king, all three of them would one day be kings of Egypt. "They are at this time in the womb of a wife of a priest of Re, but their father is none other than the sun-god himself."

The scene switches to the birth o the divine children, who are delivered by the great goddesses of Egypt disguised as dancer-musicians. As the children come forth, the goddesses address them with speeches involving puns on their names; this leaves no doubt that the kings in question are really Fifth Dynasty rulers.

Obviously this story was not composed during the reign of Khufu; it was a pretty piece of propaganda commissioned by a Fifth Dynasty king to give mystical sanction to his dynasty. Why the new dynasty should need such support is a mystery, for it seems to be distantly related to the royal family of the Fourth Dynasty. Perhaps the "religious coup d'etat" was really a political usurpation, by a lesser branch of the Khufu-Khafre family. Speculation—but that's the stuff of which much of Egyptian history is made.

But what a wealth of information we can infer from such sources as these regarding social customs, attitudes, and ethics! From the composite tale of Khufu and the Magicians we can begin to sense something which is almost impossible to get except by indirection—the whole moral attitude of a long-dead culture. We are accustomed to state our views on ethical and spiritual matters in long tomes and in short essays; we verbalize them, and analyze them, and criticize them. The Egyptians did write books of wisdom literature, but for the most part these consist of advice to aspiring young men, and one is never certain that the smooth-tongued precepts are really sincere. It is in the actions, the daily responses, of human beings that we can see the ethical sense at work; and in the tale of Khufu there are several striking examples. The maiden who dropped her ornament was only a concubine, but when she spoiled the god-king's pleasure, he did not order her thrown to the crocodiles; the patience with which he humored her unreasonable demands evidently did not strike the Egyptians as unusual, or worthy of comment. (It is interesting to note that the amiable monarch was none other than good King Snefru, whose reputation for benevolence may be well deserved.) The tale of the unfaithful wife reminds us of themes from Boccaccio and Chaucer, but there is no mockery of the cuckolded husband in Egypt. But it is in the story of Djedi that the attractive qualities of the Egyptian conscience are most clearly demonstrated —the reverence paid the wise old man by king and prince, and, most significant of all, Djedi's swift response to the king's command that he use a criminal for his experiment—"Not a man, O sovereign, my lord!"

We are far from the subjects which are ordinarily thought of as the proper study of archaeologists—pottery and tombs, mummies and hieroglyphs. Yet material objects are only the naked bones of history; the ideas, and ideals, of a people are the flesh and blood of their culture, which animate the dry details and give them meaning. When we study the past we try to see the ethics, the doubts, and the hopes that moved men's minds, as well as the products of their hands. And, as we tend to identify ourselves just a bit with the people we study, we like to find signs that our remote ancestors cherished to some extent the same notions which we have accepted as universal moral values. One of the reasons why the ancient Egyptians have interested so many people is that they are a rather amiable set of human beings. We are seldom shocked by their activities, as we are by the cold-blooded ferocity of the Assyrians or the sickening brutality of the Aztecs. We sometimes think of the Egyptians as being preoccupied with death, yet actually the converse is true. They enjoyed life so much that they took every means possible to continue its pleasures after that change which men call dying.

The pyramids of the Fourth Dynasty represent the greatest effort ever made by any people to insure survival through material means. The kings of the Fifth Dynasty were less fortunate, or less prosperous; they lavished much of their substance on their imposing sun temples, which survive today only as crumbling foundations hidden in the sand. Their pyramids were not built of stone throughout, but of rubble and sand held together by stone facings and covered with the usual handsome white limestone. Today these tombs no longer hold even the pyramid form; they are mounds of gravel which look like natural hills upon the great plateaus of Sakkara and of Abusir. The rubble of the superstructure of the pyramid of Unis, last king of the Fifth Dynasty, stands close by the towering steps of Djoser's pyramid—the great beginning and the degeneration of a noble architectural form. However, Unis's pyramid is visited by most tourists to Sakkara because it is the earliest known pyramid to be inscribed with the so-called Pyramid Texts. The white walls of the burial chamber and antechamber are completely covered with incised hieroglyphs painted a pale blue. The ceiling is star-inlaid, and the total effect is quite lovely.

The Pyramid Texts are very ancient. The language is archaic, and the religious beliefs which are described are confused and contradictory, suggesting an accumulation of generations of changing dogma. The Egyptians were broad-minded, and the idea of logical exclusiveness never troubled them. In the same body of texts the dead king is described as occupying *all* of several Afterworlds. He may (rather beautifully) "become one with the imperishable stars," the pole stars which, in this latitude, never set; he may become a *"ba,"* a human-headed bird which flits from tree to tomb; he may journey to the Land of the West or inhabit a lovely Paradise called the Fields of Yaru, located in the northeastern heavens, where the grain grew taller than earthly grain and the dreadful ferryman "Turnface" waited to carry the souls of the just to their reward.

In later times these texts, and the magical protection they

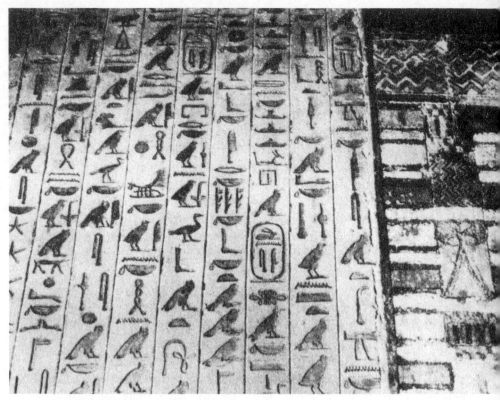

Pyramid Texts. Wall of the burial chamber of the Sakkara pyramid of King Unis, Fifth Dynasty. *Photo by Dr. Josef Vogt.*

provided, were taken over, in a slightly altered form, by the humbler folk, who had them painted inside their wooden coffins. In this stage they are called the Coffin Texts. During the Late Kingdom period, the texts were written on papyrus scrolls, and were changed even more. Today these texts are often lumped together under the general name of *The Book of the Dead*, but in ancient times there were several different collections, such as *The Book of Coming Forth by Day*, referring to the emergence of the soul from the tomb.

The Pyramid Texts are often described as "religious" in nature, yet their primary function was not the affirmation of a faith or a belief. Like the pyramids, they were designed to serve the end

Coffin Texts. Interior of the coffin of the army clerk Ipi-ha-ishutef. *The Oriental Institute, University of Chicago.*

"Book of the Dead." The Judgment, from the papyrus of Queen Maat-kare of the Twenty-First Dynasty, now in the Cairo Museum. Left to right: the Queen; Anubis, the jackal-headed mortuary god; Thoth, the divine scribe, who records the result of the Judgment; the monster who devours the guilty; Osiris enthroned; Isis. On the right pan of the scales, the feather of truth; on the left, the heart of the queen. *Photo from The Metropolitan Museum of Art.*

of survival. The pyramid protected the body of the dead king, and the texts assured his soul of continued life—life as a god, as a ruler of gods, or even as a humble rower in the boat of the gods—but life, at any cost and in any role. In the strictest sense, the Pyramid Texts are magical rather than religious. "What I tell you three times is true," said the Bellman; and, like much of Lewis Carroll, this is more than just a solemn absurdity. It is actually a good expression of one of the basic principles of magic (and that other pseudo science, advertising), in which the Word, spoken or written, can affect actuality. If saying a thing three times makes it true, then saying it more than three times makes it even truer— neither Madison Avenue nor the necromancer's textbooks worries about comparative degrees of absolutes. Repetition is important, but the Word itself has great significance. Primitive peoples know the import of a man's name, and they guard their own with care lest an enemy learn it and use it against its owner. Incantations and "spells" are elements of most magical formulae. The Egyptians, who were known to later ages as great magicians, used written words to produce the real thing in their mortuary activities. In case the regular offerings made to the dead by their posterity were neglected, lists of food and drink could make good the lack. There is a constant harping on the word "living" in all the funerary texts; the dead man lives, he is living, he lives forever and ever. By inscribing the texts which describe the future life, or lives, of the soul in the very chamber where the mummy lay, the magical significance of the Word was made stronger, and the dead man had further assurance of immortality.

It was logical enough that, having considered other means of insuring life everlasting, the Egyptians should have turned their attention to the preservation of the body itself. The air and the soil of Egypt are in themselves excellent preservatives, and it may have been the sight of the naturally mummified bodies of the more ancient dead, baked into leather by the heated sand, that gave the early dynastic Egyptians the idea of helping the process along by artificial means. The development of civilization made artificial aids necessary; bodies laid in the sand need no other means of preservation than the heat and dryness of the medium, but when tombs were built, and the bodies of the dead were shut away from the sun, the processes of decay were unhindered. So we have the development of mummification, and the production of that typically Egyptian object, the mummy, which is inseparably connected with Egypt in the minds of most people despite the fact that mummies are found in other areas and other periods. When I was studying Egyptology, some of my more distant acquaintances thought it the height of humor to chortle, "So, you're studying to be a mummy"—a remark which failed to amuse me even at the first occurrence.

The best description of the process of mummification comes from those helpful Greeks, Herodotus and Diodorus. According to the former, there were three methods, which differed in elaboration and in price. In the cheapest type, the intestines were cleaned out by means of a purge and then the body was placed in natron, either dry or in solution. Natron, a naturally occurring compound of sodium carbonate and sodium bicarbonate, is a dehydrating agent, so its use, in the dry or solid form, would be understandable. But Herodotus says the natron was used in solution, as a bath in which the body was soaked. The evidence of the mummies themselves supports Herodotus to some extent. Quite often most of the epidermis, including the roots of the body hairs, is missing, and in some cases one or more limbs may be absent, having been replaced by sticks. Prolonged soaking—seventy days, according to Herodotus—in a natron bath might produce loosening of the epidermis and even, in extreme cases, dismemberment. However, these phenomena might have been caused by other factors. If the corpse were not sent to the embalmers immediately after death, decomposition might set in and produce both loosened skin and loss of limbs. Modern research supports the idea that dry natron was used.

It is curious that Herodotus specifically mentions certain cases in which embalmment was deliberately postponed. "The wives of men of rank are not given to be embalmed immediately after death, nor indeed are any of the more beautiful and valued women. It is not until they have been dead three or four days that they are carried to the embalmers. This is done to prevent the embalmers having intercourse with them." Modern experts agree that some of the mummies which have come under their examination were in an advanced stage of decomposition before being treated by the embalmers—and that in almost every case this condition applied to women.

The application of natron was the penultimate process in all three types of embalming. In the second type the corpse was injected with oil of cedar before it was placed in the bath; the injection dissolved the stomach and intestines. Modern authorities question the word "cedar," claiming that the substance in question came from a juniper or other coniferous tree; and there is some doubt as to how this "oil" was employed.

The fanciest, and most expensive, method of mummification employed during the New Kingdom involved the removal of the internal organs, except for the heart and kidneys, which are almost always found in place. The brain was drawn out through the nostrils with an iron hook and the viscera were removed through an incision made in the lower abdomen. The internal organs were treated, and placed in four containers called "canopic jars" which were, in turn, placed in a square canopic box. The empty body

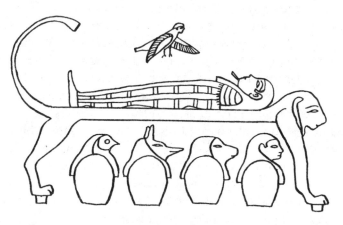

The mummy

It rests on an elaborate bed designed with the fore-and-hind-quarters of a lion; above hovers the *ba*, a human-headed bird which has some aspects in common with our concept of the soul. Beneath are the four canopic jars with lids shaped like the heads of four mortuary gods.

cavity was cleaned and anointed and natron was applied, as in the other two methods. The abdomen was filled with linen packing, or with sawdust. Then the body was washed and treated with oil or precious ointments, and, finally, the wrappings were applied.

The wrappings were of fine linen, torn into strips and wound around limbs and body; sometimes even the fingers and toes were separately wound. The cloth padded out the shriveled body, which had suffered from the desiccating procedures of embalmment. Occasionally, additional pads of linen were inserted to fill out sunken areas, or the external contours of the body, such as a woman's breasts, might be modeled in plaster.

After the mummy was wrapped and placed in the coffin, another ceremony might be performed, consisting of the pouring of a liquid preparation of resin or pitch over the wrappings and coffin. This may have been a kind of anointing, or it may have been intended to preserve the body. Ironically enough, it had the reverse effect. In certain cases the pitch fused the tissues or produced a chemical reaction in which the flesh was consumed.

Yet the greatest threat to the dead man's hope of immortality in the flesh was not putrefaction, but the tomb robber. Mummies were often destroyed by thieves in their search for the jeweled ornaments with which the bodies were adorned. The Egyptians of the Old Kingdom developed a way of dealing with this terrible possibility: they carved statues of themselves which were placed in the tomb and which could, if necessary, assume the vital functions. No man was entirely obliterated if anything of himself remained—his likeness, or even his name, carved on stone.

The kings of the Fifth Dynasty were the first monarchs, so far as we know, to add the carved Pyramid Texts to their varied forms of insurance of life everlasting. This, and the rise of the cult of Re are the most outstanding features of the dynasty. The beautiful painting and sculpture of the preceding dynasty continued during the Fifth, and some of the private tombs of the period are handsomely designed and decorated. The most striking of these tombs is that of the great noble Ti, at Sakkara, which has two great columned halls, a large storechamber, and a portico fine enough for a villa. The interior has some stunning bas-reliefs which show the daily activities of the nobility with grace and humor. Birds

Egyptian hippopotami

After reliefs in the tomb of the noble Ti, at Sakkara

and animals are depicted with particular elegance; there is a scene of hippopotami, wallowing around in the marsh, which is my special favorite. It is hard to imagine a hippopotamus as charming, but these little animals are just that.

The Doors of the South

The Sixth Dynasty began with a king with the rather comical name of Teti, and gathered steam under his son, the competent and powerful Pepi I. Externally, the picture has the same unity and solidarity that we saw under the mighty monarchs of the Fourth Dynasty. Pepi's officials paid him proper homage, carving his picture on the walls of their tombs and bragging about royal favors received. But there is a difference. The tombs of the nobles no longer huddled around the pyramid of their royal master; they were built in the local capitals, which their owners ruled as powerful hereditary princes. We might compare the situation, superficially, to the Feudal Age of Western culture. When a strong king held the throne of Egypt he could control his ambitious under-

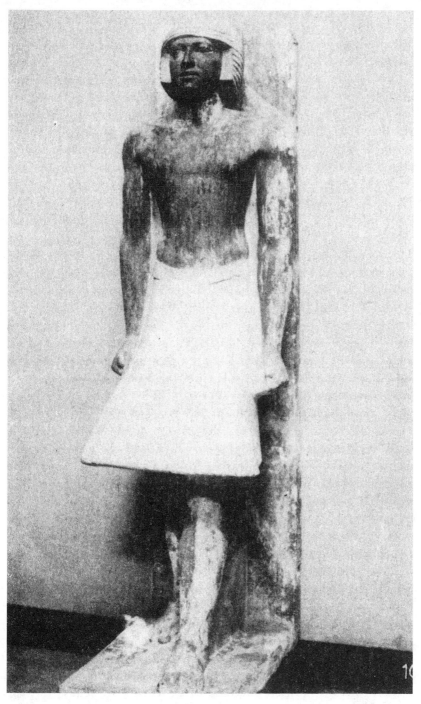

Statue of the nobleman Ti, from his tomb at Sakkara. *The Cairo Museum.*

lings. But when a weak monarch wore the Red and White Crowns —then woe to the throne of Horus!

The most interesting of the local princes were the lords of Elephantine, an island located at the region of modern Aswan. Here ended the land of Egypt and here began Nubia; here also was the first of six cataracts, which interrupt navigation to the south. The granite quarries at Aswan are now a tourist spectacle; they contain the skeleton form of what would have been the tallest obelisk ever erected, if the great spire had ever been cut from its rocky bed. Aswan granite was highly prized for statues and for building; it was brought by barge all the way downriver to Memphis.

The island of Elephantine is in the middle of the river, but the tombs of the men who ruled this frontier post were cut into the western desert cliffs. They look to the south, to Nubia, as the fortresses of the Lords of the Welsh Marches faced the direction from which danger would come. Nubia had long been a source of interest to the adventurous Egyptians. There were expeditions to the area as early as the First Dynasty, and later kings managed to impose a semi-political control. In time, Nubia became an Egyptian province, with Egyptian manners and customs. This occurrence was to have very odd results indeed a few millennia later.

But Elephantine was only the "Door of the South," and beyond that door lay other countries which had even more to offer than did Nubia. From the farther Sudan came ebony, ivory, gold, ostrich feathers; somewhere to the south was the mysterious, half-legendary land of Punt, God's Land, which supplied myrrh and spices and other precious things. The tribes of the region were barbarous and fierce, but for the greater glory of Egypt they must be controlled, if not conquered.

The first of the great barons of the Door of the South was named Uni, whose career began under Teti and continued under Pepi I and his son Mernere. One of his duties was to oversee the working of the granite quarries, but his primary function was to protect the southern boundaries and to keep the region peaceful so that trade could be carried on without hindrance. So well did he accomplish this that he was able to quarry the granite for the royal sarcophagus with "only one warship"! The boast speaks volumes about the pre-Uni situation.

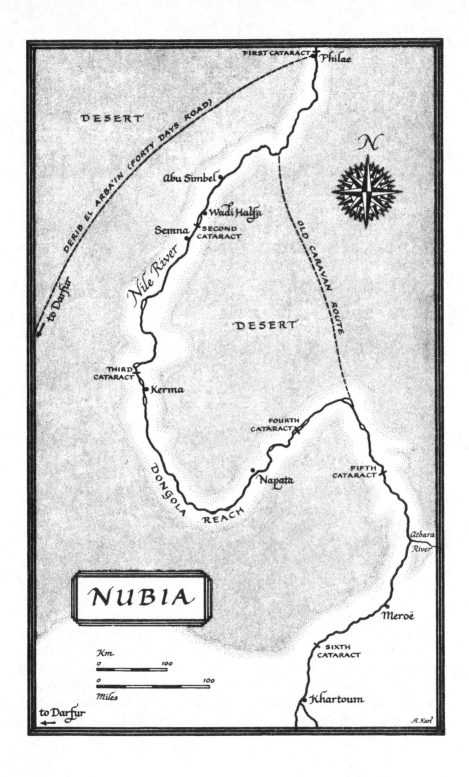

DESERT

FIRST CATARACT — Philae

DERIB EL ARBA'IN (FORTY DAYS ROAD)

to Darfur

N

Abu Simbel

Wadi Halfa

Semna

SECOND
CATARACT

Nile River

OLD CARAVAN ROUTE

DESERT

THIRD
CATARACT

Kerma

FOURTH
CATARACT

Napata

FIFTH
CATARACT

DONGOLA

REACH

Atbara
River

NUBIA

Meroë

Km.

0   100

0   100

Miles

SIXTH
CATARACT

to Darfur

Khartoum

A. Karl

When Uni passed on to his reward he was laid to rest in the tomb he had excavated high in the cliffs, where he left a biographical inscription which does his deeds only justice. He was succeeded by another man called Harkhuf, whose name is even better known. Harkhuf and his colleagues were the first African explorers; two of his associates died far from home, among strange and barbaric peoples, carrying out the king's commands. It is with obvious pride that each adds, after his conventional princely title, the words *Caravan Conductor, who brings the products of the countries to his lord.* After lives of danger and adventure, they came home to die—or were brought back from the distant lands where they had been murdered—and were buried in the tombs above Aswan. On the walls of their tombs these explorers inscribed the record of their deeds, and as we read them we have the feeling that they were not driven into the Unknown by duty alone. They went "because it was there," in the words of a modern representative of the courageous fellowship of which the lords of Elephantine were such notable members.

Harkhuf began exploring when he was only a boy, accompanying his father on a trip to the distant land of Yam. On the second trip he commanded his own men. These trips took seven or eight months, and were major expeditions. After Harkhuf's third trip, the reigning king died and was succeeded by his young half brother, Pepi II, who was a child of only five or six. Harkhuf was confirmed in his post by the little king and his advisers, and went again to the south. His next trip to Yam produced one of the most delightful documents which has come down to us from ancient times. Harkhuf enjoyed it so much that he had it copied on the walls of his tomb. The original, doubtless written on papyrus, was a letter from the king. Harkhuf had brought back all sorts of rich loot from the gold-bearing south, but it was not gold which produced the excited letter from the six-year-old king.

"Thou hast said, in this thy letter," wrote Pepi, "that thou hast brought a dwarf from the land of spirits. Come northward at once to the Court, and bring with thee this dwarf, alive, sound and well! When he comes down with thee into the vessel, appoint trustworthy people who shall be beside him on each side of the vessel; take care lest he fall into the water. When he sleeps at night, appoint trustworthy people who shall sleep beside him in his tent—inspect ten times a night! For my Majesty desires to see this dwarf more than the products of Sinai and Punt!"

This was the high point of Harkhuf's life, although we never learn exactly what royal reward was given him for the gift the king prized so highly.

Harkhuf was not the only noble to venture his life in inner Africa. Another governor of the south, named Sebni, tells of his trip upriver on a more tragic errand. His father had been killed by the wild tribes of the Second Cataract area. When Sebni got the news he gathered his men and marched south, on vengeance bound. He dealt with the killers, collected his father's body, and brought it back to Elephantine. He was met at the border by messengers of the king, who had sent his own corps of embalmers, priests and mourners, equipped with all the necessities for burial. When he had paid his last respects to his father, Sebni went north to thank the king—and to deliver the goods his father had collected. Personal sorrow had not made him forget his duty.

Other names deserve mention—Eneenkhet, the naval commander, slain by the Bedouin on the shores of the Red Sea; Pepinakht, the prince of Elephantine, who rescued the commander's body and brought it back to Egypt. Men like Pepinakht did not risk their necks for the sake of a *beau geste*. If a man's body was destroyed he died a second time, finally and forever; there was no eternal life for a soul which had no mortal tenement to which it might return for nourishment.

The adventures of Harkhuf bring to mind another of the varied subjects which are the concern of the Egyptologist. Remember the nebulous knowledge we have of the predynastic period; it would seem that at this point in history, with the aid of inscriptional material, we ought to be able to solve all our problems. We know a great deal about the lords of Elephantine— their names, their business, the products they sought, and even where they were going. To the land of Yam.

There lies the rub. Where on earth is the land of Yam? Or, more precisely, where *was* it? Some archaeologists like to play with words; they produce long articles about the derivations and meanings and pronunciation of Egyptian nouns. Others like numbers;

from them we get thick volumes on such subjects as chronology or Egyptian science. Then there are the people who prefer maps. Most of us number map addicts among our acquaintances; they can pass an evening quite contentedly with no more vivacious volume than an atlas. If they were Egyptologists, they would probably be arguing about Yam.

The details of mileage and distance so dear to modern travelers did not interest Harkhuf and his friends, and there was no reason why they should specify the location of the countries they visited when everybody who would read their autobiographies knew quite well where they had been. The divine gods certainly knew, and it is likely that all the literate inhabitants of Elephantine did too. The only figure given by Harkhuf is the length of time a trip to and from Yam took—about seven months. Since we do not know how long he stayed there, nor how fast he traveled, nor even in what direction he went (except that it was generally "south"), this figure is obviously not much help. But do not delude yourselves. Egyptologists have tried to use it, as they use every scrap of evidence they can get their hands on. Harkhuf gives the Egyptian names of the areas through which he passed on his way to Yam; but since the location of these places is also uncertain, this piece of information is equally indecisive.

Most Egyptologists have assumed that Yam lies on the Nile, but Harkhuf never actually says so. One interesting omission in his story may provide a clue—Harkhuf does not mention the use of boats. Since the Nile is easily navigable up to the Second Cataract, it is strange that he did not go by water if Yam is to be located in that area. Yet some archaeologists place Yam *above* the Second Cataract.

If we study our map, we can see other reasons which make this location of Yam unreasonable. In the first place, we know that as early as the First Dynasty the kings of Egypt had made military excursions into this very region. By the Sixth Dynasty the area must have been traversed many times by Egyptian troops and traders; a journey there could not have been the momentous and arduous enterprise that Harkhuf's trip to Yam surely was. Nor could it have taken seven months, unless he went by way of Timbuktu.

The most daring suggestion to date has come from A. J. Arkell, an authority on the Sudan and its archaeology. As an Egyptologist he is familiar with the inscriptions; as a former Commissioner of the Sudan he knews the area as few Egyptologists can claim to do. He gives Harkhuf credit for real enterprise, for he would locate Yam in the region of modern Darfur, which is far to the west of the Nile at about the latitude of the Sixth Cataract.

There is an old caravan route leading from the Nile, near Elephantine, to the Darfur region, which has been used at least since Medieval times. Arkell thinks it was used much earlier, and that Harkhuf was one of the pioneers of the route. Today it is an agonizing journey through arid regions which would appall most travelers. Yet it is still being made by camel and donkey caravans. Arkell points out that the region was less arid in ancient times, and adds that even today the trip could be made with 300 donkeys, 100 carrying goods for trade, 100 carrying forage, and 100 carrying water. Harkhuf had 300 donkeys on at least one of his trips.

Arkell's most ingenious bits of reasoning concern the names of the areas through which Harkhuf passed on his way to Yam. He has identified some of them with modern tribes who live between Darfur and the Nile, though he does not claim that these people are necessarily living today where they did in ancient times. Another point is that the ancient caravan route was probably the most famous route by which ivory came into Egypt from the south. And Harkhuf says, in one section, "I set forth upon the Ivory Road."

I find Arkell's theory perfectly fascinating. It has been accepted by some scholars, not by all—which can be said about almost every "factual" statement one might make concerning ancient Egypt. Since the location of Yam is one of those subjects that worries me almost as much as the problem of Hetepheres, I had hoped, a few years back, that we might find some clues during the extensive survey of Nubia that accompanied the construction of the second Aswan Dam. The news of the dam prompted a flurry of activity in Nubia, whose sites, it was believed, would be threatened by rising water. The temple of Abu Simbel, built by Ramses II, was the most publicized of the endangered temples; a truly monumental project cut it free of the rock in which it had been built and raised it high atop the cliffs, to a new position. But the publicity given Abu Simbel overshadowed a far more impressive accomplishment—the wholehearted, worldwide response to an appeal by UNESCO for aid in saving the less spectacular Nubian remains. Over twenty nations, from Argentina to Yugoslavia, sent teams to work in Nubia. There was a certain amount of bickering, naturally. But as an example of what can be accomplished when people turn their energies to preserving instead of destroying, the Nubian campaign was an inspiration. Many smaller temples were dismantled and moved, dozens of cemeteries, town sites, temples and churches were excavated and recorded.

However, they didn't find out where Yam was located.

The little boy who wrote with such rapture about a dwarf to play with could not have been much of an administrator at first. The country was controlled by Pepi II's mother and her brother Djau, prince of Thinis. But the fiction of divine rule was maintained; the bronzed, hard-bitten explorer-counts of Elephantine, and the proud princes of other nomes, reported to their child-king and received his orders with becoming humility.

Prince Djau was not a wicked uncle. He administered the kingdom ably, and cherished his small nephew with such care that Pepi II reached his majority and lived on . . . and on . . . and on! He ruled for over ninety years, the longest reign attributed to a king of Egypt or any other country. Hence he must have reached the century mark, or near it, before he died.

Pepi might have said, with far more truth than Louis XV, "After us, the deluge." For when he died, the whole vigorous, complex, coherent structure of the united kingdom of Egypt fell in ruins, and a time of anarchy ensued. We have noted the beginning of the trend; a strong ruler cannot permit equally strong subordinates, and even at the beginning of Pepi's reign his barons had taken unto themselves a degree of independence which contrasted ironically with the lip service paid to the power of the god-king. During the years of Pepi's young manhood, the central power was in good hands. But for the last thirty or forty years of his reign, the hands grew more and more palsied with age.

The last kings of the Sixth Dynasty are little known. The ultimate ruler of the dynasty was a woman; any man, including Manetho, could tell you that this was a bad sign. If it were not for a reference to this lady, whose name was Nitokris, in the Turin Papyrus, I would be inclined to suspect her of being as apocryphal as are the stories the Greeks collected about her. "She was the noblest and loveliest of the women of her time, of fair complexion, the builder of the Third Pyramid," said Manetho romantically. Herodotus adds a melodramatic story which tells how she avenged the murder of her brother by inviting the villains to a banquet and then flooding the dining room; she followed up her watery revenge by committing suicide. No comment is necessary upon the historical validity of either story.

Nitokris is called the builder of the Third Pyramid, but we know that this particular monument at Giza was the tomb of Menkaure. However, there is another structure at the same site which may have some bearing on the problem. It is a mastaba, but of such huge proportions that it is sometimes called the Fourth Pyramid; and it was built by a woman. Unfortunately for Manetho, this woman belongs to the Fourth Dynasty instead of the Sixth, and her name was Khentkaus. It would take a wild leap of the imagination to derive the Greek form *Nitokris* from this Egyptian name. We must also consider another Fourth Dynasty queen named Hetepheres II, granddaughter of the lady of the same name whose empty sarcophagus was found by Reisner. The second Hetepheres built a tomb for her daughter, in which the color of the original reliefs has been preserved to a remarkable degree; here Hetepheres II is shown with her hair painted yellow and crossed by fine red lines.

Egyptologists, who are just as imaginative as the next man, had a wonderful time with the redheaded queen Hetepheres. Since blondes are fairly uncommon in Egypt, they proposed that Hetepheres or one of her ancestors came from the Libyan people of north Africa, who lived not far from the Delta in the eastern desert. They suggested that the legends of Nitokris might represent a composite from a lot of different sources: a real Sixth Dynasty queen of that name, the "pyramid-builder" Khentkaus of the Fourth Dynasty, and the redheaded Hetepheres, whose memory could survive in the "fair complexion" description of Manetho.

Nitokris may be a compound, or even a man, but the Titian-haired queen is no longer fact. A friend of mine once mentioned the Hetepheres II story to an anthropologist acquaintance, and was taken aback when the latter gentleman exploded. There were, he said, no fair-haired Libyans; there were no fair-haired people in north Africa at all. Yes, he knew that Egyptologists had been talking about them for years, everyone he met told him the story of Hetepheres, and he contradicted it every time; but a good story seemed to have better survival value than the truth. (There is some justice in this claim.) Of late, Egyptologists have had to discard the redhead for other reasons. Several Fourth Dynasty queens are depicted wearing headdresses of the same shape as the wig or hair of Hetepheres. The color has, in all the other cases, disappeared, but it seems more probable that what Hetepheres had on her head was a yellow wig or kerchief rather than hair. The red lines? They are the practice lines of the artist, known from hundreds of other examples, which were never erased.

III
The Good Shepherd

Senusert

Despair and Deliverance

WHEN we look back over the first six dynasties we look across ten centuries of history. We cannot avoid the symbol of the pyramid, which towers above the desert as the culture of the Pyramid Age towered above the mud huts of the barbarians of prehistoric Egypt. However much we may frown upon autocracy, we cannot see the collapse of a civilization as fertile as that of Egypt under the Old Kingdom without regret—regret not only for the artistic and intellectual enterprises that came to an end, but for the suffering which social chaos must have brought to the people who lived through it.

"The land spins around like a potter's wheel; noble ladies are gleaners, and nobles are in the workhouse, but he who never slept on so much as a plank is now the owner of a bed; he who never wove for himself is the owner of fine linen."

To the Egyptian, the upheaval of the sacrosanct social order would have been bad enough. But the trouble went beyond that.

"I show thee the son as a foe, the brother as an enemy, and a man killing his own father. The wild beasts of the desert will drink at the rivers of Egypt and be at their ease. Men will take up weapons of warfare, so that the land lives in confusion."

99

These quotations come from two great laments composed by prophets named Ipuwer and Neferti. Like the Old Testament prophets, and in similar language, these men came before the king and cried woe upon the land of Egypt. There is a certain artificiality in the language and the structure of both compositions. It is unlikely that either was composed under the stress and agony of the events they describe, and in fact we know that one was intended as a compliment to a later king, who brought order out of the chaos, according to the contents. But the chaos was real enough. The country broke up into small states which warred against one another. Violence of all sorts was rife, and the dead and the living alike were viciously attacked by thieves.

Naturally the Egyptians looked around for a scapegoat, and they do not fail to mention the presence of intruding Asiatics. But these people always trickled down into the fertile Nile valley when they could get past the border guards. They were the result of the collapse, not the cause. The trouble lay within the state itself, and arose from the failure of centralized government.

Tragedy usually has an effect upon the character of an individual, for good or ill, and it must have had an effect on Egypt. I personally view with suspicion most attempts to characterize a national "ethos" or spirit—if such a thing can be said to exist at all. Yet the written documents from this troubled period differ profoundly from the inscriptions of the stable eras that preceded it; the spectacle of a mere wise man administering a verbal drubbing to the god-king would have left a Fourth Dynasty Egyptian speechless with shock. The disillusionment and vigorous criticism of the prophetic texts represent only one of the ways in which the men of this unhappy age expressed their reaction to catastrophe. One of the most curious texts of the period is a long poem in which a man debates with his soul the problem of suicide. Life has become unbearable; "the slings and arrows of outrageous fortune" have overwhelmed the poet and only death seems sweet. At first his soul seeks to dissuade him, pointing out, as does the prince of Denmark, that death may hold terrors greater than any evil of life. But at the end, the arguments of the misanthrope prevail; his soul agrees to accompany him wherever he may go, even into the shadows. Death, then, is one solution to the pain and disillusionment of the time of troubles. Here, expressed with the concise eloquence of true poetry, is another:

> The gods who lived formerly rested in their pyramids;
> The beatified dead also, buried in their pyramids, and they
>   who built houses,
> Their places are no more.
>
> I have heard the words of Imhotep and Hordedef
> With whose discourses men speak so much;
> What are their places now?
> Their walls are broken apart and their places are no more,
> As though they had never been.

See how the terrifying conclusion builds up—the vanity of temporal power is as futile as the vanity of intellectual attainment; not even their wisdom can save the famous sages of the past from oblivion. The conclusion? Eat, drink, and be merry. . . .

The minstrels who entertained the nobleman at his feasts sang this song; some of the listeners inscribed the words upon the walls of their tombs, where they became a statement of belief. Some of the nobles copied another harper's song, which expresses a different approach to life and death.

> I have heard those songs that are in the ancient tombs,
> And what they tell
> Extolling life on earth and belittling the region of the dead.
> Wherefore do they thus, concerning the land of eternity,
> The just and the fair,
> Which has no terrors?
> Wrangling is its abhorrence; no man there girds himself
>   against his fellow.
> It is a land against which none can rebel.
> All our kinsfolk rest within it, since the earliest day of time;
> The offspring of millions are come hither, every one.
> For none may tarry in the land of Egypt,
> None there is who has not passed yonder.
>
> The span of earthly things is as a dream;
> But a fair welcome is given him who has reached the West.

Either of these lovely songs would strike a strange note in a noble's tomb of the Old Kingdom, which vigorously expressed the material and naïve expectations of life to come. In the Fourth Dynasty the individual boasts of his deeds and his promotions. "I was greatly praised on account of it; never had the like been done by any noble before me." The biographical inscriptions of the First Intermediate Period still brag about great deeds. "I rescued my city," says one nobleman pointedly, "from the terrors of the royal house." (Well, really!—as Khufu might have said.) But there is a new emphasis in the texts of this period, an almost anxious affirmation of other deeds and other accomplishments which contrasts sharply with the pride in advancement or in wealth.

"I gave bread to the hungry, water to the thirsty, and clothing to the naked. I buried the aged. I was a father to the orphan, a husband to the widow. I did no wrongdoing against the people; it is what the god hates. I have rendered justice, which the king desired."

This is a composite, from many incriptions, of claims to virtue which characterize this period. It is superfluous, and needlessly cynical, to point out that some of the men who made these claims may have been sinners of the deepest dye. What is significant is the fact that the claims were made, and had to be made. The quest for immortality must be almost as old as man himself. Even the ape-faced Neanderthal hunters buried their dead with the tools they would need in another life and with food to supply them on that longest of journeys. As society became more complex, and life more pleasant and desirable, the human animal sought ever more means to ensure a continuance of pleasure—elaborate tombs, magical supplies of food and comforts, complex methods of preserving the body, gold and jewels and boasts of high office. But he could never be sure. He could never know for certain, that his gold was the proper medium of exchange in Paradise. The social upheaval and physical destruction of the First Intermediate Period gave the doubts of the Egyptian greater poignancy. So, during this time, along with cynicism and hedonism, we see an attempt to substitute other values for the ones that had proved inadequate—values which, being invisible and intangible, were not susceptible to decay.

There are vague references to a judgment of the dead as early as the Pyramid Texts, but we do not get a clear picture of the concept until after the collapse of the Old Kingdom. The judge is Re, the sun-god; and the creature that stands before the bar of justice is the human soul. "Thy fault will be expelled and thy guilt will be wiped out, by the weighing of the scales on the day of reckoning characters; and it will be permitted that thou join with those who are in the sun-bark." The image of the scales of justice requires no commentary. In the balances were weighed the sins and the virtues of the dead man; and only good deeds could insure eternal life.

The questions asked by the men of this troubled age so far in the past are not unique to their times, nor peculiar to their culture. They are the universal questions, asked by all men who have ever pondered the tragedy of life and the mystery of death. Never before nor after, perhaps, until the Hebrew prophets began their long debate with God, did men express the questions so clearly nor with such eloquence as did the Egyptians of the First Intermediate Period. With all due deference to the law of objectivity in history, I cannot help but feel that in the questions, and in the answers they found to them, the Egyptians achieved the high point of their spiritual and philosophical development.

For two generations after the end of the Sixth Dynasty we know very little about actual events. The clouds of dust that arose from the collapse of that mighty edifice, the Old Kingdom, obscure events and people; out of the fog come only the wailing voices of the prophets, telling of disaster. Manetho lists a Seventh and an Eighth Dynasty, but research indicates that they could only have lasted for about a quarter of a century, and the ephemeral "kings" have left almost no contemporary records. The names and titles of local princes appear instead, in the tombs and in the quarries.

Around 2160 B.C. the clouds thin out, in one area at least. That area was the Fayum, the great oasis-lake just south of the Delta. Here, in the city of Herakleopolis, a powerful family seized control and brought order to its own territory. The princes of

Herakleopolis soon made alliance with another noble house ruling in Assiut, in Middle Egypt. Between the two, a sizable portion of the country was brought under control, and the Assiut rulers reported: "Every official was at his post, there was no one fighting. The child was not smitten beside his mother, nor the citizen beside his wife."

If true, these achievements must have afforded considerable relief to the oppressed people, and the name of the great prince of Herakleopolis, Akhtoy, must have been gratefully praised. Akhtoy's successors retained his name, and the only way we can tell one from another is by means of their alternative appellations. Manetho gives them two dynasties, the Ninth and Tenth. Of the first dozen or so of these Herakleopolitan kings we know very little, but by the middle of the Tenth Dynasty we are on firmer ground. The third king of this dynasty, Wahkare Akhtoy the Third, was a good ruler, and he felt himself qualified to give advice to his son, who would succeed him on the throne. *The Instructions for King Merikare* is the title of the text, one of the best known of all Egyptian literary works. It is one of a general type of which the Egyptians were very fond; we call it "wisdom literature," and it consists of helpful hints to youth from an older, more worldy-wise individual.

Akhtoy was a king, so his precepts are intended for a youth who will hold the responsibilities of the highest office. There are none of the prosaic comments upon manners which amuse us in some of the other teachings, written for and by commoners. "If thou art one of those sitting at the table of one greater than thou, take what he may give when it is set before thy nose. Laugh after he laughs, and this will be very pleasing to his heart."

So runs the advice of Ptahhotep, a Fifth Dynasty vizier. There is none of this trivia in the Merikare text. Akhtoy begins with some sound precepts as to character: "Be not evil; patience is good. Be a craftsman in speech, for the tongue is a sword to a man and speech is more valorous than fighting." After some weighty comments on statescraft and the handling of officials, the royal author rises to genuine heights of feeling and expression when he speaks of the judging of the heart in the West, the land of the dead.

The council which judges the deficient—thou knowest that they are not lenient on that day of judging the miserable. A man remains over after death, and his deeds are placed beside him in heaps. Existence yonder is for eternity; and he who complains of it is a fool. But as for him who reaches it without wrongdoing, he shall exist yonder like a god, stepping out freely like the Lords of Eternity. More acceptable is the character of one upright of heart than the ox of the evildoer.

Unfortunately for Merikare, his father was a better poet than he was a politician. The older king does mention the domestic situation, warning his son about the wretched Asiatics of the north and assuring him that "it is well with thee with the Southern Region." That statement comes into the category of Famous Last Words. We cannot blame the king because he was unable to predict the future, but he might have remembered the past. Once before there had come a conqueror, stepping with long strides down the Nile to unify the Two Lands. He had come from the south.

This is one of those cases which almost lead us to suspect that history can repeat itself. For three millennia the kingdom of the Nile would exist, its unity broken from time to time by internal strife and by foreign invasion. And from the beginning, even with Menes the Unifier, the force of renewed cohesion would come from the south. Why? We do not know. In fact, if we were trying to predict from which area the conqueror would originate, we would in most cases choose the north. The success of Upper Egypt at the beginning of the dynasties, under Menes, is inexplicable if the north was really more sophisticated, more highly developed. The same is true of the situation after the first great breakdown at the end of the Old Kingdom. Herakleopolis during the Tenth Dynasty was the most effective of all the city-states of the divided country, and she seemed well on the way to leading the reunification. In art and in military power she was ahead of her contemporaries; the literature she produced is of an astonishingly high quality. Yet—once again—the conqueror came from the south.

Four hundred and fifty miles south of Memphis the frowning cliffs retreat from the river edge, leaving a broad and fruitful plain. At the end of the Old Kingdom there were a few small settlements in this plain. The villagers worshiped Montu, a war-god—a suggestive choice, in view of what followed. There may also have been a temple—a small and unimpressive one—to a petty local godling, Amon, a form of the fertility god Min. From these scrappy beginnings came a phenomenon—Thebes of the Hundred Gates and her patron god, Amon-Re.

The rise of Thebes can be traced back to about 2250 B.C., at which time a lady named Ikui in one of the villages of the Theban plain had the happy fortune to be blessed with a son whom she called Intef. He was a prince and a count, and his immediate descendants held the same titles.

A century or so after the birth of Intef, son of Ikui, the insidious air of the southland inflamed the ambitions of one of his descendants. The Theban princes had not been sitting supinely in their local capital while the Herakleopolitans expanded their influence; they had been engaging in a little expansion, too, and they soon extended their control as far south as the First Cataract. Prince Mentuhotep declared his independence of the kings of Herakleopolis, but it was not until the reign of his younger son, Intef II, that the rivalry flared into bloody conflict. Wahankh Intef drove the Herakleopolitans north. A stela describing his prowess from Wahankh's tomb at Thebes, is mentioned in a Twentieth Dynasty papyrus which records the results of an inspection of the royal tombs. Depredations among the tombs had grown increasingly bold, and the investigating committee reported that Intef's pyramid, which must have been a small affair of brick, had been "removed"—a pleasant verb—but that the stela was still in place, and that "the figure of the king stands on this stela with his hound named Behek between his feet." Three thousand years after the inspection, in A.D. 1860, Mariette, then Inspector of Antiquities, found the lower part of the stela, still intact. He left it there (one can almost hear Petrie's remarks on this negligence) and the inevitable happened. When Mariette's successor, Maspero, ran across the stela again in 1882, it was in fragments. The pieces were finally collected and brought to the Cairo Museum. The king was a true lover of caninity; he had not one but five of his favorite hounds shown on his stela so that they could enter the Western paradise with him.

A truce followed the first stage of the war. Then, in 2060 B.C., a new man came to the throne of the southern city. His name was Mentuhotep, and he was the greatest warrior of his warlike line. Within twenty years he conquered the rest of Egypt. His opposite number in Herakleopolis was Merikare, who found his father's philosophy small comfort in defeat.

We would certainly like to have a contemporary account of this war, but none has been found. There is indirect evidence of a unique kind bearing on the last great battle, the siege of Herakleopolis. This evidence was discovered by H. E. Winlock, working at Deir el Bahri for the Metropolitan Museum of New York.

Deir el Bahri is part of the great west Theban necropolis area which includes such marvels as the Valley of the Kings, a large group of nobles' tombs of the New Kingdom, and the huge mortuary temples of the Ramses. At Deir el Bahri itself is the beautiful temple of Queen Hatshepsut, undoubtedly the finest and most graceful piece of architecture in all of Egypt. There was an earlier temple at the same site, built by the conquering Mentuhotep. Winlock deserves the credit for the excavation of this temple, which was in very poor condition. But it must have been an impressive sight when it was built. A walled avenue of approach led from the green cultivated land to a huge shield-shaped court in front of a pillared temple which was surmounted by a small pyramid. The king laid out his tomb under this monument, and he buried his family in other tombs nearby. Winlock found some twenty-odd graves in the temple itself, including the burial place of Mentuhotep's chief queen.

But the most interesting tomb of all was not that of a courtier or royal lady. Built in a place of honor, near the tomb of the king himself, this grave contained a mass burial of sixty soldiers, with their weapons beside them. They were commoners; we do not even know their names. From the nature of their injuries, Winlock deduced that they had been slain in an attack on a castle or fortified place. Some had died at once. Others, wounded by the defenders on the walls, had been left behind when their comrades retreated before an assault of the besieged garrison. The assault being temporarily successful, the wounded men were "picked up by their bushy hair" and clubbed to death by the defenders. Their bodies lay upon the field long enough to be mutilated by carrion birds; then a final attack on the castle gave victory to their comrades, who took up the battered bodies of the slain and gave them burial.

It is a grim, and surprisingly vivid, picture to have been recreated from a group of unidentified mummies. But the most interesting feature is that Mentuhotep honored these Unknown Soldiers by burying them near his own tomb, in a proximity usually reserved for royalty or for high nobles. No less a battle than the final siege of the enemy capital, says Winlock, could have merited such favor. I like his deduction, not only because it is reasonable, but because it is so romantic. However, some scholars believe the men were killed during a battle in Nubia. If the Unknown Soldiers did die at Herakleopolis, one can only wonder at the scant numbers—only sixty men lost their lives in the decisive battle of a great war! These men might have been selected from the slain because of unusual bravery; but we must remember that war was a less efficient killer in ancient times than it is today.

These men went into battle unprotected except for the bushy hair Winlock mentions. The carefully cultivated mop atop their skulls might have been some help against clubs or maces, which were often of no harder substance than wood. Egyptian soldiers of this period also used axes and daggers. The boomerangs which have been found were probably used for hunting rather than war; we have both right- and left-handed models, and one which was tested performed exactly as a boomerang is supposed to perform. The most common weapon was the simple bow, with arrows tipped with flint or ebony—so unsophisticated in the art of war were the pre-Empire Egyptians that they did not usually use even copper arrowheads. The ones they used could kill a man just as dead as a metal point could; one of the slain soldiers had been hit in the back by an arrow which stood out eight inches in front of his body.

We know of the equipment of soldiers of this period from two sources—the burials of the veterans, and the models of soldier bodyguards found in tombs. The most attractive example of the latter comes from Assiut, and consists of two companies of some forty men each. They are wonderful models, and would drive a boy-child wild with covetousness. The men of one group are painted red-brown, the standard body color for Egyptian men, and they carry tall spears and shields painted with various insignias. The other company is black—Nubian auxiliaries, evidently—and its weapon is the bow, which is carried in one hand, with a fistful of arrows in the other. The individual figures are relatively crude, but the craftsman has caught the martial bearing and determined stride of the fighting man; Count Mesehti of Assiut could have started his journey through the unknown dangers of the Afterworld feeling secure, with such soldiers to protect him. They are lovely warriors, and they are now in the Cairo Museum; if I thought I could burgle that admirable institution with impunity, I would certainly load them onto my truck.

This is the time of tomb models. Americans are fortunate in that they do not have to go to Cairo to see some of the best, which come from the Eleventh Dynasty Theban tomb of the Chancellor Meketre. The Metropolitan Museum, which conducted the excavations, was allowed to keep most of them. They reproduce, in faithful miniature, the estate of a wealthy nobleman. The estate was almost a small village, containing numerous shops or workhouses in which various specialized activities were carried on. In the Met models one can see the little serfs and craftsmen working away, some in the brewery-bakery (bread and beer went through the same initial process of fermentation), some in the butcher shop, where kicking cattle are given the *coup de grâce*, others in the stable and the weaver's shop. A nobleman had to have a regular fleet of boats, so the tomb models included reproductions of several types, including the last bark of all—the barge of the dead upon which, gilded and stiff with resinous oils, the mummy of the noble lord made pilgrimage to Abydos, the home of Osiris. The journey may have been purely symbolic; but with the model in his tomb the noble could claim that he had performed this useful ritual act.

So skillfully made are these little models that we view them

Model soldiers from a First Intermediate Period tomb at Assiut, now in the Cairo Museum. Egyptian spearmen. *Photo from Dr. S. H. Horn.*

with the delight we would feel for elaborate toys. Of course they were more than toys to their owners. The model symbolized the actuality, and the presence of the miniatures in the tomb assured its owner that the real thing would be supplied him in the next world. The models are equivalents of the paintings on the walls of the tomb or the written lists of offerings.

We have a good deal of Eleventh Dynasty tomb material, but the greatest tomb of them all was empty. The alabaster sarcophagus of Mentuhotep was found in his burial chamber under his temple, but the crafty thieves of ancient Thebes had found it long before. Nor was Mentuhotep's mummy among the royal bodies reburied by the priests of the late Empire. Presumably it was destroyed by the thieves.

Mentuhotep ruled for some fifty years, and his son was a middle-aged man when he came to the throne. The records of this king are records of peace; the old struggle with Herakleopolis was evidently finished. He was succeeded by another Mentuhotep.

Nubian bowmen, from the same tomb. *Photo from Dr. S. H. Horn.*

The most interesting fact about this king, whom we usually call by his Horus name of Nebtawi, is not how he gained the throne, but how he lost it.

The inscriptions of the Wadi el Hammamat quarries begin in the Old Kingdom. The quarries lie along the shortest route from the Nile to the Red Sea, which leaves the river at the great eastward bend just below Thebes, and many of the expeditions that visited them, on their way to the sea or in search of stone, left inscriptions there. King Nebtawi sent an expedition to Hammamat to get stone for his sarcophagus, and the commander of the troop had a long inscription carved on the rock, which told of a marvel that there befell them. A gazelle, great with young, came bounding across the desert and stopped to deliver upon the very stone that had been selected for the lid of the sarcophagus. The gratified gentlemen of the expedition repaid the gazelle by cutting her throat. The inscription does not mention what became of the baby gazelles.

The name of Nebtawi's commander was Amenemhat. He accomplished his task efficiently, bringing back his force without losing so much as an ass. What intrigues us about the man, though, is not his talent as a servant of the king, but the fact that he did not remain a servant long. Within a few years after his return he finished the job he had begun by putting the king's body inside the sarcophagus whose construction he had supervised, and then taking the throne of Egypt for himself.

Binder of the Two Lands

Let us admit at once that there is no evidence that Amenemhat shoved the old king over the threshold of eternity. He was no doubt a usurper, but he was qualified for kingship by talent if not by blood. He was regarded as the founder of the Twelfth Dynasty, and he sired a long line of Amenemhats and Senuserts, who restored the glory of Egypt under the so-called Middle Kingdom.

One of the first acts of the new ruler was to move his capital northward. Menes had done the same thing, perhaps for the same reason: it was easier to control the princes of the Delta and northern Egypt from there. The Twelfth Dynasty capital was not at Memphis, although this city continued to be important; it was just north of the road into the Fayum, and was called It-tawi, "Binder of the Two Lands." Egyptian names were appropriate and not particularly esoteric.

Amenemhat's first job was restoring proper order in Egypt. The cyclonic upheaval of the First Intermediate Period had left a lot of debris in its wake, and the independent princelings needed more than the few years of the Eleventh Dynasty to teach them their place. It did not take Amenemhat long to regulate internal affairs to his satisfaction, and then he could turn his mind to other things. One project he began was the official conquest of Nubia. He also started a new series of pyramids, which are poor objects indeed compared to the splendors of Giza. They cluster around the old capital of It-tawi, at three cemeteries now known as Lisht, Hawara, and Lahun, and at the site of Dahshur, near Snefru's big pyramids. Amenemhat I's pyramid was of limestone. His quarries were not in the hills of Cairo, but in the older monuments of Giza and Sakkara. The pyramid is badly ruined, so we can see that the internal blocks include sculptured stones from the valley temples of Khufu and Khafre, among other sources. Some archaeologists have suggested that this pyramid be dismantled; as it stands it is not worth much, and if we could get at the core blocks, all from Old Kingdom temples and tombs, we might learn a great deal.

Amenemhat had time to finish his pyramid and temples, but he had no time to spare. Perhaps he had a premonition of what was to come, for during his last years of rule he made his son, Senusert I, co-regent. This joint kingship was a common and practical procedure, but it has confused chronology considerably. Each king dated events by his own years of reign, and only rarely, when we have an inscription that gives simultaneous year dates for both kings, can we be sure how long the co-regency lasted, or even whether a co-regency existed at all.

Thirty years after he had seized power, Amenemhat sent his son off on a campaign to "chastise" (a favorite Egyptian word) the Libyans of the western desert. While the younger king was gone, disaster struck. Probably it was planned to take advantage of the absence of the younger, more virile ruler; Amenemhat was getting old. It is unlikely that a conspiracy aimed at his life could have been formed without his knowledge during his palmier days.

Entering the royal bedchamber in the dead of night, the conspirators fell upon the king as he lay helpless and half-asleep. Although he fought for his life, hand to hand against the grim shadows in the night, he succumbed at last to the daggers of his foes. But corruption had not attacked the entire court. Certain loyalists sent swift messengers to Senusert, now sole king of Egypt. He had already accomplished the purpose of the campaign and was on his way home. The news reached him in the evening, as he made camp somewhere in the desert. Swearing the messenger to silence, the young king waited until dark had fallen and then set out with all speed for It-tawi. He reached the royal residence so soon and so unexpectedly that he was able to nip the conspiracy in the bud and ascend his throne without further difficulty. Undoubtedly his prompt and decisive action had saved the day for the royal house.

This story is known to us, not from historical documents but from two literary texts. The one that tells of the assassination is called *The Teaching of Amenemhat*, and purports to be a series of admonitions from the king to his son. There is bitterness in Amenemhat's words; he gave to the beggar and nourished the orphan, but those whom he trusted rose against him and those to whom he gave his hand came by night to murder him. "Fill not thy heart with a brother," he concludes. "Know not a friend, nor make for thyself intimates. When thou sleepest, guard thine own heart thyself, for a man has no adherents on the day of evil."

To us it may seem somewhat startling that this discourse is written in the first person, by the murdered king; and it has led some scholars to believe that Amenemhat was not killed by the conspirators, but lived on to write his admonitions. However, poetic license allows a voice from the tomb even in our own literature. The death of the king by assassination fits in with the second half of the story, for it is unlikely that, if Amenemhat had died peacefully in his bed, his son would have received the news with such alarm, or hurried away from his army to take possession of the throne unless that throne had been threatened.

The dramatic night march of Senusert is told in one of the most famous of all Egyptian literary works, *The Story of Sinuhe*. Sir Alan Gardiner, the doyen of Egyptian philology, considered this a tale which should rank as a world classic, and he quoted a letter from a man whose judgment carries considerable weight on such matters:

> DEAR MR. GARDINER:
> Thank you ever so much for the book of Egyptian literature, and I quite agree with you as to your estimate of the tale you specially admire.
>
> Very truly yours,
> RUDYARD KIPLING

At the beginning of the tale we find Sinuhe, the overseer of the king in the land of the Asiatics, taking his ease near the royal tent as the army makes camp on its way back from the war with the Libyans. He saw the messengers from Thebes arrive, and heard them speak to Senusert. The results were electric. "My heart was troubled," Sinuhe admits. "My arms fell away from my body, trembling fell upon all my limbs."

Such bodily enfeeblement might be due to shock—very proper when hearing of the death of one's king. But Sinuhe's next move makes us wonder: "In leaps and bounds, I removed myself to look for a hiding place; I put myself between two bushes in order to separate myself from the road." Having made a good start, Sinuhe did not stop; he crossed the Nile and kept right on going, through the Wall of the Ruler which marked the eastern boundary of Egypt, and out into the wilderness of Sinai.

The rest of the story is wonderful fun to read, but we will have to pass over it briefly because it has no bearing on political events. Sinuhe rose to great eminence among the "Asiatics"; at last he settled down somewhere in Syria and took himself a wife or two. But although he was honored in his adoped country, his heart increasingly yearned for home. And, with the pleasing harmony found only in fairy tales, the all-knowing king of Egypt got wind of his old servant's *Heimweh*. He sent messengers to invite Sinuhe back to Egypt.

The king's letter is marvelously tactful. It asks a question to which we ourselves would like to know the answer. "What hast thou done, that something should be done against thee? Thou hast not blasphemed, thou hast not spoken against the council of nobles. . . ."

Whatever their cause, Sinuhe's apprehensions were removed by the letter. To return to his home was no small thing, but his greatest reason for rejoicing was the prospect of laying his bones within the blessed soil of Egypt. He was so moved when at last he was brought face to face with the majesty of the king that he was on the verge of collapsing, and could not speak. The king received him kindly, and sought to relieve the tension by summoning the royal children and the queen, whom Sinuhe had once served. "Here is Sinuhe," said royalty affably, "returned as an Asiatic, a true son of the Bedouin." The queen shrieked aloud, and the royal children exclaimed, with one voice: "Surely, this is not he!"

This is a real Egyptian happy ending, but we cannot help wondering what brought it all about. What did Sinuhe overhear at the royal camp to send him scampering for sanctuary, as far from Egypt as his legs could carry him? We may be excused for suspecting that he was involved in the conspiracy himself. There are too many protestations of innocence, from Sinuhe and from the king, for him to be wholly guiltless. If so, the maganimity of the king is admirable. Even though he had been ruling in peace for many years, he could have no motive except mercy for granting the heart's desire of an old enemy.

While Sinuhe was swashbuckling around among the Arabs, his king was carrying on the traditions established by Amenemhat I. He built his pyramid near that of his father and pushed the borders of Egypt farther south. He continued the co-regency policy, as did his successors, under whom the country enjoyed peace and prosperity. Another Amenemhat and another Senusert held the throne for fifty years, during which time all was well.

All the kings of this dynasty were competent rulers. But with the number three, the Twelfth Dynasty hits its high point materially. Senusert III was the greatest of all the Middle Kingdom rulers. In all his enterprises he showed the talent we have come to expect from the men of his house; but in no project do his abilities shine so brightly as in his conquest of the Upper Nile.

Like their predecessors in the Old Kingdom, the first kings of the Twelfth Dynasty had gone into Lower Nubia, as far as the Second Cataract, but it remained for Senusert III to put the conquest on an organized basis and extend Egyptian control to limits hitherto undreamed of. He was, in later times, regarded as the patron saint of the whole region, and probably the resentful natives of Nubia never forgot his name.

At this time there lived in the regions south of Egypt a group of people whom we know only by the unsatisfactory name of the "C" peoples. (The alternative would have been to call them after one of the sites at which their culture was discovered, as was done with prehistoric cultures in Egypt and in Europe.) These people were members of the "Brown race," with curling dark hair and only slight Negroid characteristics. They entered Lower Nubia during the time of the weakness of Egypt between the Old and Middle Kingdoms. Though primitive, they were not barbarians. They made good pottery, raised cattle, and buried their dead in stone tombs circular in shape and with a chapel for offerings on one side.

These were the people whom the kings of the Twelfth Dynasty encountered as they pushed south. The Egyptians were not received with shouts of joy. Today, when we travel along the Nile southward from Aswan, we can see the ruins of great buildings located at strategic spots beside the river, all the way to the Third Cataract. They are the remains of the forts built by the Egyptians to hold the river route to the gold lands of inner Africa. Fourteen of these fortified towns were built during the Middle Kingdom. In the heavy walls and the strategic location of each we see recognition of an enemy of no mean quality; the forts were close enough so that they could reinforce one another in case of an attack.

The forts are badly ruined today, but it does not take too much imagination to reconstruct them, or to imagine the life of an Egyptian outpost garrison in the years two millennia before Christ. The heaviest fortifications were on the land side. The Egyptians held the river, and the forts could be supplied and relieved by water. A low wall and ditch served as the outer ring of defense; then came a forewall with bastions, inside which was a narrow passageway. The innermost wall was very high and thick, built of mud brick strengthened with timber insertions, and supported by towerlike projections at intervals. A narrow street ran around the inside of the wall. Within the defenses was the garrison town itself, with a big house for the commandant and smaller ones for the soldiers. There were also storehouses and a treasury, plus a small temple.

Most of the forts up to the Wadi Halfa region of the Second Cataract were built by Senusert III's predecessors. He built eight more in the fifty miles—as the crow flies—which lie south of Wadi Halfa. Senusert III fixed his boundary by formal decree at the most southerly of these forts, Semna. But this is not the limit of Egyptian penetration into Nubia, though it may have been the end of concentrated military efforts.

After Semna, the Nile runs through a district called the "Belly of the Rocks," where the difficulties of navigation are immense. Rocks and shoals threaten the boats, and the river runs almost at right angles to the prevailing northwesterly winds. There is an easier stretch after this, and then more cataracts—the Third—after which the battered boats come out onto a stretch of river known as the Dongola Reach, which is safe for navigation. At the head of this smooth stretch, just beyond the fanged rocks of the Third Cataract, stands an amazing structure. The modern name for it is the Western Deffufa.

We are now at the site known as Kerma, which Reisner excavated in the early twenties. It is 150 miles south of the Twelfth Dynasty frontier at Semna—150 miles in a straight line and much farther if one follows the bends of the river. But the Egyptians were here during the Middle Kingdom. They built the great mound called the Western Deffufa, which looks less like a man-made structure than a peculiar wind-carved formation in a desert region.

I remember reading about Reisner's work here when I was a student, and I remember too that his conclusions were generally accepted. He thought that Kerma was the provincial capital of an Egyptian governor of the far south. Several generations of such governors controlled the area during the Middle Kingdom, died there, and were buried where they died. If Reisner's theory is correct, Senusert III was indeed a mighty conqueror.

What are the actual physical remains upon which Reisner based his ideas? It is difficult to know the precise functions of the Western Deffufa. The top part, which contained the buildings or rooms, has been worn away by erosion; the lower section is simply a gigantic brick platform raised for defense. But a group of rooms on a lower level has survived, and the litter found in these rooms is significant. It included scraps of imported Egyptian articles and also local products such as ostrich eggshells, rock crystal, and copper oxide.

East of this mound is another ruin called the Eastern Deffufa, beside which is a large cemetery. The bigger tombs consist of a central chamber, where the body of the deceased was laid upon a bed, and a long corridor running through the mound past the central chamber. In the corridor of each of the largest tombs Reisner found the bodies of several hundred people, most of them women and children. They had been buried alive. Some lay with their faces hidden in their hands or protected by a bent arm; one poor girl had crawled under the bed on which her dead lord lay, thus prolonging the agony of death by suffocation.

In one of these big multiple graves Reisner found an object which was of primary importance for his theory. This was the statue of an Egyptian lady who was the wife of a Twelfth Dynasty prince of Assiut named Hapdjefa. The lower part of a life-sized statue of the prince himself was found in the same grave-mound. This, said Reisner, must mean that the chieftain for whom this court of the dead was assembled was none other than Hapdjefa himself. Hence the theory of the Egyptian governors of the south, buried in the land they had ruled, with the bodies of their Nubian harem around them in true Nubian fashion. This was "going native" with a vengeance.

Let's look at the rest of the evidence which bears on the situation. There is a tomb of this same Hapdjefa at Assiut, in Egypt. Some scholars assert that he was never buried in it, but it is a nice tomb—as tombs go—with a particularly elaborate set of mortuary contracts inscribed on its walls. The titles of Hapdjefa do not include any epithet which would indicate a governor of Nubia, and he is the only Egyptian whom Reisner could really connect with Kerma. (The occupation of the site must have covered a period of at least three generations, probably longer.) Last of all, I should mention Reisner's statement that the statues of the Egyptian prince and his lady were carved from native Nubian rock; they were not, then, imported objects.

Well, there it is, such as it is—the evidence. What can we do with it?

Arkell, whose work in the Sudan I have mentioned before, disagrees with Reisner. He pushes the point, which has been recognized before, that the burial mounds differ from standard Nubian funerary practice only in the magnitude of their size. Since only great chiefs could have squandered so many slaves in death, Arkell wants to identify Kerma with the capital of Cush, the most powerful native kingdom in the Sudan after the Middle Kingdom. He thinks the imported Egyptian objects were preserved, as being particularly valuable, long after they were first brought into the area. Kerma, he says, was a trading post during the Middle Kingdom, but the Egyptians did not have political or military control over the region.

The big stumbling block in the way of this interpretation is Reisner's claim that the significant statues were carved of native stone. Reisner was a fine scholar and it is unlikely that he could be mistaken about such a point. But we can get around the difficulty, if we want to, by suggesting that the statues were made by an Egyptian, living at Kerma, for a native prince who didn't care what the inscription said as long as it was in the language of the sophisticated traders. As an explanation, this is not very good; but I really would like to get around the difficulty, because Reisner's view seems to me even less tenable. The turning-home of the Egyptians as the time of death approached, which we see illustrated in *The Story of Sinuhe*, is a strong psychological point against the burial of Hapdjefa in Nubia. Equally formidable as an objection to the theory of Egyptian political control so far south is the long, unfortified stretch of river between Kerma and the frontier fort of Semna. It is hard to believe that a strategist of the caliber of Senusert III would build a military establishment so far from potential reinforcements.

Kerma is a fascinating site, and the man who commanded it for Egypt, whether he was a lofty prince-governor or a simple trader, deserves high honor. The post was possibly built by the grandfather of Senusert III. The region must have been peaceful during his time, but Senusert III led several military expeditions to the south, so we many presume that the C peoples were giving him trouble. He "pacified" the region so energetically that there was peace for the rest of the dynasty. But when the inevitable end came in Egypt, it was marked by fire and fury in Nubia. All the forts of the Second Cataract area were burned, and the trading post at Kerma fell to the natives.

Senusert III's greatest military exploits were in Nubia, but he led at least one expedition into a part of Palestine. The Egyptians of the Middle Kingdom probably did not have a military empire in Syria, as they did in Nubia, but contacts increased during the Twelfth Dynasty. Excavations in the Syrian cities of antiquity have turned up a goodly number of imported Egyptian objects, so Egypt must have carried on considerable trade with the east.

It is no wonder that the Greeks thought highly of Senusert, whom they called Sesostris. He had settled Nubia, ventured into the rich lands of the east, and quenched the ambitions of the noble families of Egypt—their tombs at the provincial capitals disappear during his reign. Toward the end of his life he associated his son with him on the throne, as his ancestors had done, and when he died, after thirty-eight years of unceasing activity, he sought a well-deserved rest in his pyramid at Dahshur.

Senusert's pyramid was built of mud brick. A casing of fine white limestone hid the deficiencies of the construction for a time, but when the outer stone was removed the brick collapsed into ruin. Shortly before this time the kings had abandoned the traditional northern entrance to their tombs; that was as good as drawing a map for the ubiquitous tomb robbers. The entrance to Senusert III's pyramid was far to the west of the structure, but as a subterfuge it was not very successful. When the French archaeologist Jacques de Morgan entered the pyramid in 1894, he found that he had been anticipated. The body of the king was no longer in the huge red sarcophagus. But de Morgan proved once again that careful excavation can turn up material which the tomb robbers missed. In a gallery under the northwest corner of the pyramid he found a collection of wonderful jewelry which had belonged to princesses of the royal family. De Morgan seems to have had a sixth sense for gold; it was he who found the second great cache of jewels near the pyramid of Amenemhat II, also at Dahshur.

Both collections included collars and bracelets, pectorals, crowns and rings which had belong to the daughters and wives of the Twelfth Dynasty kings. The pectorals consist of inlaid gold plates, several inches square, which are cut out into elaborate designs, with cartouches of the kings flanked by hawks and supported by little kneeling gods. The workmanship is superb; sometimes there are as many as three or four hundred separate bits of semi-precious stone in each of these small masterpieces, each bit cut to fit within a space outlined by fine gold wire. The effect is that of cloisonné enamel. The colors are rather bright—red-orange of carnelian, deep lapis blue, turquoise. The pectorals were worn on the breast, suspended from necklaces of large beads.

The prettiest of all the pieces of Twelfth Dynasty jewelry is a crown made of strands of fine gold wire, starred at irregular inter-

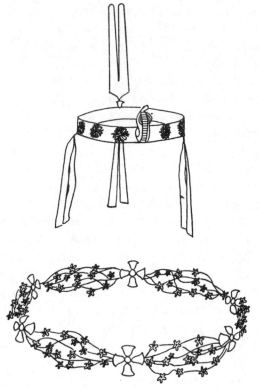

Crowns of Twelfth Dynasty princesses

vals with tiny five-petaled turquoise flowers with carnelian centers. The wire was caught here and there by cross-shaped pieces of gold, and the effect of the dainty flowers against the shining black hair of the princess must have been lovely.

Most of this jewelry is in the Cairo Museum. However, another such hoard, from the pyramid of Senusert II at Lahun, was found by Petrie in 1914, and this magnificent example of the ancient jeweler's art is now in the possession of the Metropolitan Museum. Except for the crown I have described, which is a uniquely lovely thing, the Met's jewelry is the equal of anything in the Cairo collection. It belonged to a lady named Sit-Hathor-Iunet.

When archaeologists find anything as valuable as this jewelry, they like to deal with it personally. But when the news of the find reached Petrie, he was in a quandary; he had strained himself and was unable, physically, to excavate the jewelry himself. This was not a question of going down into the tomb and lifting up a jewel box. The box had decayed, as had the thread on which the beads and separate elements were strung, and the resulting mess looked like the burial chamber of Hetepheres on a miniature scale. Petrie's standards demanded that each individual bead be cleared and recorded on the spot; otherwise, all hope of restringing the necklaces and bracelets in something like their original order would be lost. Petrie's assistant at that time was Guy Brunton, who, like most of his students, was to become a prominent Egyptologist in his own right. Brunton spent a solid week in that tomb, curled up on the bare floor of the corridor at night (to guard against thieves) and digging beads out of petrified mud by day, until the find was cleared and recorded.

Once the jewelry was restored (thanks to Brunton), it was obvious that Petrie had made a superb discovery. The Cairo Museum was a lot more relaxed about releasing objects in those days, and they already had a magnificent collection of Twelfth Dynasty jewelry, thanks to de Morgan. Petrie was allowed to keep what he found. He had been excavating under the auspices of the British School of Archaeology, which was composed of individual members as well as institutions such as museums and universities. Up to this time the discoveries which the Cairo Museum relinquished had been divided among the members in proportion to the amount of their contributions but it was obvious that the jewelry was too valuable and too important to be included in the usual seasonal division. Petrie decided to offer it to the member who (or which) would pay properly for it, the proceeds, of course, going to the School's excavation fund. Being a loyal Englishman, he offered it first to British museums, but was chagrined to discover that none of them could, or would, take advantage of the proposition. Finally he had to expand the offer overseas, and the rich Americans got into the picture. Thanks to the generosity of private donors, and the solvency of its funds, the Metropolitan Museum was able to acquire Sit-Hathor-Iunet's jewels. The Met's

Egyptian collection, incidentally, is one of the finest in the world next to that of the Cairo Museum; everyone interested in Egyptology ought to see it.

Senusert III's son was another Amenemhat, the third in number. He too was well known to the Greeks, but his achievements were in the arts of peace rather than war.

The capital of Egypt at this time was, as we have said, It-tawi near the entrance to the Fayum. The Fayum might be called a large oasis; it is a depression in the desert which, in prehistoric times, was filled by the Nile to produce a large lake. In shape the depression is strikingly leaflike; the narrow stem is the connection with the Nile valley, which leads to the river through an opening in the western cliffs. Early in the Middle Kingdom an anonymous genius conceived the idea of controlling this great mass of water for the benefit of the irrigation system, which was always a matter of interest to kings and people alike; the whole internal prosperity of the nation depended on it. The unknown genius need not have been the king, although court fiction credited him with every talent. The king does deserve credit for seeing the value of the suggestion. Great regulators for controlling inflow and outflow were built, and an immense wall was begun inside the Fayum to hold back the lake and reclaim land for cultivation.

Amenemhat III was not the initiator of this great labor, but he did more than any other king before him; his wall was probably about twenty-seven miles long, and opened some seventeen thousand acres to cultivation. In a country such as Egypt, where every square foot of irrigated land is worth a fortune, these new acres were a great addition to the country's agricultural potential. One cannot help comparing this monumental public works system with the Fourth Dynasty undertaking which was its equivalent in extent and in labor, if in nothing else—the Great Pyramid of Giza. Not that the Senuserts and the Amenemhats were altruists. The reclaimed land was not distributed to the humble peasants, but was kept by the crown. Hence we may see the Pyramid and the dam as examples of ostentation vs. practicality, rather than exploitation vs. charity.

Many buildings sprang up on the new lands of the Fayum—temples, statues, towns. They have vanished today into the soil that gave them birth, but we know about one structure in some detail. It was still standing in Greek times, and as a world-famous tourist sight was visited and described by both Strabo and Herodotus. The building was known as the Labyrinth, which gives some indication of its size and complexity. Today only a mass of limestone and granite chips, covering the surface of the grounds for hundreds of square yards, shows where this wonder of antiquity once stood. But Strabo tells us that the ceilings of the chambers each consisted of a single stone, and that the passages were walled with monolithic slabs. Herodotus says the Labyrinth contained twelve walled courts and no less than three thousand rooms. The historian himself saw the 1,500 rooms which were above ground—he says—but he had to take the word of the priests as to the existence of the corresponding 1,500 underground chambers, since they were burial places, and sacred. We know enough to discount about fifty percent of what any Egyptian told Herodotus. He was a marvelously receptive audience for a good story, whether he believed it or not, and the ancestors of the dragomen must have fought over who was to guide the Greek; if they resembled their descendants, they liked appreciation almost as much as they did baksheesh. Yet Herodotus is not a bad source when he is describing things he actually saw. Such a construction was perfectly possible for the Egyptians of this period. They worked massive blocks for the pyramids and carved sarcophagi and even burial chambers out of one gigantic square of stone. So we need not doubt the word of the Greeks—in this case. A modern archaeologist has calculated the size of the Labyrinth as 305 meters long by 244 meters wide—big enough to contain the enormous temples of Luxor and Karnak.

The resources and effort which the Old Kingdom monarchs had put into their tombs the Twelfth Dynasty kings used elsewhere; their pyramids were unimpressive. Amenemhat III's pyramid was adjoining the Labyrinth, at a site called Hawara. The Labyrinth, then, may have been in part a mortuary temple.

The Hawara pyramid is a labyrinth on a small scale. Built of mud brick like that of Senusert III, its interior is fantastic; no-where during the Middle Kingdom did a royal architect so chal-lenge the ingenuity of the tomb robbers. The entrance was on the south, opening onto a flight of stairs leading down to a vestibule. There was no apparent way out of this little chamber; the hidden exit was in the roof, of all places, where one of the slabs slid back to reveal another room. The passage leading from the second room was completely filled by huge blocks of stone. One thief had laboriously chiseled a tunnel through these blocks, thus falling for one of the oldest of all practical jokes—this passage was a blind. The real one led to another chamber which had all the appear-ance of a dead end. A hidden sliding door led to a second dead-end chamber; from this a trapdoor opened onto a passage which led, not into the burial chamber, but past one side of it. Two false burial shafts descended from the floor of the passage (one can almost work up some pity for the thieves, chipping their way through all the extraneous stone provided for their befuddlement, and uttering fulsome curses in ancient Egyptian). The far side of the same passage was filled in with stone, in order to suggest that something important lay beyond. The real entrance to the burial chamber was concealed in the middle of the passage. If a thief actually did get this far, he found himself staring in dismay at a burial chamber which was hollowed out of a single block of stone and was roofed with a gigantic stone slab that weighed forty-five tons. This stone had sealed the chamber after the royal mummy had been placed within.

It is hard to believe, but thieves did penetrate into the burial chamber. They took everything they could carry away and then set fire to the remainder—including the king's body. Their an-noyance is understandable.

When Petrie investigated this pyramid in 1880 he had as much trouble as the robbers. He found the burial chamber by digging right into the pyramid, and realized that he would have to import some expert masons to chisel through the roof block. The masons came, but the tunnel through which they had to pass was dug through sand and kept caving in. Petrie, typically, regarded the possibility of being buried alive as one of those occupational hazards an archaeologist has to put up with, but he was sufficiently aware of the foibles of lesser human beings to know that the masons would have quit on the spot if they had known how dangerous the sand tunnel was. So while the experts from Cairo were employed, Petrie spent his nights in the tunnel, shoring up the worst spots and repairing what had fallen in during the previous twenty-four hours. Finally the masons finished and Petrie wriggled, head down, through the hole. The chamber was full of water; Petrie cleared the floor by pushing chips of stones and small objects onto a hoe with his feet. When the chamber was cleared, the eminent archaeologist found the original entrance by traversing the passages in reverse, from the burial chamber out. They were filled with mud, and there was just room for him to slide, stripped and lying on his back, through the traps and complications, in absolute darkness and miasmatic air, and in slime up to his ears. From this perilous and repellent trip Petrie gained nothing except the knowledge of the location of the entrance. He never dreamed of questioning that it was worth it.

We have, from time to time, talked about methods in archaeology. Here, in Petrie's exploit, is a method which is not for the faint of heart. Let us quickly add that few Egyptologists of today have to undergo discomforts even remotely like those Petrie and his contemporaries had to endure. But the spirit that animated the pioneers is, and must be, an integral part of the archaeologist's character. He may never have to hang by one hand from the edge of a cliff in order to copy an isolated inscription, or slither through the boggy bowels of a pyramid on his belly. But he should be ready to do so if the necessity ever arises; his is the responsibility, and his the expert eye. And if he is willing to relinquish to another the glory of being the first to gaze upon a new page out of the past, he lacks the spirit of adventure which is part of the quest for knowledge.

Amenemhat III built another pyramid at Dahshur, though he was probably buried in the labyrinthian structure at Hawara. Once again we find this strange and as yet unexplained phenomenon of two tombs, which appeared at the very beginning of the dynasties. We can be relatively sure that we have not yet found the true explanation for such lavishness.

Amenemhat III is the last of the great Twelfth Dynasty kings.

The end of the dynasty is lost in obscurity, and the impact of its collapse put an end to stable government for two centuries. A period of upheaval, which we call the Second Intermediate Period, followed the fall of the Middle Kingdom, as the First Intermediate Period followed the Old Kingdom. We may talk glibly about the failure of centralized government as a cause of the anarchy, but the more basic question—what caused the centralized government to fail—is still unanswerable.

Superficially, the broad sequence of events at the end of the Old Kingdom is paralleled by what happened after the fall of the Middle Kingdom. There is even a repetition of that most ominous of all portents, the appearance of a woman on the throne of Horus. The Twelfth Dynasty lady, Queen Sobekneferu, was apparently the last of her line; if there had been an eligible male around, he would have married her and taken over the throne. What is surprising is that no ineligible male (speaking from the legitimist point of view) came to carry out this procedure. We might learn a great deal, not only about the rules of inheritance in Egypt, but about the causes of the fall of the Middle Kingdom, if we knew more about this lady. Unfortunately, she is hardly more than a name. Even her tomb has disappeared, unless it is one of the two disintegrated pyramids between Dahshur and Lisht, at Mazghuna. Both these pyramids were explored by—guess who? Petrie. But he found no identifying marks. There is never enough money for excavation, and one of the obvious methods of pyramid identification has never been tried at Mazghuna—the excavation of the tombs around the pyramid. It would be illuminating to find the tomb of Queen Sobekneferu's vizier with a long account of his career and hers. It is more likely, however, that these pyramids date from the Thirteenth Dynasty.

What were the accomplishments of the Middle Kingdom, as compared with the Old? In one sense they were not as profound or as dramatic. The men of this second great period may have climbed as high as did their ancestors, but they did not have to start so far down on the ladder. Writing, monumental building, a state religion, a philosophy of kingship and the social order, and many other basic elements of civilization were defined in the Old Kingdom and re-used by its successor. But there are changes. One

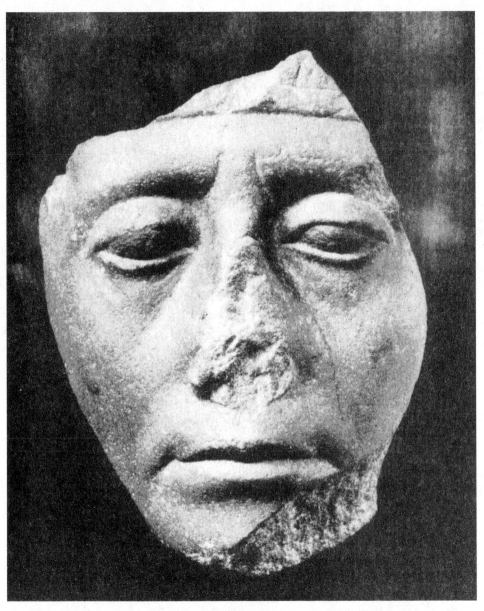

Fragment of a head of King Senusert III. *The Metropolitan Museum of Art, Carnarvon Collection, gift of Edward S. Harkness, 1926*

of the most striking details is the alteration in the face of kingship, as it appears in the statues. Look at the portrait of Senusert III— the deep lines from nose to mouth, the unsmiling, somber set of the mouth, the heavy furrows in the brow. The face of Khafre, of the Fourth Dynasty, is truly the face of a god; the features show supreme confidence, in himself and in the universe. The faces of the Middle Kingdom rulers show the weight of grave responsibility, if nothing more tragic.

We may see in these faces, and in the contrast between egocentric pyramid and public irrigation works, a sign of a change in the notion of the role of the king. Is he now the shepherd of his people rather than a remote godling; the *primus inter pares* of a feudal state rather than a being unique in his divinity? There is no easy answer to this question. At best, any conclusion is affected by the old temptation to see the bright side (from our angle) of the people we have selected as the object of our study. Even so, there is some justice in the claim that this period developed a stronger sense of social and moral responsibility than had formerly existed. Nowhere is this claim supported more strongly than in the literary works of the period. Let us examine just one more story, in order to nail down the point.

The Tale of the Eloquent Peasant must have been the special bane of little Egyptian schoolboys. It was copied extensively, and used as a school exercise; its style is so confoundedly literary and artificial that a translation cannot be read by a non-Egyptologist without pages of commentary explaining the figures of speech. Some of these, let us add, are not precisely clear even to an Egyptologist. As the reader may have deduced, I am here making an apologia for not translating the text. We will look at a synopsis instead, because the story does have something to say about social attitudes.

A peasant of the Fayum is on his way to market with a train of donkeys when he encounters a petty official belonging to the household of Rensi, the great steward of the king. This petty official, whose name is Thutinakht, covets the peasant's property, and concocts a dastardly plan; he spreads linen across the path, forcing the peasant to lead his donkeys along the edge of the field. One of the small sad animals succumbs to temptation and snatches

a bite of grain, whereupon Thutinakht confiscates the whole caravan and drives the protesting peasant away. After several days of
fruitless appeal to the unscrupulous official, the desperate peasant
seeks out the grand steward. He addresses this mighty man in a
speech so eloquent and so poignant that the steward is loath to
relinquish the pleasure of listening to him speak. So he makes no
answer to the plea. The peasant, who can certainly count persis-
tence among his character traits, returns again and again to the
seemingly indifferent steward and addresses him in no less than
eight fine speeches. In the meantime the steward has reported the
peasant's plight, and his eloquence, to the king, who orders that a
copy be made of each beautiful word. He also orders that the
peasant's family be fed while the orations are being delivered—a
nice touch, which we might not have expected from a tyrant. The
story has a happy ending and even a touch of poetic justice: the
peasant gets his property back, and is further enriched by the
goods of the greedy official who robbed him.

In the course of his travail, the peasant makes use of every
device to sway his impassive audience—threats, pleas, exhorta-
tions, flattery. Among his arguments is an appeal to a more solemn matter: justice for the sake of justice. "Righteousness
descends with the doer thereof into the tomb, and he is remembered because of it." The argument of the peasant, and the events
of the tale, pronounce the same conclusion—justice is the same for
rich and poor alike. It is a conclusion which may startle us, coming at this time and this place; perhaps in no other culture did the
monarch enjoy such absolute power as in ancient Egypt, where
dogma proclaimed him a veritable god. But we have seen hints of
this ideal in other texts and in other areas of life, so we can understand why some scholars venture to use the word "democratic"
about certain aspects of this particular period.

Even Paradise begins to look like a people's republic, for the
prerogatives of immortality have been usurped by the non-royal
dead. Here a peculiar twist is given to our notion of equality; all
men were equal, because every man was a king. The Pyramid
Texts of the Old Kingdom had assured the ruler of life everlasting; the Coffin Texts of Middle Kingdom commoners endow
them with a similar privilege. The soul of the dead man must face

a judgment, but the judge is no longer Re, as in earlier times. He is now Osiris, ruler of the kingdom of the dead. Since the deceased was also Osiris, imitating the status of the dead king, this presents a picture which may be confusing to modern eyes—Osiris the deceased being judged by Osiris the god. But it did not bother the Egyptians. Very few things bothered them.

Of course when we talk about commoners we are really talking about the nobles, petty and otherwise, and about a few of the craftsman and tradesman class. Real commoners—peasants—had no coffins to write texts upon and no tombs to put the coffins in; all they had was a hole in the sand and a few pots containing food. Even so, Paradise was democratized in the sense that any man who could afford to have a coffin painted could be Osiris. The name of the god became a sort of epithet, applied to the deceased—the Osiris Hapdjefa, prince and count, or the Osiris Sanakht, carpenter.

IV
The Fight for Freedom

Ahmose

Invasion

There was a king of ours whose name was Tutimaois, in whose reign it came to pass, I know not why, that God was displeased with us, and there came unexpectedly men of obscure birth out of the eastern parts, who had boldness enough to make an expedition into our country, and easily subdued it by force without a battle. And when they had overpowered our rulers, they afterward savagely burnt down our cities and razed the temples of the gods, and used all the inhabitants in a cruelly hostile manner, for they slew some and led the children and wives of others into slavery. . . . All this nation was styled Hyksos, that is, Shepherd Kings; for "hyk" in the sacred language denotes a king, and "sos" in the vulgar tongue signifies a shepherd.

THIS is one of the few surviving quotations from Manetho; it was copied by Josephus, for reasons of his own. I may have given the impression that Manetho is not to be trusted; and, in fact, I don't think he is. Three statements in the account given above are correct. Egypt was invaded, the conquerors came from "eastern parts," and some of them—not all—were styled Hyksos.

Obviously, the fact that we are able to sneer at Manetho means that we have other sources of information. These are almost entirely archaeological. Certain Egyptian texts mention the great humiliation inflicted by the Hyksos—whom they call "Aamu," or "Asiatics"—but all of them were written long after the event. The Egyptians suffered from a sort of official amnesia with regard to unpleasant facts; one has the feeling that the conquest would never have been mentioned at all if there had been a reasonable way of glorifying a king for liberating his country without referring to what he was liberating it *from*.

Who were these "Asiatics," who are never more explicitly named? How did a tribe of crude barbarians manage to invade and subjugate the mighty kingdom of Egypt?

Manetho's etymology, among other matters, is a bit inaccurate. The word Hyksos does not mean "Shepherd Kings," but is derived from two Egyptian words which mean "Rulers of Foreign Countries." The foreign countries were probably the lands of southwest Asia, which had been a source of trouble to Egypt before. Asiatics were always seeping down into Egypt; they had taken advantage of the nation's internal weakness after the Old Kingdom just as the Hyksos profited by the same weakness after the fall of the Middle Kingdom. There was considerable restlessness in Asia in this period, and great movements of tribes and ethnic groups. New faces and names appear in other areas of the Near East, and it may be that the Hyksos were part of the wide *Völkerwanderung*, which originated, perhaps, in the steppes of the Caucasus and picked up additional components as it wandered.

The conquest was not so bloody nor so destructive as the melodramatic Egyptian writers claimed, even before Manetho. The Hyksos rulers became thoroughly Egyptianized, using the hieroglyphic writing, assuming the Egyptian royal titulary, and worshiping the old gods. They particularly honored Set, the enemy of Osiris. This may be explained by Set's resemblance to one of their own gods. It was not the affront to Egyptian sensibilities that one might think; as we have said elsewhere, Set was a perfectly good god in his own time and place, and that place was the northeast Delta, where the Hyksos entered Egypt. Hyksos culture is questionable; it is hard to assign many artifacts or culture traits to this people. Pottery of a certain type, and a form of earth fortification were once attributed to the Hyksos, but there seems to be some doubt about both of these elements. The certain contributions of the Hyksos to Egyptian life were in the realm of warfare. They probably introduced the horse and chariot, and the compound bow. These and other effective new weapons may account in part for the ease of the conquest. We cannot add much more to our picture of the mysterious people called the Hyksos, except for one small fact. Some of these people had Semitic names.

Asiatics—men of Semitic speech—in ancient Egypt; here Biblical scholars pricked up their ears. The connection of the Hebrews with Egypt has been the subject of long and wearisome discussion among historians; few Egyptian records even mention Israel, and none of them are particularly informative about that nation or the people who founded it. There is no Egyptian reference to Moses, nor to Joseph; no text contains even a faint echo of the long captivity, which began with the enslavement of the Hebrews by a pharaoh who knew not Joseph and ended with the miracles of the Exodus. It is no wonder that the theories about the Hebrews in Egypt vary considerably. One school of thought would place the Exodus in the fifteenth century B.C., another in the thirteenth; a third version contends that there was no single, large exodus of enslaved peoples, but a series of small exodi, so to speak, which were coalesced by Jewish tradition and historians into a single event. More of this later; what we are concerned with now is how the Hyksos can be fitted into the story.

If we suppose that it was during this period that Joseph was brought down into Egypt by the slavers to whom his wicked brothers had sold him, we find it easier to understand the speed with which he, a slave, rose to power. He was a man of Semitic speech and customs serving a king from the same sort of ethnic background. If this sounds plausible, let us not forget that the ancients were not so conscious as we about the ties of "blood and birth"; social distinctions were very important, and a slave was a slave wherever he came from. We can hardly envision the Egyptianized Hyksos king taking a slave to his bosom just because the fellow came from his home town. Still and all, it may be more likely that Joseph could have overcome the handicap of his servitude under a non-Egyptian ruling class. The position he came to hold was equivalent to that of vizier, the highest nonhereditary post in the land and the most powerful, under the king. The people who made up the Hyksos consisted of many different tribes and ethnic groups. One of these groups, say some Biblical scholars, could have been the Hebrews. Later, when the Egyptian royal family recovered its birthright, the men and groups which had been favored by the conquerors would have been in disrepute, and so new kings might indeed be called "kings who knew not Joseph." So, the advocates of this theory claim, the servitude of the Hebrews began. How it ended we will see in due course.

At first the Hyksos conquest was limited to the Delta region, at whose eastern end the Asiatics had entered Egypt. The Thirteenth Dynasty continued to rule most of Egypt, except for an area near Xois, whose princes belong to Manetho's Fourteenth Dynasty. Then, about 1675 B.C., a new impetus, perhaps in the form of a more energetic Asiatic prince, prompted further Hyksos expansion, which ended in the conquest of a great part of Egypt, under King Dudimose (Manetho's Tutimaois). Manetho called the second period the Fifteenth Dynasty, and its rulers he termed the "Great Hyksos." There were six of them and they ruled for over a century. Each of the great six is given the title "Ruler of Foreign Countries," in one of the Egyptian king lists, which makes the etymology of Manetho's "Hyksos" certain. Their power extended at least through Middle Egypt, and at one time over the rest of the country as well. A Sixteenth Hyksos Dynasty was probably contemporaneous and inconsequential.

The last Hyksos king of all Egypt was named Apopi (Apophis). During his reign a well-known pattern repeated itself. There must have been a peculiar quality in the air of the southland, centering around the city of Thebes, which rendered the men of the south impatient of subjugation. Again, as at the end of the First Time of Troubles, the standard of rebellion was raised in Thebes.

"Now it happened that King Sekenenre was ruler of the southern city [Thebes]. Prince Apophis was in Avaris, and the whole land was tributary to him. Now a messenger of King Apophis reached the prince of the southern city, saying: 'It is

King Apophis who sends to thee, saying: "The pool of the hip-popotami, which is in Thebes, must be done away with. For they permit me no sleep, day and night; and the noise of them is in my ears!" ' Then the prince of the southern city was dumfounded, for he did not know how to answer the messenger of King Apophis."

The conclusion of the story is lost, but the intent of the pre-posterous message is obvious. Apophis, three hundred miles from Thebes and the bellowing hippopotami, was trying to pick a fight. He succeeded—or someone succeeded, for it is quite possible that the haughty and ambitious princes of Thebes actually began hos-tilities.

Apparently there were two kings called Sekenenre during the Seventeenth Dynasty, which is Manetho's name for the indepen-dent, or quasi-independent, Theban family contemporary with the Fifteenth Hyksos Dynasty. Sekenenre II, appropriately called "The Brave," died a violent death; his mummy is a ghastly sight, with several gaping holes still visible in the skull, and the face contorted in a frightful grimace of pain. The wounds were in-flicted in battle, by an ax or club. The first, on the jaw, would have been sufficient to send the warrior-king reeling to the ground; his adversary finished him off with at least four crashing blows that split his skull wide open. The king's death threw his men into confusion, and probably lost that particular battle for Thebes; for several days the royal corpse lay untended where it had fallen. At last it was recovered and given a proper, if hasty, burial. The dead and withered face still seems to hold the emo-tions which were the last to animate the dying brain—fury, and pain, and the knowledge of defeat.

Not all Egyptologists agree on this version of the tragedy—and tragedy it was, for Sekenenre the king if not for Thebes. Certainly the king died violently, they say, but these were troubled times; perhaps Sekenenre fell to the assassin rather than in battle. But this theory is fairly unconvincing. The ferocity of the wounds, the nature of the weapon, the evidence of the beginning of decom-position in the body tissues—all this, added to the folk tale about the hippopotami, suggests that Sekenenre fell on the field of battle with the ax of a Hyksos warrior in his skull, after he had decided to answer the insulting demand of Apophis with war instead of words. Folk tales may contain a true fact buried among yards of embroidery, and popular memory would long preserve the name of the first prince of Thebes to take up arms against the barbarians.

Liberation

With the last ruler of the Seventeenth Dynasty we reach the point the Egyptians did not mind talking about, and so we have a historical text. King Kamose, the son of Sekenenre, took up the battle standard his father's dead hand had dropped. He caused his achievements in the War of Liberation to be carved upon two great stelae. One of them survived only in a late copy which broke off right in the middle of a battle, thus tantalizing Egyptologists for years. In 1954, excavations at Karnak turned up the second stela, which carried the story of Kamose's campaigns to its triumphant conclusion. The discovery caused quite a stir, for this kind of luck does not occur very often in archaeology.

The first text begins with the king meeting with his council and holding forth in great passion upon the ignominy of his position:

"To what avail is my strength, when one prince is in Avaris and another in Cush, so that I sit here associated with an Asiatic and a Nubian, each in possession of his slice of this Egypt and I cannot pass by him as far as Memphis!"

In texts like these the council members are depicted as timid souls so that their caution may cause the king's impetuous bravery to shine more strongly. Kamose's council tried to soothe the king by pointing out how peaceful and prosperous the country was. "Why rock the boat?" they inquire.

Naturally this excellent advice falls on deaf ears, and Kamose goes forth to battle. When the first text breaks off, the war is going well; Kamose's advance has been unopposed and he has taken time off to punish an Egyptian collaborator named Teti.

Something is missing between the end of one stela and the beginning of the second, for when the sequel starts, Kamose is already approaching the enemy capital, the heavily fortified city of Avaris in the Delta. The Hyksos king had prudently shut himself up in the fortress, and none of Kamose's taunts and insults could induce him to come out and fight. He was the same Apophis who had sent Kamose's father, Sekenenre the Brave, that outrageous message about the hippopotami, and he may have suspected that Kamose's antagonism had a personal as well as a patriotic cause. Kamose devastated the fields and villages around the capital, and got so close to the enemy palace that he was able to see the women of the harem looking down at him and his army from the roof. He sent more threatening messages to Apophis via these ladies, but nothing, it seemed, could shame the Hyksos king into taking action. Before long, Kamose found out why.

One day Egyptian soldiers captured a messenger heading south from the besieged city. The dispatch he carried was an urgent appeal for aid to the prince of Cush, or Nubia. The terms of the letter made it clear that the Asiatic and the Nubian were in cahoots; Apophis volunteered to keep Kamose busy until the Cushite army could arrive, whereupon the allies would crush Kamose and divide Egypt between them. The Hyksos king may thus be the first diplomat in history to use an ancient device—how ancient we did not know until this text was deciphered—for he says that Kamose is planning to attack Cush, too—"Help me now, or you'll be next."

Kamose arranged that the ingenious appeal would never reach Cush. Still, he was not in sufficient strength to attack so formidable a fortress as Avaris; he went back to Thebes, where he was met by cheering crowds. He had won the battle, but it was not given to him to win the war. We do not know what cut the courageous prince of Thebes off in his prime; a Hyksos weapon, in some later and unrecorded battle, or one of the diseases to which the ancients were prey? We can be sure that if Kamose had lived he would have taken another crack at Avaris; he was succeeded by his younger brother Ahmose, who completed the work he had begun.

The later campaigns are recorded by two soldiers who fought under King Ahmose in the concluding years of the War of Liberation. These men were not historians or scribes; in evaluating their stories we must allow for the normal amount of exaggeration in the case of a man who is recounting his exploits for the admiration of posterity and the consideration of the immortal gods. (Like the Greeks, the Egyptians could consider their deities omniscient in theory but quite capable, in practice, of being befooled by a clever man.) Even so, we have the feeling that our two soldiers did not boast extravagantly. There is an air of verisimilitude about their naïve claims which is conspicuously lacking in some of the later accounts of military prowess; and while a man might swindle the gods and lie to his descendants it would not be easy to pull the wool over the eyes of a warrior king like Ahmose. He rewarded the two soldiers liberally for valor, and under succeeding kings they rose to high military rank.

Just to keep the record straight, let us deal with the confusion of names. Both the soldiers were named after the king—Ahmose—and both came from the same town, El Kab. For the sake of clarity we call one of them Ahmose, son of Ebana, and the other Ahmose Pen-Nekhbet. Ahmose son of Ebana was a sailor, later rising to a rank equivalent to that of admiral; the other Ahmose served in the infantry and became a general. Both made a career of the service and saw fighting under the successors of Ahmose the king. Ahmose Pen-Nekhbet—General Ahmose—must have been the younger of the two, for his service under King Ahmose was limited to a campaign in a single Palestinian town. But the other Ahmose was with his king through the whole Palestine campaign, and it is from his tomb inscriptions that we learn of King Ahmose's final success in clearing the land of the Hyksos.

Ahmose the Admiral was a marine, rather than a sailor; he speaks of fighting on land and in the water. In his first fight he was so young that he had not yet taken a wife. His father had served under Sekenenre, and it is odd that there is no mention of Kamose, who certainly used the royal marines. Possibly the young Ahmose was too youthful to go to war immediately after his father died. He soon proved himself; he married, and was transferred to the northern fleet, the post of danger—for the king was about to carry out his brother's unfinished plan and lay siege to the yet unconquered Hyksos capital. Several battles were required to take the city; in one of them Ahmose the Admiral won himself a hand

—an unattractive old Egyptian custom, which is meant to be taken literally; the hand was removed from the body of the dead foe. In later battle reliefs we see great heaps of amputated hands being piled up before the stately figure of Pharaoh, and presumably they were used as a tally of the dead as well as a proof of personal valor.

Avaris finally fell; instead of hands, Ahmose the Admiral took a few bodies, which he was allowed to keep as slaves. Avaris was the last Hyksos stronghold in Egypt, but King Ahmose was not content with driving them out of the country. He wanted to break their power permanently and insure that they could never return to shame Egypt again. He chased the fleeing Hyksos host to Sharuhen, in Palestine, and there fought another great battle, after a siege which, according to Admiral Ahmose, lasted for six long years.

The battle of Sharuhen ended the peril from the north; but there was still danger from the south—from Nubia, which had been allied with the Hyksos. Ahmose the Admiral went south with his king and "made a great slaughter" among the Nubians. He was well served in those days, for he had taken a total of ten slaves.

The enemies of the south were not crushed in one campaign. Again and again they rose in rebellion. The leader of the last revolt under King Ahmose is specifically named; he was called Teti-en, which we might translate, if we are feeling romantic, as Teti the Handsome. He must have been a particularly annoying opponent, for the Egyptians ordinarily designated their enemies only by opprobrious epithets—That Fallen One, or, That Enemy. The magical import is clear; the name was a part of a man's identity, and to deny him his name was to destroy him in part. Perhaps Admiral Ahmose had a sneaking admiration for "that fallen one, Teti-en," who was eventually slain by the king. We can spare him a little sympathy too; he was a rebel only because he failed. If he had succeeded, he would have become a liberator, like King Ahmose and General George Washington.

The Hyksos were gone—but not forgotten. They left a mark on the mind of Egypt which would never wholly disappear, and a seed in the body politic which would bear strange fruit in future years. Whether she liked it or not, Egypt was now a military power. Not as yet had the army become the sharp, professional tool it would become a few generations later; but it had gained a lot of practice and several new weapons. The horse may have been known before the Hyksos, but records from that period are the first mention of its use in war; and what an appalling weapon the chariot must have been, with its pounding snorting steeds, thundering down on a group of unarmored foot soldiers! Each chariot held two men, the warrior and the driver, who also shielded his companion with the long heavy body shield. The compound bow, another Hyksos contribution, was considerably more powerful than the old simple bow which the Egyptians had always used.

Besides these military additions, and the foreign experience gained by many men of Egypt, the Hyksos added a more important and less tangible factor to Egyptian life. "The wretched Asiatic" was no longer a figure of contemptuous fun. No more could the Egyptian feel secure in his green "island," isolated by sea and sand. The walls had been breached, and never again would Egypt feel the complete superiority she had enjoyed under the Old and Middle Kingdoms.

At least, this is how some scholars interpret the situation. Psychoanalysis of a whole nation is a tricky business, especially when all the members of that nation have been dust for millennia. And it is very hard to find visible signs of a persecution complex during the brilliant centuries which are to follow. Materially the height of Egyptian culture is yet to come. Spiritually and intellectually—that is another question, and a rather complex one.

The founder of the Eighteenth Dynasty, which begins the New Kingdom or Empire period, was modestly laid to rest among his ancestors, in the old Eleventh Dynasty cemetery at Thebes, which is almost totally destroyed. Almost nothing of Ahmose has survived except his mummy, which was found in a great secret cache of royal mummies in the late nineteenth century. It is now in the Cairo Museum.

One of the things that strikes us about the new Theban family of kings is the unusual importance of their women. Ahmose was especially devoted to his womenfolk; not only did he honor his wife and his mother, but he took time out of his many wars to think nostalgically about his grandmother. A stela from Abydos shows Ahmose and his queen sitting in conversation in the great audience chamber; they are speaking of ways in which they may honor the dead. "I have remembered the mother of my mother and the mother of my father," says the king reflectively, "the great king's wife and king's mother, Teti-sheri." Although she already has a tomb and tomb chapel, Ahmose decides to build her a bigger and better one, "because he so greatly loved her, beyond everything."

She was a charming young maiden, this Teti-sheri, before she became a grandmother. There is a little statue of her in the British Museum which shows a slender body and a delicate wistful face framed by the queen's vulture crown. This, say the art critics pontifically, is an example of the new, elegant artistic style of the New Kingdom, but one does not think of scholarly criteria when one looks at it; its charm is universally appealing.

The genealogies of the period are still being debated, but it is probable that the king who delighted in so lovely a young wife was the first Sekenenre—or maybe his name was Senakhtenre. At any rate, Teti-sheri survived him; she lived to see her daughter marry her own brother, Sekenenre the Brave. Her granddaughter, Ahmose-Nefertari, also married *her* brother, Ahmose. (The period certainly has a plethora of Ahmoses; I have mentioned only a few of them.) Ahmose's queen was a lovely woman, and a great lady, who was deified in later times.

Since Teti-sheri was the ancestress of this line of royal ladies, we can assume that they inherited her dainty features and her charm. But it was probably not for charm that they were remembered so long and honored so highly. Was it for their importance in the inheritance of the throne? This is the generally accepted theory. I don't accept it, myself; other queens of other periods had the same importance, if the notion of inheritance through the female is correct (I don't accept that, either), and they are no more than names to us now. I suspect that the quality that distinguished the queens and princesses of the early Eighteenth Dynasty was that elusive thing called personality; in the

Queen Tetisheri. *The Trustees of the British Museum.*

next chapter we will see what happened when Teti-sheri's great-great-granddaughter decided to exert her share of the family character. These women were the wives of kings and of soldiers; the fragile Teti-sheri, while still a young woman, may have seen the mutilated body of her son borne home from the battlefield and watched from a window of the palace as her grandsons marched out to war in their turn. Maybe she egged them on, as did the equally fragile and bloody-minded ladies of the Confederacy. According to a stela found at Karnak the queen Aahhotep, wife of Sekenenre the Brave and mother of two great soldiers, upon one occasion had to rally the troops and put an end to rebellion. This is one of the most tantalizing references in Egyptian history; and we know nothing more about it. Historical novelists, take note!

Ahmose's son bore a name which the Eighteenth Dynasty was to make famous—Amenhotep. Like the similar dynastic name of the Middle Kingdom, Amenemhat, it honored the patron god of Thebes. But, unlike the Twelfth Dynasty kings, the new rulers of unruly Thebes did not move their capital to the north. From this time dates the rise of Thebes, whose monuments still awe the visitor.

Ahmose left his son a united Egypt, free for the first time in centuries of foreign oppression. He also left to him, and to us, his two soldier-namesakes from El Kab. We are grateful for the legacy, since the tomb inscriptions of these men have given us much useful information. General Ahmose and Admiral Ahmose served, in all, six kings of Egypt. Both fought in Nubia under Amenhotep I, in the campaign which regained all the territory formerly held by the Twelfth Dynasty, and perhaps more. "I fought incredibly," says the admiral modestly. He also rushed the king back to Egypt upon the news of a threatened invasion by the Libyans, a distance of two hundred miles in two days. We can say little more about Amenhotep I; he fought in Nubia, he probably fought in Asia, he built monuments. Then he died.

His successor is a more interesting character, if for no other reason than because he was the father of one of the most fabulous personalities who ever sat upon the throne of Egypt. He was a man of no mean accomplishments in his own right—Thutmose, the first to bear the second famous family name of the Eighteenth Dynasty.

"From the Horns of the Earth to the Marshes of Asia"—such were the boundaries of the empire Thutmose I gained for Egypt. The Asian marshes are the swamps of the Euphrates—a grandiose claim, but we have abundant evidence for its accuracy. The tomb autobiographies of the two gentlemen from El Kab describe their valor in the Asiatic wars, and Thutmose I's stela on the banks of the Euphrates was found by his grandson when he came that way. The Horns of the Earth, then, must lie to the south. How far south we cannot be sure. The Old Middle Kingdom boundary at the Second Cataract was passed, and the former trading post at Kerma as well. An inscription of Thutmose I was found even farther south, near the Fifth Cataract. But there are no striking topographic features in this region which could be called horns, if this term means tall hills. Some scholars think Thutmose I got down as far as the site of Meroë, beyond the junction of the Nile with its first tributary, the Atbara. Admiral Ahmose commanded the flotilla that sailed upstream to—wherever it was in Nubia— and acted with his usual amazing bravery. The king's military exploits in the south were substantial enough to warrant the creation of a great new bureaucratic office, comparable in importance to the vizierate. The prince, or king's son, of Cush (Nubia) was thereafter the right hand of the king in the region south of Elephantine.

It was a goodly territory, from the far cataracts of the Nile to the Euphrates. The tribute began to pour into Thebes. Thutmose used it to beautify the city and to honor the gods, and also to provide for his good name in the Hereafter. His royal architect, Ineni, is one of the officials who left rich tombs filled with inscriptions boasting of their own prestige. Ineni tells of his work in the great Amon temple at Karnak, and in the desolate valley where Thutmose had ordered his tomb to be built. The pyramids were impressive and enduring, but it had become evident that they had certain drawbacks as true Houses of Eternity. Thutmose I decided to sacrifice publicity for safety. His tomb was dug out of the rock in a remote valley, far from the river; it consisted of a series of chambers and corridors, beautifully decorated and richly equipped within, but completely hidden from sight. "I supervised the excavation of his Majesty's tomb," says Ineni. "I was alone, no one seeing, no one hearing."

Obviously the aristocratic official did not wield pick and shovel himself, but he was responsible for all the arrangements. He chose a spot some seven miles from the river, on the west bank; it is now known as the Valley of the Kings. How secret the operation really was is open to doubt. There is no indication that the king had all his workmen executed when the tomb was finished, as some bloodthirsty writers have suggested. Some of them, the talented artists and sculptors who decorated the walls, were too valuable to be tossed away, and it is probable that only a slave could be summarily murdered without a trial. The fact that all the royal tombs in the Valley—with one famous exception—were robbed in antiquity is a good indication that some of the workmen survived. Once the exact location of a tomb was known, it was as good as robbed; the hidden passages and massive barriers bothered the thieves no more than did the similar devices in the pyramids—and small wonder, when we remember the magnitude of their eventual reward.

The king was laid to rest in the tomb which he had built with such high hopes of secrecy. He could, at the end of his life, view his accomplishments with pride and the future with few misgivings. His chief wife had borne him four children. Three of them had predeceased him, but the fourth, Hatshepsut, was a fine proud girl, of pure royal blood. By marrying her to her half brother, Thutmose II, the old king had settled the question of the succession and given Egypt a new Horus to take his place on the throne. The empire was stable; the Two Lands were at peace, prosperous, healthy. If any man could give up his last breath with the consciousness of leaving all his affairs in order, Thutmose I was that man. He had no way of knowing that the next few years would see a strange phenomenon, unparalleled in all the fifteen centuries of history that had gone before.

V
The Woman
Who Was King

Hatshepsut

HATSHEPSUT and Cleopatra; Zenobia; Catherine of Russia, Elizabeth the Great.

The reader knows most of these names—all of them, probably, except the first. History blazons out the names of many famous women, and many famous queens, but the women in the brief list above share one attribute in addition to their royalty and their fame. Born into one sex, they carried out the traditional duties of the other. Further—all of them succeeded, at least temporarily, in the difficult and conventionally masculine task of directing the affairs of a great nation.

Hatshepsut of Egypt heads the list because she is the earliest of that impressive group. She merits the highest place for another reason. In her assumption of the king's role, she dared to do something which none of her spiritual kinswomen ever dreamed of attempting: she cast off the trailing skirts of a woman and put on the kilt and crown of a king.

She was beautiful, of course; all great queens are beautiful. The statues we have of her do not give much of a clue to her actual appearance. One of them shows a small, rather gentle face, with a pointed chin and broad forehead, but the sculptured body of a queen of Egypt was always as slim and graceful as that of a goddess, just as a king's body had to be the ideal of masculine beauty. Since she was an Egyptian, we can assume that Hatshepsut was slim and fine-boned, with small hands and feet; she must have been dark, with black hair and the oblique, tilted black eyes of most Egyptian women. If, in middle age, she acquired a double chin and the harsh-lined face of royal responsibility, we need not take official cognizance of such a disillusioning idea.

From earliest childhood she had been taught the duties of the high position she would one day fill. She was the daughter of a king of Egypt and his chief royal wife; inevitably as sunrise, she would be queen of Egypt in her turn. The king? He would be her husband. At first she might have expected to wed one of her two brothers, but after they died the choice was limited to her half brother, named Thutmose, after his father and hers. Thutmose II's mother was a noble lady, one of the secondary wives of the king, but not the chief wife who had borne Hatshepsut.

There is an impression among archaeologists that Thutmose II was not the man his father had been. In part the idea stems from the description of his mummy as that of a "diseased" man who died young; in part from the contrast of his two minor campaigns with the warlike prowess of his father; and perhaps in part from the mere fact that he was married to Hatshepsut, whose personality overshadowed stronger men than her young husband.

The picture may be unfair to Thutmose II. The mummy may not be his, and it may not be diseased. Opinions as to the length of his reign differ, and if he only occupied the throne for a few years he would not have had time to do much. Still, the impressive figure of his wife towers above him and all he did; and there is a faint hint that even before her husband died, Hatshepsut had taken one step which was not in accord with the dignity of a queen, or even the honor of a wife.

Thutmose II died. Whatever his potentialities, this is just about the most important statement of fact we can make about him. He left, with regard to the problem of the succession, a domestic situation similar to the one which had prevailed after his father's death. His chief wife, Hatshepsut, had borne no sons, only

daughters. By a woman of lowly birth, a palace concubine named Isis, Thutmose II had sired one son. The situation, and its solution, were not unusual. The child Thutmose III was betrothed to his little half sister Nefrure and, upon his father's demise, the toddler became the Horus, Lord of the Two Lands, Beloved of the Two Ladies, Menkheperre, Thutmose III.

They were heavy titles for a very small boy, and the weight of the Red and White Crowns was a burden no infant could assume. Again, the situation had precedent; but in this case the mother of the king was no fit person to assume the regency. A peasant girl— perhaps a slave—to administer the affairs of the Two Lands? That was against propriety, particularly when Egypt had so fitting a regent available in the person of the Great Royal Wife Hatshepsut, Wife of the God, Daughter of the King and his Great Wife.

So far, the affair had been conducted in a perfectly respectable and dignified fashion, consistent with tradition and—as the Egyptians might have said—"in keeping with *ma'at*," the universal order of justice and correctness. Hatshepsut was now Dowager Queen and Regent of Egypt, as we would say; the Egyptians had no equivalent titles, and Hatshepsut simply retained the ones she had used when her husband was living.

Then, two years after the little king had climbed the high stairs to the throne, the universal order received a shock that rocked it to its foundations.

> Came forth the king of the gods, Amon-Re, from his temple, saying: "Welcome, my sweet daughter, my favorite, the King of Upper and Lower Egypt, Maatkare, Hatshepsut. Thou art the king, taking possession of the Two Lands."

The King of Upper and Lower Egypt.

The Egyptians were tolerant people, and they were seldom troubled by inconsistencies. But here was an utterly astounding event, so unparalleled that the very structure of the language rebelled against it. The word we sometimes translate from the

Queen Hatshepsut. She wears a masculine headcloth, but the body is that of a woman, wearing the long woman's robe. *The Metropolitan Museum of Art, Museum Excavations, 1926–29; a contribution from Edward S. Harkness and the Rogers Fund, 1929.*

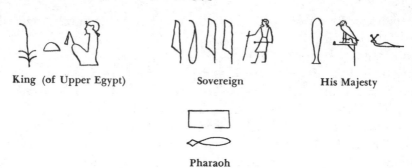

King (of Upper Egypt)   Sovereign   His Majesty

Pharaoh

Certain titles of the Egyptian king

hieroglyphs as "queen" literally means "king's wife." There are a number of words which refer to the king; the most common was originally the title of the king of Upper Egypt only. It was written with the heraldic plant of that area, and meant something like "the one of Upper Egypt." The king was also called "sovereign" or "his Majesty." During the last years of the Eighteenth Dynasty we first find the famous word "pharaoh" as a title of the king. It comes from two Egyptian words meaning "great house," and first referred to the palace.

But the point is that all these titles were masculine! Egyptian has two genders, the feminine ending being a "t"; and there were no words for a reigning monarch that were feminine in gender. The bewildered scribes were forced to some strange expedients in order to deal with her Majesty, King Hatshepsut. They usually employed the feminine pronoun, but now and then, in the middle of one of the long, flattering texts which they could have written in their sleep, they would forget, and a "he" or "his" might creep in. Sometimes they added the feminine ending to the word for "lord" or "majesty." But they still had to face such grotesque descriptions as "The (female) Horus."

The literary confusion is one of the few signs we have which suggest the bafflement of Egypt at its female king. Hatshepsut is shown in a man's kilt (and body!) wearing the king's crown and the artificial beard; and she is also shown as a woman, with feminine dress and the queen's crown. The dichotomy carries over

King Hatshepsut. Note the masculine headcloth and short kilt. *The Metropolitan Museum of Art, Rogers Fund and Contributions from Edward S. Harkness, 1929.*

into other spheres: two tombs, one in the Valley of the Kings and the other in a lesser spot; two sarcophagi, one for a king and one for a queen.

Hatshepsut might deny her femininity verbally, but in two ways it inevitably affected her life and her reign. She could not wage war; and she could not deny her heart. Elizabeth of England remained a spinster all her life, but even her cold and unemotional brain was affected by emotional commitments. The Earls of Leicester and Essex have an Egyptian counterpart. His name was Senmut.

He was a parvenu, an upstart, a nobody; he was not even particularly good-looking. His long aquiline nose and flexible, rather cynical mouth were distinctive rather than handsome. Who and what he was originally we do not know; he appears among the servants of the queen even before she proclaimed herself king— possibly before her husband, Thutmose II, died. From that time on, Senmut's meteoric rise to power parallels that of Hatshepsut. He held over twenty different titles, and he was singled out by the queen as was no other official. In justice to Hatshepsut's reputation, we must admit that there is no direct evidence that her relationship with Senmut went beyond that of mistress and servant; but we cannot help suspecting. . . .

Next to Hatshepsut herself, Senmut's is the dominant figure of her reign. Yet he was not her only prop and support politically. We have not yet tried to explain how she succeeded in the fantastic coup which seized the throne of Horus for a woman; and in fact it is very hard to understand how she did succeed. She must have had that indefinable quality which is called *"charisma"*; it blazes at us now over a gulf of four thousand years, and we can imagine what the impact must have been at first hand. But personality alone is not enough to explain a phenomenon such as Hatshepsut. She must have had the help of powerful organized forces in the state. There were a number of possible power groups —the nobility, the bureaucracy, the military, the priesthoods. We have not mentioned the people, for they were a negligible force, illiterate and unorganized.

The most influential of Hatshepsut's adherents was a man named Habusoneb, who was, early in her reign, both vizier and

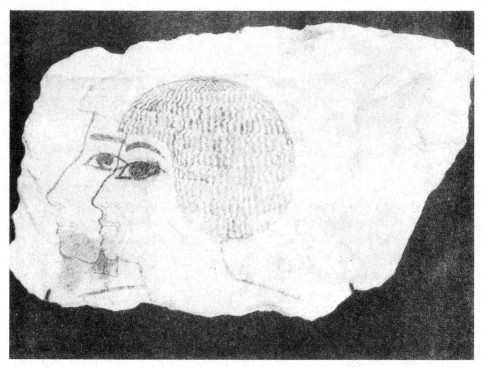

Sketch of Senmut. *The Metropolitan Museum of Art. Anonymous gift, 1931.*

High Priest of Amon. One is tempted to see in this man, rather than in the parvenu Senmut, the power behind the throne, the Cardinal Richelieu of the reign. It is hard to see Hatshepsut in the role of Louis XIII; her husband, Thutmose II, might have fit the part better. But certainly a woman in her position needed all the help she could get, and Habusoneb represented a lot of help. Hatshepsut's alliance with the High Priest was one of political expediency; he never presumed on the royal favor to the extent that Senmut did. An interesting, and as yet unexplained, point is that a number of Thutmose I's favored officials transferred their allegiance to Hatshepsut when she supplanted her nephew—Ineni the architect and Ahmose Pen-Nekhbet, the old soldier from El Kab, among others. Another of her officials had the unusual name "Nehsi," which means "the Nubian."

Hatshepsut knew her position was precarious, and she bolstered it with propaganda as well as with picked allies. The propaganda was based on two major pieces of evidence, both of which are totally fictitious. One of them claimed that she had been chosen by her father as his successor, and raised to the throne by his own hand. The other proposed the magnificent notion that she was the physical daughter of Amon-Re, the god.

There was nothing new about this idea; all kings were called "son of Amon" and "son of Re." But Hatshepsut's reliefs depict the process by which she became the daughter of the god in some detail. They are the earliest of this type of scene to survive, although the fiction must have been current much earlier.

On the walls of the temple of Deir el Bahri we can see the god on his way to visit the queen Ahmose, Hatshepsut's mother. "He [Amon] made his form like the majesty of this husband, the king Aakheperure [Thutmose I]. He found her [Queen Ahmose] as she slept, in the beauty of the palace. She waked at the fragrance of the god, which she smelled in the presence of his Majesty. He went to her immediately. . . ."

At this point Breasted, who first translated these inscriptions, breaks into Latin, but the sense is clear without any translation at all. Afterwards, Amon made a little speech to the delighted queen: "Hatshepsut shall be the name of this my daughter, whom I have placed in thy body. She shall exercise the excellent kingship in this whole land."

Successive scenes show the matters, physical and religious, which have to do with the birth of the divine child. Khnum, the creator of men, is instructed by Amon to fashion the baby and its ka—a sort of protective genius—on his divine potter's wheel. Both the little figures are unquestionably male—another of the unconscious slips of the confused artist, who probably copied the whole series from more ancient reliefs, now destroyed. Then the queen is shown holding the newborn infant and attended by the traditional goddesses of birth and midwifery. There are other scenes, most of them badly broken.

Except for the little error of the male babies, this sequence makes an impressive story. How impressed anyone actually was is open to question. Whatever the combination of propaganda and

Obelisks of Thutmose I (left) and Hatshepsut (right) at Karnak. *The Oriental Institute, University of Chicago.*

power, Hatshepsut succeeded not only in gaining the throne but in holding it for more than twenty years. Under her reign the land prospered. She built magnificently, adding handsomely to the Temple of Amon at Karnak, where one of her huge obelisks, the largest to be quarried in Egypt up to that time, still towers into the sky. These tall, four-sided spires were usually erected in pairs near the gateway, or pylon, of a temple. The obelisk form suggests majesty and ambition, and the ancient Egyptians were not the only ones to appreciate these qualities. The Washington Monument is an obelisk, and many of the biggest Egyptian obelisks were carried off by foreign conquerors to augment the grandeur of their native capitals from London to Constantinople. The second obelisk of this pair of Hatshepsut's collapsed in antiquity. When they were first erected, both monuments were ornamented with fine gold. The inscriptions on the sides and base of the obelisk, from which our facts are obtained, state that the queen measured out the precious metal by the bushel, like sacks of grain. From this, and from other evidences of wealth, we can be fairly sure that the queen's inability to lead her armies into battle had no adverse effect on the Egyptian economy. The lack of military exploits was felt most keenly when Hatshepsut came to the problem of the carved reliefs which glorified a monarch's great deeds. Since she could not show herself wielding a mace and bashing the heads of enemies, she gave great prominence to an economic triumph—a trading mission to the distant, almost fabled land of Punt.

No one knows for sure where Punt lay; the latest guesses put it somewhere on the Somali coast. The products of this country included goods highly coveted by the luxury-loving Egyptians—apes and ivory, gold and spices, fabulous animals and exotic plants—and dwarfs like the one Harkhuf brought to his king during the Old Kingdom.

The scenes showing Hatshepsut's expedition to Punt, which was organized and led by Nehsi, the Nubian, occupy more of the wall space at the Deir el Bahri temple. The great ships are shown setting out, with sailors hanging like monkeys from the rigging. When they finally reached Punt they were greeted by the astounded natives, including the wife of the chief—an enormously fat woman seated on a very small donkey. (The Egyptians undoubtedly thought this was very funny; even in so solemn a venture as the Punt expedition, their typical sense of humor could not be restrained.) After a successful trading mission the ships returned, bringing not only gold and ivory, but a collection of myrrh trees, zealously tended on the long journey, to adorn the terraces of the temple of Amon and the queen.

All this energy—the expedition, the obelisks, and other undertakings—were carried out to the glory of Amon. "Her Majesty did this because she loved her father Amon so much, more than all other gods. . . . I have done this from a loving heart for my father Amon." It looks as if Hatshepsut were trying to propitiate someone—the god or the priests or both.

We have mentioned the great obstacle of her sex, and the sullen weight of tradition, which Hatshepsut had to overcome in her quest for power. But we have not yet discussed another handicap, which makes her success truly inexplicable. All the time Hatshepsut was wielding the scepter so energetically, there was another king of Egypt in the background. It is easy to forget about him because apparently the Egyptians themselves did so for many years. He was to be one of the greatest and most forceful kings who ever ruled Egypt; a conqueror who, in breadth of vision and martial prowess, may legitimately be compared with the great Alexander. To be sure, Thutmose III was only a child when Hatshepsut stole his throne. But she ruled for over twenty years; long before the end, the boy would have become a man and begun to show the stubbornness and intelligence which are so conspicuous in his character later on.

This is one of the greatest mysteries of the queen's life, which holds so many mysteries. How did she manage to suppress and control a personality which was, in strength, equal to her own, and which was handicapped by none of the problems she had to overcome? If the young Thutmose had been like his father, he might have taken the arrogant usurpation meekly. But he was not; he was a chip off an older block, a block of hard Aswan granite. His grandfather, the conqueror of Syria and Nubia, would have been proud of him.

To what tasks did Hatshepsut set the aspiring warrior? She let

him burn incense before Amon when her Punt expedition returned in triumph.

This scene would make a good subject for historical drama.
The queen, brilliant in her gorgeous regalia and robe of sheer
pleated linen; conspicuously near her, the no-less-gorgeous figure
of that upstart Senmut, loaded with the ornaments of gold and
precious stones with which the queen's bounty had provided him;
above all, the towering statue of the god, wreathed in blue, sweet-
smelling smoke. And behind them, obscure and unnoticed, the
slender figure of the boy king—he must have been in his early
teens by then—smoldering with suppressed fury and aquiver with
thwarted ambition, his sullen black eyes glowering at the intricate
shape of the Red and White Crowns upon the head of his hated
aunt—those crowns which should have been his. The air must
have crackled with tension.

Hatshepsut and Senmut probably felt no emotion stronger
than contempt for the helpless young king. They were at the
height of their power, unchallenged, with great influence and
power behind them—the nobles, the old bureaucracy, the priesthoods. Trade flourished, great building works gave employment
to the people, there was no lack of food. The military as a strong
force was not yet fully developed; the large professional armies of
the later Empire, who turned to looting and violence when foreign conquests failed, had yet to be formed. The great campaigns
of Thutmose I lay years in the past. And if there were men who
chafed at the boredom of peace, and yearned to continue the
imperial designs of the queen's father, no doubt there were men—
and women—who cherished the peaceful years and found hap-
piness in the simple activities of family and crops. The life of the
peasant was hard, but it *was* life; and almost any kind of existence
was preferable to dying far from home and being buried at a
distance from the gods and temples of Egypt.

Many of the peasants, and all of the artisans and craftsmen,
were busy with Hatshepsut's main interest, the construction and
restoration of temples and monuments. She was, she claims, the
first ruler to restore the damage which had been done by the
Hyksos to many of the sanctuaries of the gods, and her own building works were numerous. In the thick of it all was Senmut, who

held, among other offices, that of royal architect. Most of his other duties probably were administrative—which does not necessarily speak for his talent as an administrator. We can be sure of one thing, though. Senmut may have resembled Essex and Leicester in the place he held in the affections of a queen, but he had a lot more behind his face than did those handsome but ineffectual gallants, and one of his offices, at least, was no mere sinecure. If we can believe Senmut's claims—and there is no reason why we should not—he was one of the most talented architects the ancient world ever produced. To him we owe the marvel of the queen's temple at Deir el Bahri: the most beautiful temple in Egypt, and one of the finest of all ancient buildings.

Deir el Bahri lies directly across the Nile from modern Luxor. In its bay is the temple which Hatshepsut built for her mortuary cult and for the glory of Amon and other gods. The external design is dramatically simple; in form and in mood it echoes the strong, severe shape of the cliffs which rise behind it. The temple consists of rows of pillared colonnades on two levels, which are reached by long sloping ramps. The central halls are flanked by wings, at right angles; their fluted circular columns irresistibly suggest Greece, rather than Egypt. The first impression of this noble building is, somehow, non-Egyptian, although the basic inspiration for its design was drawn from the earlier, Eleventh Dynasty temple nearby. But Senmut was not an imitator. His design is as superior to the older building as the Parthenon is superior to the graceless, stubby old temple at Corinth. The implied comparison with the Parthenon is not inappropriate, for both structures—the Parthenon and the temple of Deir el Bahri— have one major triumph in common: the observer is instantly struck with a sense of harmony in the proportions. No dimension could be altered without damaging the whole. The graceful colonnades of the Egyptian temple show that the Greeks were not the first to comprehend this particular architectural form. The architect of Deir el Bahri also made full use of the terrain, and of the peculiarly brilliant Egyptian climate. The overhanging cliffs do not diminish the handiwork of man, but support and frame it; and the contrast of strong shadow and sharp sunlight is deliberately made a part of the design.

Hatshepsut's temple at Deir el Bahri. *Photo by the author.*

Though this temple, which was named Djeser-djeseru in Egyptian, was dedicated to Amon and other gods, its primary function was to serve the funerary cult of the king Hatshepsut. Other kings had constructed mortuary temples at the foot of the cliffs. Some of them had built tombs there too; but Hatshepsut's father took the momentous step of separating tomb from temple, for greater security. Hatshepsut's tomb was in the Valley of the Kings—another monstrous intrusion into the prerogatives of men. The seven-hundred-foot-long corridor of the queen's tomb was in a direct line toward the temple; evidently the original plan had been to drive the corridor straight under the mountain ridge which separates Deir el Bahri from the Valley of the Kings, so that the royal sarcophagus would lie under the temple. This ambitious plan was never carried out. But there was a tomb under the holy sanctuary of the temple of Djeser-djeseru. It was the tomb of the commoner, Senmut. In this, and in certain features of the temple, we have the clearest presumptive evidence that Senmut was more to his queen than a loyal and talented servant. Only the uncrowned consort who shared the queen's couch, if not her throne, would have dared so much.

Like every other ancient site in Egypt, Deir el Bahri is haunted by the ragged, self-appointed "guides" who arouse pity and irritation in almost equal measure. You cannot walk through the colonnades of this temple for long without thinking of its inspired builder; and if you mention his name aloud, one of the guides will surely pounce on you, nodding eagerly and making imperative gestures. "Senmut! Senmut!" he exclaims, and leads you back into the shadows of the inner rooms. The darkness thickens, and the floor beneath your feet is rough and hazardous. You stumble over a loose stone and wonder if you should not turn

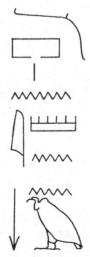

Senmut's name and title

back; then your "guide" stops and lights a pitiful little stub of candle. There is an open doorway to your left, leading into a small windowless room which was once, perhaps, a storeroom. The doors which closed it in have long since vanished. You must squat in an awkward position to see, by flickering candlelight, the thing you have come to see—the small carved figure of a man, in the space which would have been hidden by the opened door. He is kneeling upon one knee, in the infinitely graceful Egyptian position of worship, with hands uplifted; and above him is the name which, with incredible insolence, he dared to intrude into a shrine reserved for divinity: SENMUT, STEWARD OF AMON.

The small carving is rather rough, and the conventionalized profile probably bears no resemblance to its supposed model. It is impossible to explain why the sight of it should create such an unforgettable impression. Perhaps it is because we sense something about the man in the very position he presumed to occupy. Outside the temple the brazen sun blisters down out of a hard, hot sky; but the corridor beside the little storeroom is black and breathless, just as it must have been on that vanished day when Senmut the architect supervised by lamplight the insurance of his survival among the gods. To what trusted servant would he entrust the carving of this piece of blasphemy? Was it done with the knowledge of the queen, or did he risk her divine anger in his anxiety for life everlasting in her company?

Senmut's tomb under the temple is another piece of matchless impudence; only members of the royal family could hope for such a favor. It is fantastic to assume that he could carry out a project as large as this without Hatshepsut's knowledge; she was a woman of great energy, and undoubtedly visited her mortuary temple often while it was abuilding. Some archaeologists have suggested that she found out about her lover's presumption and dismissed him from favor (possibly from life); but this seems unlikely to me. The tomb was badly disfigured later, but it still preserves some remarkable reliefs. It was meant to have truly royal proportions; the corridors are over 100 yards long as they stand.

The royal architect's gamble for eternity did not pay off. He never occupied his gorgeous tomb; we do not know where his bones were laid to rest, if they found rest at all. He had another tomb, more suited to his official rank, on the slopes of a hill not far from Deir el Bahri. Perhaps Senmut was buried here. His magnificent sarcophagus certainly was; it is very like Hatshepsut's sarcophagus, and was probably made at the same time. (Is there no limit to this man's ambition? asked the scandalized nobility.)

Senmut may have been a "man on the make"—one of the most successful of all time—but he did not lack finer feelings. He buried his family—mother and father, brother and sister—near him so that they might share his good fortune in the West. One of the pleasantest things we know about Senmut comes from his own small private cemetery. He must have been a lover of music, for he caused his minstrel to be buried near his own tomb, with the singer's harp laid in the coffin. His pets were buried too—a pet ape and a little mare, enclosed in coffins and provided with food and water to last them until they reached the West.

To a real aficionado of detective stories, no fictitious crime holds the fascination of the many unsolved mysteries with which history abounds. Did the little Dauphin die in prison, or was the child who perished a substitute? Was Richard III really the murderer of his nephews in the Tower? Did Leicester push his wife down the staircase at Kenilworth, in the overweening hope of marrying Elizabeth the Queen? Whose gold hired the cutthroats who stabbed Cesare Borgia's brother and threw his body into the Tiber? To these delightfully ghoulish questions we might add another, with equally dark implications: How did Hatshepsut meet her end?

We have a lot of material about the other mysteries of history (at least it seems quite a bit to an archaeologist); enough for a strong presumption in most cases, if not a certainty. But an inquest on the death of Hatshepsut would be a brief affair. We know that she died (all men must die), and that her nephew, Thutmose III, became king in fact as well as in name. But the lack of information only whets our curiosity. How did Hatshepsut die? What part did Senmut the royal architect play in the last days and years of her reign? What event liberated the frustrated young Thutmose from the bondage which had held him for twenty years?

If the queen died from purely natural causes, the removal of

her dominant personality would inevitably bring about the downfall of her party; Hatshepsut, like certain other political leaders,
was the party. Her supporters could put forth no successor, and
Thutmose III would naturally gain the power.

But there are factors which argue against so tame a conclusion.
There is a sense of mounting tension toward the end of Hatshepsut's reign, the conflict of two forceful minds in bitter, if un-
spoken, competition for the same goal. Our sense of drama
demands a resolution of this conflict in dramatic terms.

The feeling has more behind it than the poetic urge. We may
not know much about events, but we know something about the
characters of the people involved. And if there was ever a time in
history when events were shaped by individuals, rather than vice
versa, this must be that time; Hatshepsut's career is inexplicable
in any terms except those of her personal ambition and character.
In the case of Thutmose III, we can quibble. Behind the seemingly placid façade of Hatshepsut's Egypt there may have seethed
a furious resentment of the queen's blow against the universal
order; dissatisfaction might have selected Thutmose as its agent,
just as it would have selected any available strong man. But
Thutmose III was not just any strong man; he was one of Egypt's
mightiest kings. No one has ever proposed a satisfactory explanation for his long silence, a silence which lasted for twenty-two years,
while a woman ruled his heritage. Certainly he was no weakling.
Though intelligent and even imaginative, he was not a prey to
that sort of philosophical reasonableness which often ends in inaction because all alternatives seem equally good. He was only a
child when Hatshepsut first usurped his throne, and was in no
position to resent the deed. But he was not always a child. Surely,
we insist, a collision was inevitable between the maturing strength
and resentment of the young king and the waning powers of the
queen. We are not satisfied with a tame and bloodless ending for
the haughty spirit of Hatshepsut. And, perhaps, we would like to
see Thutmose enjoy his revenge.

He enjoyed it, in every sense of the word. The land of Egypt
trembled under the fury of Thutmose's wrath, and the mute evidences of it still speak from the walls and from the tombs. His
wholesale destruction of anything Hatshepsut had ever touched
rules out one of the hypothetical explanations for his long years of

inaction—that he willingly acquiesced to the usurpation. I keep coming back to the question of Thutmose's silence because for me it is the most tantalizing, the most vexing, of all the small mysteries in the great mystery of Hatshepsut; how *did* she ever control Thutmose III? Some scholars try to explain the mystery by denying that Thutmose resented his aunt's occupation of the throne; they claim he did not destroy her monuments. Somebody did, though. Personally, I can't believe that any normal, chauvinist male—much less Thutmose III—would accept the theft of his heritage by a mere woman. Either there is something horribly wrong with our interpretation of the royal succession in Egypt, or Hatshepsut had some means of blackmailing Thutmose. It would be too much to hope that we could find definite proof of the true answer, but I would even be satisfied with a fictitious answer if it made sense. I can't think of one. Can you?

I am personally, if illogically, convinced that Thutmose did away with Hatshepsut. It is possible that he did away with her mummy; no trace of it has ever been found unless the unidentified mummy found in the tomb of Amenhotep II, along with the bodies of other monarchs rescued from their desecrated tombs, is in fact hers. The techniques of mummification suit the period, and the investigators described the body as that of an "elderly woman." I would like to take leave to resent the adjective; the lady was probably between thirty-five and forty-five when she died. At any rate, the new king was careful to insure that Hatshepsut would die the second and final death, by obliterating her name and her carved image from every spot he could get at. One of the first places which echoed to the blows of sledgehammers smashing stone was the temple at Deir el Bahri. The Metropolitan Museum Expedition, working at that site, found the pieces of dozens of statues of Hatshepsut dumped into a pit before the temple, and fragments of others were strewn over a wide area. Hatshepsut's titles and portraits were erased from the walls of the temple. In some cases they were replaced by the name and figure of Thutmose III, but more often by those of his father and grandfather—anybody but Hatshepsut! The great obelisks at Karnak were not overthrown, but Thutmose ordered them sheathed in masonry which would cover up the queen's name and her proud inscriptions.

Thutmose II had good reason to dislike his aunt, but it is possible that he hated Senmut even more. Not only was the man a commoner and a traitor to the true king, but he had occupied the place in Hatshepsut's affections that Thutmose's father ought to have held, but probably never did. The young king went after the architect with a fury that made his treatment of Hatshepsut look comparatively tame. The queen's sarcophagus was left intact, but Senmut's, the mate to hers, was literally broken to bits. Over twelve hundred fragments of it were found, scattered broadside over the ground near his tomb, and these pieces represented only about half of the original sarcophagus. It took genuinely royal fury to reduce stone of this hardness to such a state. Of the mummy that lay within it, there is no trace, and it is not hard to imagine what Thutmose must have done with it. I have not given up hope of finding Hatshepsut's mummy. Family feeling, unwilling respect, piety—any of these emotions might have restrained Thutmose from actually destroying his aunt's body, but there was no reason why he should not have dismembered Senmut personally, and enjoyed every minute of it. Someone had even betrayed the secret of the little images behind the doors of Djeser-djeseru, and Thutmose sent his agents after them. Luckily for us, the human tools erred. They had no strong feelings one way or the other about Senmut, and in the heat of the day it was pleasant to snatch a nap in a secluded spot where the overseer could not see. . . . Four of the hidden figures escaped Thutmose's vengeance, and it is these that we see today if we venture into the recesses of the great temple, which still shouts aloud the genius of Senmut, and his royal impertinence, louder than any inscription could do. In this aspect of his revenge Thutmose failed.

With other followers of Hatshepsut he was more successful. Habusoneb, the high priest and vizier, lost his name, on tomb walls and statues. So did Senmen, Senmut's brother. The most dreadful fate of all fell upon one of Hatshepsut's henchmen who had been buried in distant Silsileh. His tomb was so badly battered that we do not even know his name. In this anonymity lay oblivion; there would be no offerings in the Afterworld for a nameless soul.

We have been talking all this time about people and quite rightly, because Hatshepsut and her successor are figures which cannot be ignored. But there were other elements involved in the struggle for power; they probably affected Hatshepsut's seizure of the throne, and they were, equally probably, connected with her downfall. Hatshepsut's devotion to Amon, and the position of her ally Habusoneb as High Priest of Amon suggests that this mighty spiritual power supported her. But Thutmose III also honored Amon; and how he honored Amon! After he assumed power, he caused to be circulated a curious and suggestive story.

As a youth, or "puppy," he had served in the temple of Amon as a minor priest. One day came the occasion of a great festival of the god, in which the shrine was carried in procession through the north colonnaded hall of the Karnak temple. The reigning king (who is not named) made the offering, while the young priest stood humbly in his place, unnoticed, Then, to the amazement of all beholders, the shrine which held the god began to wander about as if in search of something. It made an unexpected circuit of the hall and finally stopped before the gaping young priest. When that worthy prostrated himself, the god raised him up and led him to the "Station of the King." Thereafter the god "opened for me [Thutmose speaking] the doors of heaven, and I flew to heaven as a divine hawk that I might see his mysterious form."

And so on. The god Re himself crowned Thutmose, his titulary was fixed, and he was seated at the right hand of Re.

The last part of this tale, one need hardly say, is a fine example of poetical fiction-making. But the first part is significant—and perhaps no less fictitious. It is hard to believe that such an event really happened at the time Thutmose says (or implies) that it did. He can hardly have been more than a toddler when his father died, too young to have even a minor temple position; and if the unnamed "king" of the inscription was Hatshepsut in her prime, I, for one, would not like to have been one of the priests who guided the movements of the god under her furious eye. All ruling kings blandly claimed the favor of the god, and Hatshepsut was assiduous in honoring Amon—with good reason, since according to her version that divine spirit had fathered her. What we may see in these tales is an attempt, conscious or not, to use the symbol of the god as a polite substitute for the political support of the priesthoods. There are only two possible explanations for Thutmose's story. Either it is pure fiction, like Hatshepsut's divine birth, or the event took place at a later date and may have been the signal for a *coup d'état*. This implies a political shift, or split, in the priesthood itself.

Habusoneb, the politician-priest who had supported Hatshepsut's claim, was not the man who led the transfer of allegiance to the rising sun of Thutmose. Habusoneb is significantly absent after Thutmose assumes power; in fact, his memory was bitterly persecuted. No. If Amon decided to switch to Thutmose, the oracle who voiced the god's decision was another man.

But why switch at all? The Egyptians never heard of the adage about the horses and the middle of the stream, but no people were ever more satisfied with the status quo. Was the queen getting old? Then Thutmose would succeed to the throne in any case (in theory he already held it, and had for more than twenty years). Why rush things in an undignified and violent manner? A plausible answer is that the cannier of the priests knew quite well that nobody who had been popular with Hatshepsut was going to be a bosom companion of her nephew's. It would be good policy to assure the coming king of one's loyalty before allegiance became a necessity.

Conspiracies have been formed for less logical reasons, but in this case there may have been a stronger motive. Let us anticipate a trifle and look at Thutmose's first official act as king *de facto*. Within a few months of assuming power, Thutmose had left Egypt. He was on his way to Syria, where a powerful confederation of local princes was threatening the supremacy of Egypt, established in that area by Thutmose I.

We have no records of disaffection or of rebellion under Hatshepsut. But it would be naïve to suppose that there were none just because she did not choose to mention them. We know, from later cases, that the "pacified" territories of Syria did not stay pacified very long without a display of force from Egypt. The last major campaigns before those of Thutmose III had been those of his grandfather, some thirty years earlier. Although Hatshepsut's reign appears to have been peaceful and prosperous, we can be fairly sure that by the end of her time the local princes of northern Syria were getting ideas. They may have started getting them even earlier—"A woman on the throne of Egypt? Well, well, well!"

Thutmose III marched, not for exercise, but to face a confederation of rebels. It is tempting to suggest that it was the news of this confederation, reaching Egypt, that brought l'affaire Hatshepsut to its crisis. It has been suggested that Hatshepsut did carry out a few minor military campaigns. I find the evidence for this idea unconvincing, and I am equally unpersuaded by the argument that Thutmose III also led Egyptian armies abroad during her reign. I can't imagine how Hatshepsut would dare let her gifted nephew become a military hero, or win the allegiance of the army. The overwhelming impression of her reign is one of peace, commerce and trade, especially in contrast to the reigns of her father and her successor.

No, Hatshepsut did not wage war. So, in detective story tradition, we might ask who profited most by war, after the king himself? The beneficiary of Thutmose's generosity is clear—the god Amon and the priesthood of the god. The young king's sudden favor in the eyes of the god might have been due to the fact that he had succeeded in convincing a significant part of the priesthood that Amon would wax fat with gold if he were allowed to run things in Egypt. One can, in fancy, see the meeting, in some dark cell in the temple of Amon; the young man, eyes alight above the magnificent Thutmosid nose which so eloquently supported his claim to kingship, leaning forward and gesturing in the eagerness of his discourse; the group of slender, shaven-headed priests in their immaculate white linen robes, faces impassive at first—and then, wordlessly, a nod of agreement here, a slow and thoughtful scratching of a shaven chin there.

This is historical fictionalizing, of course. There is a difference between a theory and a possibility; neither should contradict known data, but an honest theory ought to have some little something in the way of proof behind it. Unless new facts come to light, there never can be a theory about Hatshepsut's fall because there is no evidence of any kind. You can see why Egyptologists occasionally turn to historical fictionalizing for lack of anything more solid. As a feeble justification for my own predilections in the direction of fiction, I can only add that I'm not the only one.

So ended the reign of the king who was a queen. There were other reigning queens in ancient Egypt; some of them even assumed the king's titles. But none ruled for a generation without opposition, and none mounted the throne over the prostrate ambitions of a man like Thutmose III. There are some scholars who see in this great dynastic feud a deeper meaning in terms of political philosophy. Hatshepsut's followers were the party of peace, and Thutmose, all by himself, was a good-sized "party of war." One represented growth through trade and economic development, the other dominance through conquest. Certainly these contrasting conditions were the results; but whether they were ever openly expressed ideologies or slogans of two opposing parties is dubious. We are inclined to view them rather as the inevitable consequences of the personalities of the protagonists. Whatever the Egyptian noblewoman might have been, she was no Amazon. When she accompanied her lord to the chase, she sat demurely at his feet and handed him his arrows; and she never accompanied him to war. There is no evidence that Hatshepsut ever desired to break this tradition—even if it was the only one she never flouted —and even less evidence that she could have carried it off if she had tried. Thutmose III was a warrior, born if not bred—for we can hardly suppose that Hatshepsut saw to his military training with great enthusiasm; she would much prefer to see him occupied with nice harmless activities such as burning incense before Amon. It is not unnatural to suppose that whatever warlike tendencies he had were intensified by his hated aunt's lack of ability in that direction.

They have come down to us as equals, each unique in his or her own sphere. None of his successors tried to tarnish Thutmose's glory, and his designs on Hatshepsut's name and fame were foiled by the leveling forces of time and by the brilliance of modern scholarship. The masonry with which he encased her mighty obelisks collapsed, and archaeologists restored Hatshepsut's name on the walls of her temple. It was the one petty act of a career otherwise free of malice or hastiness, this revenge of Thutmose

III's. Knowing what he must have endured we can forgive him much. Nor can we condemn Hatshepsut for her sins against the conventions of her time, which are not our conventions. Perhaps in the end she was corrupted by a power more absolute than any the modern world has ever seen, reinforced as it was by the doctrine of divine kingship. But let it be remembered, to her honor, that she never yielded to the ultimate corruption—murder. And what a temptation it must have been! Especially as the feeble boy-king gained in stature and in wisdom—and correspondingly in menace—yes, the "foul and midnight thought" would have entered the minds of most rulers, male or female, who held their thrones by such tenuous sophistries as maintained Hatshepsut the king upon the throne of Horus. Whether she contemplated it or not we will never know. But we know that she died and Thutmose lived. From that simple fact we may imagine a great deal.

The Hatshepsut Problem

Scholarly feuds are a lot of fun for laymen, and even for the scholarly world itself, with the possible exception of the combatants. The spectacle of two dignified and learned gentlemen belaboring one another over a misplaced verb form or a piece of broken pottery, with adjectives which should be restricted to political debates, is inherently ridiculous and consequently entertaining. In point of fact there is nothing more absurd about the subjects of *"Gelehrtenduelle"* than about the causes of many wars, when one considers the stakes involved; but the tragedy of warfare, which removes any possibility of humor unless it be of a macabre variety, is missing in the academic battles. They rarely descend to violence, except that of a verbal nature.

One of the most hard-fought skirmishes on the battlefields of academe was waged around the turn of the last century on the Hatshepsut question. Let not the unwary reader be misled as to the nature of the question. The problem in Egyptological minds was not why Hatshepsut did what she did, or how she got away with it; it was basically a problem of what happened, and when. The historical sequence which I have given above is now the accepted view, but it was not arrived at without a good deal of Sturm und Drang.

The protagonists in the battle were Kurt Sethe on the one hand and Edouard Naville on the other. Sethe was one of the best Egyptologists Germany ever produced, which is saying a good deal. He wrote with authority on Egyptian history, philology, and religion; his work on the Egyptian verb is still a classic. He was misled, in the case of Hatshepsut, by a particularly plausible theorem, and his version of the Thutmosid succession was accepted by many well-known Egyptologists.

In appearance Sethe was the popular stereotype of a scholar— small in size and solemn of manner, though capable of deep and genuine warmth toward his close friends. The Swiss Naville was Sethe's exact antithesis, being a big, burly man with a jovial personality. Beneath the joviality, however, was a stubbornness which his opponents might reasonably have termed "bullheadedness." When the solemn German and the bullheaded Swiss met in conflict, they met head-on.

Sethe's interpretation of the facts was based on the assumption that when King A's name is erased from an inscription and replaced by the name of King B, then King B must have followed King A. This certainly sounds reasonable. But when Sethe applied the rule to the succession of the Thutmosid kings, he came up with the following sequence:

1. Thutmose I
2. Thutmose III
3. Thutmose III and Hatshepsut ruling jointly
4. Thutmose III ruling alone after having deposed Hatshepsut.
5. Thutmose I and Thutmose II as co-rulers, having displaced Thutmose III by a coup d'état
6. Thutmose II ruling alone after the death of Thutmose I
7. Hatshepsut and Thutmose III again—coup d'état.
8. Thutmose III alone after the death of Hatshepsut

Obviously this proposal had its difficulties. Naville fell upon them with cries of contempt. So heated did the debate become that in 1902, when Sethe and Naville were both camped out at

Luxor for the winter season, they were not on speaking terms with one another. Then a domestic catastrophe befell the Naville camp—the kitchen, complete with cook, collapsed into a tomb pit—and Madame Naville was for calling the whole thing off. Sethe, hearing of the trouble and of Madame Naville's laments, gallantly offered his hospitality, on one condition—the name of Hatshepsut was not to be mentioned. For several weeks the two deadly rivals lived in amity, enjoying many discussions on Egyptological matters—all matters except one. When the Naville establishment was restored to order, the Navilles moved out and the status quo was reestablished. Naville and Sethe stopped speaking.

Naville was right in disagreeing with Sethe, but wrong about certain details. In 1928 a reappraisal of the whole Hatshepsut problem was undertaken. An American scholar—Winlock—and a German scholar—Eduard Meyer—in separate works, thoroughly but courteously demolished Sethe's theory. So Sethe revised it, as follows:

1. Thutmose I
2. Thutmose II and his wife Hatshepsut
3. Hatshepsut and Thutmose III, the latter a puppet
4. Thutmose I and II—coup d'état!
5. Thutmose II alone, after the death of Thutmose I
6. Hatshepsut and Thutmose III after death of Thutmose II
7. Thutmose III alone after the death of Hatshepsut.

The astute reader will have seen that the basic problem in the above reconstruction—which is not a great improvement over Sethe's original theory—rests in points 4 and 5, the resurgence of Thutmose I and II. He may also have deduced that it is based upon the fact that when Hatshepsut's cartouches were rubbed out they were in some cases replaced by the names of her father and her husband, as well as by that of her nephew.

The last word on the Hatshepsut problem was summarized by Professor William F. Edgerton of the Oriental Institute, who went to Egypt and looked at the monuments. He could then state definitely that Hatshepsut's cartouche, once erased, was never restored—an important point, for the queen would surely have replaced her name on the monuments if she had returned to power after being deposed by her father and husband. This fact alone is enough to rule out both Sethe's original and revised theories. We are then left with the problem of the cartouches of Thutmose I and II which are written over cartouches of Hatshepsut—and Edgerton verified Sethe's contention that this had happened. In some cases the name of Thutmose III was put in the blank spaces which had once held Hatshepsut's cartouche, but these are rare.

The solution isn't that difficult. It is not essential to assume, that when one finds a king's name inscribed on stone, the king himself put it there. When Thutmose III hacked out Hatshepsut's name from her temples and buildings, he put in its place the names of his father and grandfather as well as his own. Hence we can derive the chronological sequence we have used in our chapter, the simplest and most logical.

Such examples of filial piety are not too common in Egypt. Ordinarily the kings who proclaimed this virtue in loud voices went around scratching out everybody's name so they could put their own up. But the hypothesis is more attractive than the merry-go-round of coup and counter coup produced by Sethe, which suggests a group of stage conspirators following each other around with daggers drawn. And filial piety could be a useful thing when a king wanted to emphasize the legitimacy of his descent and the validity of his claim to the throne.

Oddly enough, the conclusive evidence on the Thutmosid succession has been known to scholars for years. Breasted, who followed Sethe's involved explanation, translated the pertinent inscription in his collection of Egyptian texts, and never seemed to notice that it contradicted the sequence he proposed a few pages later in the book. Breasted was not the only one who disregarded the evidence, and yet it is about as definite as evidence can be, coming from a contemporary witness who had no motive for concealing the truth.

Ineni, the architect who supervised the tomb of Thutmose I, began his career under Amenhotep I. After listing his efforts on behalf of that king, he says that Amenhotep "went forth to heaven." Then follows the account of Ineni's services under

Thutmose I, who "rested from life, going forth to heaven, having completed his years in gladness of heart." Next we come to Thutmose II who, after the death of his father, "became king of the Black Land and ruler of the Red Land." Thutmose II's death is specifically described: "He went forth to heaven, having mingled with the gods." And then the clincher: "His son stood in his place as King of the Two Lands, having become ruler upon the throne of the one who begat him. His sister, the Divine Consort, Hatshepsut, settled the affairs of the Two Lands."

The last sentence is probably one of the most tactful descriptions of a usurpation ever penned. The text goes on to glorify Hatshepsut, but the important part of Ineni's biography is the definite statement that both Thutmose I and II were dead before Hatshepsut and her unwilling co-ruler ever came to the throne. In fact, Ineni's description agrees precisely with the presently accepted sequence of kings.

It is hard to explain why this uncompromising witness should have been kept off the stand so long. It must be admitted that "eyewitness" accounts are not always impartial, and archaeologists have good reason for preferring the incorruptible testimony of stone and clay. However, this testimony can be corrupted because it must be sifted through the minds of fallible mortals such as scholars.

The Hatshepsut problem is a problem no longer. I don't think any reputable scholar disagrees with Edgerton's conclusions. But that is the delight of a field like Egyptology; one never knows when a barefoot fellah may uncover a new inscription which will throw all our preconceived notions into a cocked hat, and set the scholarly world to its gentle wrangling once again.

VI

The Conqueror

Thutmose

THE greatest warrior Egypt ever produced was a little man, slightly over five feet tall. The average height of the ancient Egyptians was less than that of modern men, but some pharaohs, as we know from their mummies, were about six feet tall, and Thutmose must have been on the short side even in his day. One is irresistibly reminded of Napoleon, and of the usual psychological clichés about little men and their overweening ambition. The clichés hardly seem applicable, however. Not all conquerors have been little men, and few little men have been conquerors. If Thutmose's astounding accomplishments were "compensation" for a subconscious sense of inadequacy or frustration, there is no need to look beyond the known events of the king's boyhood for the source of the frustration. He was, as his adult life demonstrates, a man of varied and profound capabilities. Soldier, strategist, statesman, administrator—in each of these roles Thutmose displayed both energy and imagination. To accomplish all he accomplished in one lifetime, he must have been one of those irritating people who sleep only four hours a night and spend their waking hours operating at the highest pitch of efficiency. The enigma of his life—which has never been, and may never be, resolved—is the contrast between his passive youth and his volcanic maturity.

He was not a passionate man; except for the one, understandable burst of vindictiveness with which he assailed Hatshepsut's memory, we find no evidence that he ever allowed personal feelings to influence policy. It is a pity that physiognomy is not a reliable reflection of character, for while we cannot explain what went on behind Thutmose's face, we know pretty accurately what he looked like. His is not a handsome face, for its regularity is marred by one outstanding feature. Thutmose III excelled his predecessors in nose as in everything else, and bore it as proudly as Cyrano bore his.

We happen to have unusually detailed records which relate the military exploits of the Conqueror. The basic source is a long inscription which we call *The Annals of Thutmose III*. It was recorded on the walls of the temple of Karnak, and there it may be read today by any visitor who can decipher hieroglyphs. The stone-carved inscription was copied from an original, probably written on leather, by a man named Thaneni. In his tomb, Thaneni says proudly that he followed Thutmose III on his campaigns and "recorded the victories which he won in every land, putting them into writing according to the facts." He was evidently the official army historian, or military scribe, and it is to him that we owe the famous tale of the Battle of Megiddo with which the *Annals* of Karnak begin. But the man who supervised the carving of the copy was a priest, whose chief interest was not in battles but in booty, much of which went to the temple. As the *Annals* continue, they gradually degenerate into a prosaic list of tribute, with only tantalizing hints of great battles and brilliant strategies. Fortunately, we have other sources. The most useful is the tomb autobiography of a soldier named Amenemhab, who was second only to the royal warrior himself in valor. In recent years other inscriptions which tell of the exploits of Thutmose the Great have been found at Gebel Barkal in Nubia and at Armant.

On April 16, 1468 B.C., Thutmose left Tharu, the last Egyptian city on the northeast frontier, at the head of his army. His purpose, "to extend the boundaries of Egypt"—a candid avowal of motive which is not found in the annals of most modern con-

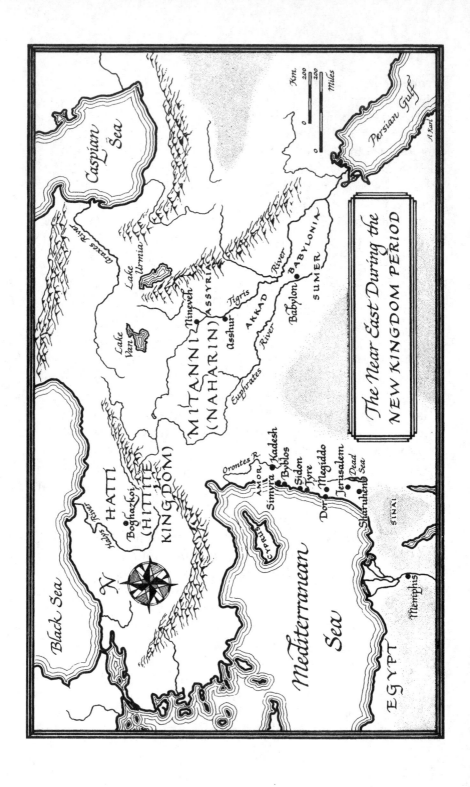

querors. In fact, the expedition marched to counter the threat mentioned in the preceding chapter, a threat posed by the great confederation of north Syrian states and their princes.

Ten days later Thutmose was at Gaza—a distance of 160 miles, not a bad pace for infantry. The date was significant: exactly twenty-two years earlier, Thutmose had been crowned king of Egypt. A good deal had happened since then; Thutmose's thought must have been both bitter and triumphant as he dwelt on his memories of the past. But he did not waste time in repining, or even in celebrating. He arrived at Gaza on the fourth day of the Egyptian month Pakhons, and he left the city on the fifth day. On the sixteenth day he encamped at Yehem, a town on the southern slopes of the Carmel Mountains.

Thutmose's goal was the city of Megiddo, in the plain on the northern side of the mountains. Megiddo had been fortified by the allies, who were under the command of the powerful king of Kadesh, because of its important strategic position as well as its reputation as an invincible fortress. The site of Megiddo had been occupied for thousands of years; it commanded the best road from Egypt to the Euphrates and was a populous city before and after Thutmose III.

Thutmose called his officers together for a council of war. The problem: how to cross the mountain ridge and reach the plain. There were three possible roads. One came out of the mountains north of Megiddo and one skirted the slopes of the city. The third route was the shortest and most direct. But the direct route had one conspicuous disadvantage, which the officers promptly pointed out.

"How can we go upon this narrow road, when it is reported that the enemy is there waiting? Must not horse go behind horse, and soldiers and people likewise? Shall our vanguard be fighting while the rear stands in Aruna, unable to fight?"

This makes very good sense, militarily. However, as we saw in the story of Kamose, the caution of the royal council is a favorite Egyptian literary device, and is intended to contrast with the valor and reckless courage of the king.

"My Majesty will proceed along this road of Aruna," the king swore, with great oaths. "Let him who will among you go upon

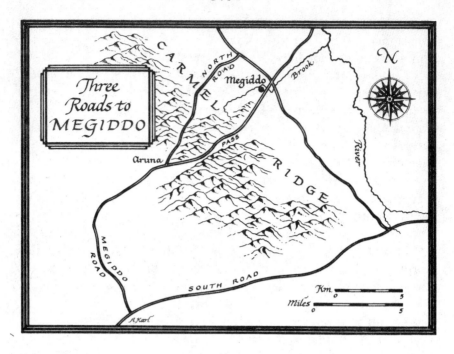

those roads of which you speak, and let him who will among you come in the following of my Majesty."

Evidently courage was a royal attribute more cherished by the Egyptians than good sense. Thutmose only succeeded in this reck-lessness because his opponents were equally careless—which, to do him justice, he might have counted upon. His courage cannot be doubted; he himself led the way through the narrow, treacherous pass, up the mountain ridge to the town of Aruna, where he spent the night. Next morning he pushed forward again and, before long, ran into the enemy. As the council had predicted, the rear of the Egyptian army was still in Aruna; but luckily for the Egyptians, the king, in the van, had reached a widening in the pass. Here the exasperated officers once more pleaded for caution.

"Let our victorious lord listen to us this time, and let our lord await for us the rear of his army and his people!"

This time Thutmose harkened. He waited till the rest of the army caught up with him. The enemy was not in sufficient force

Thutmose III. Head of a statue now in the Cairo Museum. *Photo from The Metropolitan Museum of Art.*

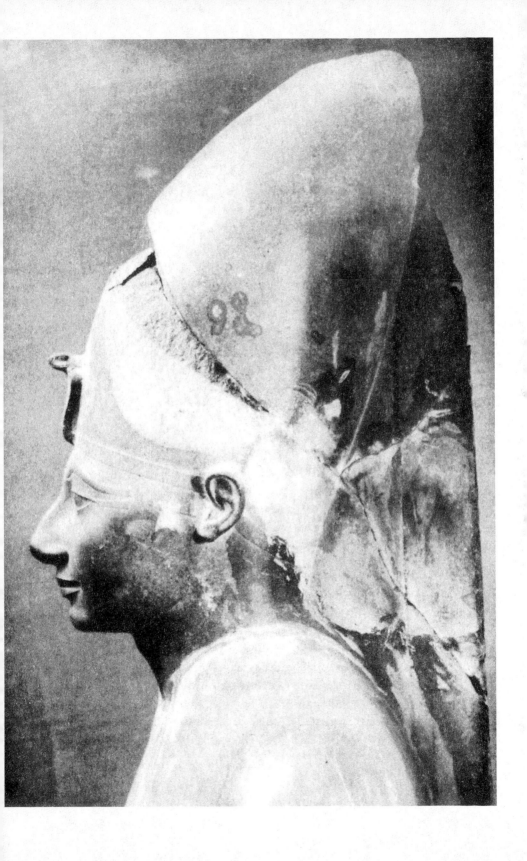

to oppose him, so he was then able to press forward and make camp on the south of Megiddo, on the bank of the brook called Kina. The time was about one in the afternoon.

Heaven knows what the king of Kadesh and his confederates were doing all this time. They might have won the battle if they had had scouts farther along the Aruna road, or had brought up reinforcements in time to deal with Thutmose when he first came out of the pass. Perhaps they assumed that no soldier of any intelligence would venture upon the Aruna road, so narrow and so susceptible to ambush. Or perhaps they counted on the strong walls of Megiddo, for when Thutmose led the chariot charge against them next morning, they broke with scarcely a fight. "They fled headlong to Megiddo in terror, abandoning their horses and their chariots of gold and silver, and the people hauled them up into the city, pulling them by their clothing."

The Egyptians enjoyed low comic touches of this sort, when the joke was on the enemy; the picture of the mighty prince of Kadesh being pulled up over the walls of Megiddo by his shirttails is rather funny. But what happened after that was not so amusing, and Thaneni, the army scribe, is bitter about it:

"Now if only the army of his Majesty had not given their hearts to plundering the belongings of the enemy, they would have captured Megiddo at this moment!" The sight of the abandoned horses (still uncommon and very valuable) and the jeweled equipment of the allies was too much for the Egyptian soldiers. They loyally carried the loot to the king, but Thutmose was not consoled. He urged the army on to victory: "The capture of Megiddo is the capture of a thousand towns!"

So the troops of Egypt had to pay for their greed by a long siege. They cut down the trees near the city and walled it in. The incompetent rebels had not planned to be besieged. They had left the very grain in the fields, and their empty stomachs must have felt even emptier as they looked over the city walls and saw the Egyptians munching their crops. Famine finally took its toll; the "wretched Asiatics" came forth suing for peace.

Somehow or other the *pièce de résistance* of the confederation, the king of Kadesh, had slipped over both sets of walls one dark night and made his getaway; it is hard to imagine how, but he did it. Despite this disastrous loss, Thutmose showed amazing clemency toward the inhabitants. Naturally, he took most of their property; but like a famous American general, he allowed the allied soldiers transport to their distant homes. "Then my Majesty gave them leave to go to their towns. They all went by donkey, so that I might take their horses."

In his haste to escape, the king of Kadesh had been forced to leave his family behind; either that "fallen one" was not bound by strong ties of familial affection or he relied rather trustingly on Thutmose's clemency. His hopes were justified. Thutmose took them as hostages but did them no harm. It was safer to be besieged and captured by Thutmose III than by most European conquerors.

After cleaning out the city of Megiddo, Thutmose took the road again, north to the Lebanon. He subdued another confederation of three cities here, and built a fortress. The season was growing late; the rains were due. Thutmose turned south toward Egypt, but not without a political stroke no less effective than his military exploits. He had appointed new chiefs for the conquered countries, to supplant the "rebellious" princes. The sons of the new rulers were taken to Egypt by the canny king, whose scribe explains: "Now whosoever of these princes died, his Majesty would cause his son to stand in his place." The heirs of the Asiatics served as hostages for the loyalty of their fathers; and when they in turn came to rule their vassal cities they had become Egyptian in custom and language and sympathy, identifying themselves with the cultured Egyptians among whom they had been raised from childhood rather than with their own humble subjects. It was a master stroke, and this is the first recorded instance of its being practiced, though later conquerors found it equally useful.

The city of Thebes was in celebration when the king returned, and Amon had the best cause to rejoice; he got the lion's share of the plunder. Not only gold and jewels, but also land in conquered Lebanon and in Egypt itself went to the god, with cattle to graze thereon and slaves to tend it.

The following year Thutmose was off again—an easy swing through the conquered territories to check up on the princes he had left in power. The chieftains' collective memory was good; they poured in with tribute and assurances of undying devotion. There were also gifts from the king of Assyria, then a young nation on the threshold of its later power. The Egyptians blandly recorded these gifts, as they would do with other gifts from more powerful monarchs, as "tribute." If a wandering Assyrian reached Egypt and was able to read the Karnak inscriptions—unlikely event—he would hardly be in a position to contradict them.

The energetic king had now worked out a schedule to which he would adhere for the rest of his life: half the year in the field, the other half in Thebes, organizing, building, and checking on what had been done in his absence. The army marched from Egypt after the spring harvests, which occurred earlier in that country than elsewhere in the Near East, and arrived in Syria just in time to swoop down on the enemy's ripening grain. When the rainy season approached, Thutmose turned homeward, reaching Thebes some time in October.

Thutmose devoted his third and fourth campaigns to further consolidation of territory already won. The records of the third campaign at Karnak are rather striking, although they do not note any great battles; instead, the walls depict long rows of plants which were brought back, at the king's command, from Syria. This suggests a certain degree of intellectual curiosity on the part of Thutmose; we wonder what other subjects, besides botany, engaged his interest. But few records touch upon this attractive trait; conquest was a more dramatic subject for reliefs than was scholarship.

In Thutmose's early campaigns we may see a leitmotif which emerges more clearly as the years pass. The great adversary at Megiddo, the leader of the allies, was the king of Kadesh. The Egyptians never gave him a name, for reasons which we have explained before, but he was a shrewd and cunning adversary and a constant thorn in Thutmose's side. We recall that the successful siege of Megiddo did not net this wily bird; he had escaped, leaving his family in Thutmose's hands. In the next five years Thutmose must have realized that he would eventually have to face and crush Kadesh and its king, but he was no longer the impetuous youth who had led his army through the dangerous pass of Aruna. His fifth campaign dealt with the Phoenician cities of the coast, hitherto unmolested. This move had its place in a larger strategy; Thutmose could not advance northward toward Kadesh with the potential threat of Phoenicia behind him. Cunningly, he avoided the southern coast and struck by sea at the wealthy northern kingdoms of Phoenicia. Two great battles, and the coast was won; the other chieftains sent messages of submission. Thutmose returned home by sea, the first part of his long-range plans completed. The next campaign was to be against Kadesh itself.

Kadesh was a hard nut to crack, even for Thutmose III. It was entirely surrounded by water, with rivers on two sides and a canal on the third; moats and formidable walls made it perhaps the strongest fortress in all of Syria. Thutmose laid siege to the city. Thanks to the materialistic orientation of the scribe who recorded this campaign, we can't even be sure whether he conquered it or not. Amenemhab, Thutmose's trusted officer, was there; but since his memoirs were designed to be carved in his tomb, they naturally concern themselves primarily with the bravery of Amenemhab. We can only conclude that he was not especially brave upon this occasion.

What happened to the adversary, that "fallen one" of Kadesh?

The records are infuriatingly silent on this point. Evidently the king of Kadesh repeated his earlier exploit and got away from the beleaguered city. He was certainly a leading advocate of the "he who fights and runs away" school of thought. We have not heard the end of him yet.

Thutmose regarded Kadesh and not its king as the major goal of this campaign, for he went on to the next stage of what had become a truly ambitious plan. Whether he had dreamed of his final goal from boyhood, or whether he dared envision it as his triumphant army proceeded, almost unopposed, through the highlands, we do not know. It was a dream worthy of a conqueror, and it had precedent. Years before, his grandfather, Thutmose I, to whom he owed not only filial respect but the admiration of one fine soldier for another, had led his armies to the banks of the Euphrates—that strange inverted water whose current actually flowed from north to south instead of in the normal, decent manner. The inverted water had now begun to haunt the slumbers of Thutmose III.

But between him and the Euphrates lay a sizable obstacle—not a loosely bound confederation of small city states, but a mighty empire—the empire of Mitanni, or Naharin.

The kingdom of Mitanni is still one of the unsolved mysteries of Near Eastern archaeology. To be sure, we know it was there, which could not have been said a century ago. But its capital, known as Wassukanni, has never been found, and its language is still imperfectly understood. Most of what we know of this flourishing country, one of the half-dozen great powers of the second millennium B.C., we know from records of other nations. During the fifteenth century before Christ, a group of alien warriors, trainers and breeders of horses came down from some unknown homeland in farther Asia and subjugated the indigenous peoples of the area near the Upper Euphrates. They spoke an Indo-European language, these cavalrymen, and the gods they worshiped have been connected with the deities of India—Mitra, Indra, Varuna. At its peak the empire of Naharin extended from the Zagros to the Mediterranean, and from Lake Van to Asshur. Its interests naturally extended to the part of northern Syria which lay near its own borders.

These were the people whom Thutmose III meant to face next. The attack on Mitanni was not out-and-out aggression; the king of that nation had backed the confederation of the chieftains of Syria which was crushed in the battle of Megiddo. However, it is not likely that Thutmose was worrying about justification.

Before undertaking his greatest battle, Thutmose took every precaution for success. He spent a year making sure that his territories in Syria were under control, and a further year in Egypt making ready. In 1457 B.C., he was on his way.

One little touch displayed during this famous campaign shows Thutmose's foresight, as well as his self-confidence. In Byblos, on the Phoenician coast, he had ships built of the famous cedar. Loaded on carts drawn by oxen, "they journeyed in front of my Majesty, in order to cross that great river which lies between this foreign country and Naharin." The river is, of course, the Euphrates, and the poor oxen must have had a time of it, all the way from Phoenicia.

Senzar, Aleppo, Carcemish—one after another the cities of north Syria fell, or sent messages of submission. Thutmose's reputation had evidently preceded him. The king of Naharin fled before him, abandoning his country to fire and the sword. Thutmose crossed the river on his cedar boats and laid waste to Naharin, carrying its people away captive to Egypt. Upon reaching the river, he erected a stela beside that of his grandfather, Thutmose I.

Thutmose must have been in his glory as he turned back toward Egypt, conquering a town here and there as he marched. By an ironic touch of fate, he came closest to disaster at the time of his highest triumph; his life was saved only by the prompt action of his devoted follower Amenemhab. This was one of the great moments of the general's life, and he remembered it vividly even when, as an old man, he sat recounting his deeds to the patient scribe who would supervise their recording for eternity. One of the cities Thutmose scooped in on his way home was called Niy. After the battle of Niy, word got around that there was a herd of elephants in the vicinity, and the king decided to take time out for relaxation. There were 120 beasts in the herd which the Egyptians hunted, and one of them—"the largest," according to modest Amenemhab—charged the king. Standing in the water between two rocks, the general placed his body between his king and danger, and cut off the beast's "hand." He was rewarded with gold—and changes of clothing. One would hope so, indeed. An elephant in a river can raise considerable surf, and if Amenemhab really did sever its trunk there must have been other stains than those of water on his linen kilt.

We know only this single narrow escape of the king's, thanks to the "shrivelled soul of the ancient bureaucrat" who recorded the campaigns at Karnak. The epithets are those of Breasted, who goes on to add, bitterly, that the ancient scribe "little dreamed how hungrily future ages would ponder his meagre exerpts." Of course, Thutmose must have had his share of wounds and danger;

he never led his regiment from behind. But the myth of the invincible king, armored in his divinity, is never questioned in the official records.

One might suppose that Thutmose could now safely rest upon his laurels. For ten years he had spent half of his time in the field; he had extended the empire further than had any king who ever ruled Egypt; and the plunder that poured into the capital at Thebes must have dazzled the eyes of the watching populace. He had enlarged the temples and built new ones, sent caravans to Punt and the Sudan, and received gifts from Babylon and Hatti.

But the conquered lands were too new to subjugation to bear it lightly, and Thutmose had to maintain his empire or give it up. He had another twenty years of life before him, and in that time he fought nine more campaigns. One need not suppose that the task was unpleasant; by inclination and by habit Thutmose may have preferred the life of the camp to that of the courtly halls of Thebes, with their rich decorations of gold and faience—and their tedious round of ceremonial duties. He had his staff, well trained and devoted; Thaneni, the scribe who recorded the exploits of his Majesty; Amenemhab, the trusted general who had saved him from the elephant in Niy; Intef the marshal, a prince of Thinis, who had the king's apartments (in tent or conquered palace) ready for him when he arrived at night; Thutiy, the prince and priest and commander of the army, who conquered Joppa by a trick straight out of the Arabian Nights, if we can believe a folk tale of a later date. Thutiy's soldiers entered the city hidden in panniers borne by a train of donkeys—the precursor not only of the Trojan Horse but of Ali Baba. This tale is fiction, but Thutiy is not. His tomb has been found, as well as a beautiful golden dish, bearing his name and titles, which was given to him by Thutmose as a reward for one of his valorous deeds—could it have been the conquest of Joppa?

With such men behind him, Thutmose could venture greatly. And he could do so with his mind at east about the welfare of the Two Lands, for he had left another trusted servant as vizier, a man named Rekhmire.

Rekhmire's tomb is one of the showplaces of Thebes today. It lies on the hill of the Sheikh Abd el Kurnah, on the west bank of the Nile, where many of the great nobles of the Empire are buried. The wall paintings of the tomb show us, in brilliant detail, how rich and how sophisticated was the life of a nobleman of that imperial age. The tomb also gives an interesting account of the duties of the vizier. And what duties they were! The vizier was in charge of *everything*. He was a whole cabinet in himself—Secretary of State, receiving embassies and reviewing tribute in the king's absence; Secretary of the Treasury, since the chief treasurer reported to him, and he was responsible for taxation; Secretary of the Interior and of Agriculture, supervising the water supply, the plowing and the canals; Attorney General *and* Chief Justice; Secretary of War, with both army and navy under his control; Secretary of Labor, for he regularly inspected the royal craftsmen, from cabinetmakers to sculptors. In his spare time the vizier wore several other hats: he was mayor and chief of police of the residence city and was also in charge of the royal messengers and the king's personal bodyguard. Rekhmire's tomb inscriptions mention all these functions and others; then, just in case something has been overlooked, the writing adds: "Let every office, from first to last, proceed to the hall of the vizier to take counsel with him."

The painted walls of the tomb depict Rekhmire in the process of carrying out many of his onerous duties—which evidently did not take every moment of his time, for there is a spirited scene of a party at the vizier's home, with wine flowing freely and the guests enjoying its effect. Since his accession to the vizierate was the high point of Rekhmire's life, it is natural that his formal investiture in office should be the subject of another relief.

Here we see Thutmose III enthroned. Before him stands the new vizier, attentive to the exhortation which the king delivers. It is a sobering speech, which must have had the same import as a solemn oath of office. "Look thou to the office of the vizier," Thutmose begins, "and be vigilant over everything that is done in it. Lo, it is the mooring post of the entire land; lo, it is not pleasant at all—no, it is bitter as gall." Foremost among the responsibilities of the vizier is justice. "The abomination of the god is partiality. So this is the instructon: thou shalt act accordingly.

Thou shalt look upon him whom thou knowest like him whom
thou dost not know; upon him who has access to thy person like
him who is distant from thy house."

If Rekhmire took his responsibilities seriously, his position as
judge must have been the most sobering of all his duties. He was,
by proxy, the dispenser of that justice which is higher than mortal. The tomb walls show him to us in this awesome task, seated in
the hall of justice; before him are the forty leather whips which
were the symbols of the discipline he could wield if he chose. For
a long time these forty pictured objects were believed to be
leather rolls containing a law code which governed the vizier's
decisions; and how Egyptological mouths watered at the prospect
of one day finding such rolls! Peculiarly enough, the Egyptians
had no such code of laws. The other peoples of the Near East did;
the Code of Hammurabi is the most famous, but there are earlier
examples from the same area. Perhaps it was not strange that the
Egyptians—to the best of our knowledge—never developed formal
codified law, since the judgment of the god-king and his proxies
was, by definition, straight from heaven.

Rekhmire implies that Thutmose kept a close check on the
activities of his subordinates; if so, he was satisfied with what he
found, for he left Egypt to their administrations half of each year
while he carried out his military objectives. Most of the king's
remaining nine campaigns were tours of inspection, gentle re-
minders to the dynasts in Syria that though they might be far
from Egypt geographically, they were only days removed from the
all-seeing eye and all-powerful arm of the king. The tenth campaign had to deal with a more serious problem—a resurgence of
the king of Naharin and his allies. The battles Thutmose fought
on this occasion daunted the proud princes of northern Syria for a
good many years. Even on the relatively peaceful inspection tours,
Thutmose maintained high standards of efficiency. Harbors were
kept permanently supplied and garrisons were trained. "Tribute"
continued to pour in, filling the treasuries of king and gods.

Thutmose had defeated Hatshepsut, crushed Mitanni, and
conquered an empire; but there was one shadow out of his past
which had never been exorcized. Once again, and for the final
time, the prince of Kadesh reappears, out of the mists which had

shrouded his activities for so long, to stand against the fighting hawk of Egypt. We have not heard of him since the battle of Kadesh, ten years before, when he mysteriously vanished from the beleaguered city. Where he had been, and what he had been up to, we do not know; but now he was ready for his last gamble with fate. He had engaged formidable support—Naharin again, and many of the coastal cities. His chief ally was the city-state of Tunip, to the north of Kadesh. Thutmose had fought in Syria for nineteen years, but if he lost this battle he might lose all that he had won.

The aging king (he must have been in his forties, which was old for that time) was prompt to take up the gage of battle. In the spring of the 42nd year of his reign, Thutmose's fleet could be seen heading for a harbor on the north coast of Syria. Instead of marching up the river to Kadesh, he had decided to cut her off from her northern ally first. Tunip held him for a time, but he took it eventually, and then led his troops up the Orontes to Kadesh. And here Amenemhab, the old soldier who had cut off the elephant's trunk, performed his second great deed.

The battle was fiercely fought by both sides. The stakes were tremendous, and the king of Kadesh knew it. In his last, desperate attempt to turn the tide in his favor, he thought up a trick that was worthy of him: he sent a mare out of the city and had her driven toward the Egyptian army. The chariotry wavered as the stallions yielded to this exciting distraction. The prize of victory hung in the balance; and Amenemhab moved to weigh the scales. Leaping from his chariot, he ran the mare down and killed her. In a gesture of pure panache, he cut off the animal's tail and presented it to the king. The assault on the city must have followed immediately; in an epic it could not be otherwise, and an epic king would have cried his army on with a great shout of laughter and a flourish of the mare's tail. Amenemhab, carried away by his success, was first over the walls. Behind him poured the hard-bitten veterans of the Syrian wars. Against such men and such a leader even Kadesh the invincible had no chance. The city fell; and with it fell the last hopes of the Syrian cities for independence.

And what of the prince of Kadesh, who did not know when he

was defeated? Once again we may invoke Breasted's curse on the withered bureaucrat who recorded this campaign only as a list of booty collected. But we can deduce the fate of Thutmose's arch-enemy from the silence that followed. Never again, in the ten years that remained to the king, did Syria rebel against her over-lord. We cannot imagine such a state of peace and lethargy with the restless spirit of the prince of Kadesh still abroad in the land. The second battle of Kadesh was not a long-drawn-out siege, as the first had been. Thutmose was behind schedule that year, held back by the resistance of Tunip, and he had not time for such niceties. Kadesh was taken by storm, and its prince may not have had the opportunity to repeat his past escapes. Did he die in battle, in the last hopeless fight to save his city when the bronzed troops of Egypt swarmed over the wall; or was he captured by Thutmose and executed, as the greatest rebel of them all? Thutmose's records do not mention the execution of enemies—who were, in the egocentric Egyptian view, guilty of rebellion and treason. It is, of course, unsafe to conclude from this silence that such executions never took place. Still, we may prefer to think of the prince of Kadesh as perishing in battle. We have a certain sympathy for him. Three times he had fought against the most invincible warrior of his age, the man to whom many of his peers had tamely surrendered without so much as a spear being cast. Megiddo, Kadesh, and Kadesh again. . . . It would be interesting to find, some fine day, the buried records of the lost capital of Naharin, and see what they have to say about their ally of Kadesh. To his own men he was probably a patriot and a hero; to the Egyptians, just another rebel.

So ended, after twenty years, the active military career of Thutmose III. He was first and foremost a soldier, and that is why we have devoted so much space to the description of his campaigns. His other accomplishments compare favorably with the activities of other kings who did not spend half their lives abroad. Rekhmire mentions the king's omnipotence; some of this can be written off as court flattery, but there is no doubt that Thutmose made good use of his annual six months in Egypt. He toured the country inspecting canals, buildings, and harvests, and he ordered careful records kept of his campaigns and their results. Of all his building activities the most famous are the great obelisks. They have had a curious history; not one of them stands in Egypt today, but they have literally carried Thutmose's name to the four corners of the earth. The obelisk in Central Park in New York once towered above Thutmose's temple at Heliopolis; its former mate stands on the Thames Embankment in London.

When he returned from the Second Battle of Kadesh, Thutmose III had another ten or twelve years of life remaining to him. During this time he occupied himself with such minor details as Nubia, which was now pouring fantastic amounts of gold into the Egyptian treasury. He himself visited the south countries in his fiftieth year, and his domains stretched to the Fourth Cataract.

Perhaps the most far-reaching consequence of the life of this man was not the empire itself, but the changes which the empire was to produce in Egypt. Almost every aspect of life was affected; and some of the changes were to bear fruit in a far future day, and in a way which even Thutmose the Great could not have anticipated.

Some of the results are fairly obvious. The army was no longer an amateur militia, hastily assembled for specific campaigns. Since Ahmose there had been a hard core of professional fighters, with the Medjay of Nubia as its elite; these men served as the royal bodyguard and city police in time of peace. But an army which has fought yearly for twenty years has lost its amateur standing; the men knew their craft and their officers, and the ones who survived brought home wealth such as their fathers had never seen. The empire, so hardly won, had to be held. This meant garrisons, though not large ones, in foreign cities. The army organization was complex; quartermaster, signal corps, and general accounting had come into being, along with chariotry, infantry, and naval forces. Now, for the first time, the professional fighting man, as a group and as an individual, becomes a force in the state.

Another obvious result of empire was the effect of the enormous wealth pouring into Egypt from north and south. The *nouveau riche* acquired expensive tastes and demanded foreign products. No wealthy household was complete without an Asiatic slave or two, and sophisticated Egyptians sprinkled their speech with foreign words and even turned to the worship of new gods.

New people and new ideas often have a favorable effect upon the culture they invade; in the optimum cases the new and the old give birth to a civilization higher than either of its parents. But one of the consequences of foreign ideas in Egypt was not so attractive. This was the effect upon Egyptian art. Craftsmen and painters had developed their skills early, and the canons of taste were beautifully harmonious. The avalanche of new techniques which came from the conquered lands and from other empires was not always assimilated easily. The contents of Tutankhamon's tomb show a certain degradation of the pure classic style; many of the objects are exquisitely lovely, all are beautifully executed; but one or two are dreadfully vulgar in taste. There is one lamp, in particular, that has always set my teeth on edge. It is an ingenious piece of craftsmanship; the alabaster vessel which forms the central portion of the object is double, and a scene has been painted, in bright color, on one of the inner surfaces. When the oil floating in the vessel was lighted, the figures were visible through the translucent stone. The central vessel is a tall, vaselike shape, fairly attractive by itself, although its lines do not have quite the grace of earlier vases. But, on either side of the vessel are added decorative elements—kneeling figures, plants, cartouches—which combine to form a clumsy design, and which are, in total, far too heavy for the size of the central vase.

We could go on describing the changes that resulted from the growth of empire, but one point is especially noteworthy. That is the fantastic wealth and power which began to accrue to the great state god Amon. Among the multitudinous gods of Egypt there were a dozen or so greater than the rest: Re of Heliopolis, the very ancient sun-god; Ptah of Memphis, patron of artisans and artists, to whom (among other gods) was ascribed the creation of the world; Osiris and Isis and their son Horus; another Horus, a falcon and a sun-god; Thoth, the ibis-headed divine scribe; and others. All of them were older in dignity than the parvenu Amon; none of them, except perhaps Re, had ever enjoyed the preeminence of the god of Thebes. By a convenient process called

Lamp of Tutankhamon. *The Cairo Museum.*

syncretism, Amon was able to absorb his potential rivals in the pantheon; among other gods he swallowed Re himself, and was known as Amon-Re. This does not mean that Re's temples were closed down. His ancient worship continued as before, but Amon could now claim the attributes and the qualities of the honored sun-god. As the conquering pharaohs went out to battle under the aegis of Amon-Re, they attributed their victories to his aid, and thought it only fitting that he be rewarded. The whole transaction made a vicious cycle: the more powerful Amon became, the greater the size of his reward; the richer he got, the more his power increased. It would be a mistake to view Egyptian history from this point on as a conflict between the temporal power, residing in the king, and the spiritual might of Amon-Re and his priests. From the Egyptian point of view, no such distinction could exist, and there were many other factors involved. Yet the shadow of Amon, hawk-headed, holding the insignia of power in human hands, began to grow long across the fertile green valley of Egypt. Thutmose III had raised up a number of unexpected monsters to plague the placid immutability of the divine kingship, but this was perhaps the most menacing of all.

Thutmose the king, of course, had no doubts about the future. The tips of his tall obelisks, shielded with gold, caught the light of the rising sun each morning and sent sparks glittering across the Nile. Slaves in strange colored garments, speaking a gabble of uncouth tongues, tended the affairs of the land and worked beside the slighter, smooth-faced Egyptians. Even the succession was in order, for Thutmose had a son.

Thutmose's military and administrative exploits so overshadow everything else in his life that we have not mentioned his domestic side. Actually, not much is known about it. The uxorious Amenhotep III had a queen who was a personality in her own right; Akhenaton cherished an almost Byronic passion for his lovely wife; and that ancient reprobate Ramses II fascinates us solely by the sheer number of women he acquired. But Thutmose III has left an impression of austerity so far as the weaker sex is concerned. Perhaps he had had enough of women after Hatshepsut.

Oddly enough, however, two of his wives may have been daughters of that overpowering lady. One of them, Nefrure, may not have lived to marry her half brother. She was certainly Hatshepsut's child, but she is a ghostly wraith of a person, and the queen Thutmose honored most is another lady. It is surprising that Thutmose should have permitted the woman who sat beside him on the throne to be called by a name identical with that of the woman he hated—Hatshepsut. We are not positive that she was her namesake's daughter; the only thing that suggests the relationship is the name. Yet this seems fairly strong proof, under the circumstances. It was not a name which Thutmose would like to have seen perpetuated for sentimental reasons.

Though he may not have found female society particularly congenial, Thutmose was no more monogamous than anybody else. Three members of his harem were found buried in a single tomb which was published by H. F. Winlock in 1948. These ladies had foreign names, which reminds us of a policy of Alexander the Great; perhaps Thutmose anticipated the Macedonian in seeing the potentialities of foreign conquest through marriage. These three young ladies were never more than junior members of the royal family, however; and in view of this fact, the wealth of their funerary equipment is quite striking. In 1948, Winlock estimated the value of the gold and silver employed as around $6,800. In ancient times its value would have been considerably greater, and the precious metals represented only part of the equipment of the tomb. What then must have been the treasure buried with the body of the king-conqueror himself!

Toward the end of his life, the aging king placed his son beside him on the throne. About a year later, on March 17, 1447 B.C., King Menkheperre, Thutmose III, "mounted to heaven; he joined the sun, the divine limbs mingling with him who begat him."

Today, when the innocent tourist visits Thebes, he may be shown the battle reliefs of Thutmose III, and regaled with tales of the deeds of the great warrior king. But when, in respectful admiration, he asks the name of this mighty man of war, he will be informed that the warrior was none other than Ramses II. Of course he may get a reliable guide; there are many of them in Egypt. But the average dragoman and guide still associates the word "great" with Ramses, whose one famous battle was a triumph of egotism and poor planning. There is a reason for this error, since Ramses managed to get his name up in every blank space remaining on every wall in Egypt. But the epithet "the Great" surely belongs to Thutmose III, if to any king of Egypt, even if we judge him only by the material results of his campaigns. In an age which saw brutality—though not on so grand a

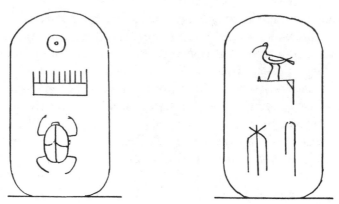

Cartouches of Thutmose III
The left reads: Men-kheper-Re; the right: Thut-mose.

scale as Christian Europe was able to work up—he showed clemency; at a time when death was the proper portion of the defeated, he spared the fallen. At the very least he deserves to regain the prestige he has lost to bombastic old Ramses II. Therefore, I am appending a copy of the cartouches of Thutmose III, so that the reader of this book may recognize them when he pays his first visit to the land of the Red and White Crowns. The ability to identify a cartouche or two has utility; it gives the tourist prestige in the eyes of his fellows, and will sometimes worry a guide enough to make him control his imagination in future. The cartouche may have a further utility if the reader-tourist wants to take home a scarab as a souvenir of his visit to Egypt. The royal name most often found on the little amulets is that of Thutmose III, for his fellow countrymen, then and later, knew full well the magical value of such a name. Only be sure that you buy an imitation scarab, not a genuine one. There is no difference between the two types, as sold in the antique shops in Cairo, in origin or in appearance; the only difference is in the price.

And do not forget to add Thutmose's tomb to your repertory while in Thebes. The central attraction of the Valley of the Kings, across from Luxor, is the tomb of Tutankhamon. During the "season" this part of the Valley is almost too populous, for in the same immediate area are other tombs which are popular with visitors. But if you are wearing sensible shoes you may take a short hike, only a few hundred yards, to a small canyon in the cliffs, apart from the swarming center of things; and here you will have a genuine feeling for the secrecy and loneliness that these houses of eternity once conveyed. Today you may climb by rickety wooden stairs to the hole in the cliff where once the swaying funeral cortege carried the embalmed body of Thutmose the Great. In location and in atmosphere it is one of the most impressive tombs in the Valley of the Kings, and it has another claim to fame. The funerary chamber is one of the most beautifully decorated in all of Egypt. But don't forget those sensible shoes.

Thutmose's mummy was not found in his tomb. The members of the second oldest profession had gotten to it, long before any of our immediate ancestors were born. But his body survived, thanks to the frantic efforts of a group of devoted priests in the last dying days of Egypt's greatness. This story will be told in due course. Today Thutmose's mummy lies in the Cairo Museum, with those of his peers. There is nothing particularly majestic about the withered face. Battered by impious tomb robbers, even the once-imposing Thutmosid nose has lost its panache. You may draw your own moral.

VII

The Power and the Glory

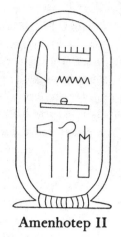

Amenhotep II

WE have exhausted our superlatives on Thutmose III, but that is all right; we will not be needing them for a while. Not that the Conqueror's son was not a fair enough fighter himself. If we can believe the stories that have come down to us—which we probably should not—he surpassed even his renowned father in feats of arms. Thutmose III had driven an arrow nine inches out of the back of a copper target two inches thick; Amenhotep II drove his arrow clean through a target *three* inches thick. He trained his horses so ably that they did not sweat, even when galloping. He rowed a boat (with a 34-foor oar) four miles without stopping, and then landed it alone; his 200-man crew had collapsed long before. He could outrun anyone in Egypt, and no man could draw his bow.

All this braggadocio is harmless, if mendacious. But Amenhotep II was not a Nice King. Soon after his father died, he had to lead a campaign into Syria to suppress a "rebellion" of the local princes there; these worthies soon acquired the habit of trying out a new king to see whether he would be as competent or as interested as his ancestors had been. The account of Amenhotep's first

Syrian campaign leaves an unpleasant taste in the mouth. Probably the actual events did not differ greatly from what had happened under his father; but there is a noticeable difference in the selection of the details which Amenhotep II wished to commemorate. After capturing seven of the rebel princes, Amenhotep brought them back to Thebes, hanging head down at the prow of the royal barge. He then bashed in their heads personally, and hung six of the bodies on the walls of Thebes. The seventh was sent down into Nubia to be draped over the battlements of the city of Napata as a lesson to the Nubians.

As an act of barbarity, this is pretty tame compared with the daily activities of the Assyrians or the morning prayers of the Aztecs. The technique was still being used in enlightened England, during the enlightened eighteenth century A.D. The English were more economical with their corpses; they took them to pieces in order to spread the effect—a head here, a torso there—it all added up. One of the most popular artistic motifs in Egyptian reliefs was the bashing of enemies or of captives by the king, and it may have represented a ritual act which was performed before Amon-Re at the end of a successful campaign. But Amenhotep's father had better things to record than smashing in skulls.

However we may deplore Amenhotep II's techniques, they were eminently successful. A few campaigns into Syria and Nubia settled those areas, and the king spent the rest of his life in a normal royal fashion—quarrying obelisks, building at Karnak, excavating his tomb—and, one presumes, shooting arrows through targets. He also amused himself with certain pursuits which might be genteelly summarizd as "wine, women, and song." One day when Amenhotep was sitting around in the palace, making a happy hour for himself (as the saying went), he got to feeling nostalgic and decided to dash off a note to an old comrade and drinking companion. This official, who was at one of the forts in Nubia, was so impressed by the letter, written in the king's own hand, that he had it reproduced on stone. It was found by George Reisner at Fort Semna.

I do not propose to translate this text; to be candid, I doubt if I could even if I wanted to. Authorities differ as to the interpreta-

tion of some of the more interesting sections, and the whole document gives an impression of remarkable incoherence. We often
have this feeling about mutilated inscriptions; but in this case I
am inclined to wonder how much of the incoherence might be
due to Amenhotep's condition when he wrote it. What are we to
do, for example, with the ladies who are familiarly referred to as a
servant girl of Byblos, a little maiden of Alalakh, and an old
woman of Arapha? Is Amenhotep insulting his rivals, the princes
of these cities, by derisive epithets; or is he reminding the friend
of his youth of certain memories they have in common? I suppose
this peculiar letter could be interpreted more favorably as a touch
of good fellowship from one jolly soldier to another; but I am
prejudiced against Amenhotep II. We should, however, say one
nice thing about him before we leave the subject. So let us add
that there may be a grain of truth in the king's claims about his
archery. Not much more than a grain, though.

His bow was buried with him in the tomb in the Valley of the
Kings, where his body was found, one of the few royal mummies
which survived to our times in their original burial places. Tomb
robbers had been at it, and had removed everything of value from
coffin and body. Then, when Egypt went into its last illness, and
the depredations at the royal tombs passed the bounds of en-
durance, priests moved the bodies of the ancient kings into secret
hiding places for safety's sake. One of the places chosen was the
tomb of Amenhotep II, and eventually he had thirteen other
royal bodies for company. When this cache was discovered in
1898, Amenhotep's body was left in its sarcophagus after the other
mummies had been removed to the Cairo Museum. The reasons
were sentimental; there has always been a vociferous minority
who feel that the mortal remains of Egypt's kings should be left in
honorable burial, not exposed to the gaze of curious sightseers.
The procedure ought to be safe, since everyone knows that nothing worth stealing would be left on the mummies. However, the
ancient and honorable profession of grave robbing is one Egyptian tradition which has been handed on from father to son, down
to the present day; and some of the boys near Thebes evidently
failed to read the newspaper accounts which explained that
Amenhotep no longer owned anything worth stealing. They

broke into the tomb again in 1901, and slit through the mummy wrappings, to find—nothing but a mummy. It is surprising that they bothered, since the grapevine among the brothers of the less-legal crafts operates more efficiently than archaeological newsletters, and thieves, of all people, ought to "case" a place before they rob it. Perhaps it was just a matter of old habits, which reputedly die hard.

Amenhotep's successor was another Thutmose—the Fourth. His is a more elusive personality; it fails to convey any positive image, pleasing or the reverse. He made the usual excursions, with army, into Syria and Nubia, in order to put down the usual revolts, and he piously finished and erected the obelisk which his grandfather and namesake, Thutmose III, had begun at Karnak. The largest surviving obelisk, it is now in Rome, and commemorates the names of both Thutmoses. The only other record of interest left by Thutmose IV is the stela which nestles between the paws of the Sphinx at Giza, where it may be seen today upon the payment of a bit of baksheesh. The stela tells the story of how Thutmose, as a young prince, lay down to rest in the shadow of the great stone beast after a tiring hunting trip. As he slept, the sun-god, of whom the Sphinx was then believed to be the image, appeared to him in a dream and begged him to clear away the sand which had covered most of the huge statue. As a reward, Re would see to it that the young man inherited the throne. Thutmose got the crown, and carried out his part of the bargain. Some Egyptologists have interpreted this story to mean that Thutmose was not the original heir. Divine intervention was a popular substitute for legitimacy, so the theory may have some foundation. But our very uncertainty on this point, at a period in Egyptian history which is relatively well documented, serves to indicate how little we really know, and how much we have yet to learn.

By now, one point should have been made clear—that it takes more than a sun helmet and a shovel to make an Egyptologist. Most of the books on archaeology which are written for the "layman"—an opprobrious epithet, for whose use I apologize—tell and retell the accounts of excavations as if that one activity were the sole source of an archaeologist's data. Now and then an attempt is made to give the linguist his due by mentioning the

Rosetta Stone, and by recounting the life of Jean François Champollion and the process by which he deciphered the hieroglyphs. Philology and excavation are certainly important subfields of archaeology, but, as I have tried to demonstrate, there is hardly any aspect of knowledge which is not grist for the mill of the archaeologist. One of the unexpected subjects he has had to contend with—in Egypt, at least—is genealogical research. Generally, family trees are interesting only to the twigs of the particular tree. But the genealogies of the ancient Egyptians can give an archaeologist vital information about such matters as inheritance, marital customs, and family life. Royal family trees, of course, are a legitimate subject of historical study. An English historian would have a hard time discussing the Wars of the Roses and the advent of the Tudor dynasty without bringing up the marital— and other—activities of the sons of Edward III. In Egypt, royal genealogies are particularly important because they shed light on a problem which is still in dispute—the problem of the inheritance of the throne.

We are familiar with the relatively modern solutions to this problem, in which the right to rule descended from father to eldest son. Sometimes royal daughters were acceptable, in lieu of sons, and sometimes not; but ordinarily it was the offspring of the reigning monarch, whether king or queen, who acquired the mystical sanction of the crown.

This procedure was not universal. In Nubia, to the south of Egypt, the crown went to the brothers of the king before reverting to his eldest son—a practical procedure, which tended to avoid minority rule and the evils which attend upon it. Anthropologists have collected examples of even stranger rules of royal inheritance; there are even rumors of societies in which queens were preferred to kings.

Since kingship, until very recent times, included among its duties the leadership of a nation's military forces, it is not surprising that male rulers were preferred in most eras and most areas. A queen's primary biological function would interfere periodically with her military duties, however Amazonian her personality and talents. We can be sure about one thing. The Egyptian queen was not, and could not be, a reigning monarch. Hatshepsut is the exception which proves the rule, and we have already seen the curious expedients to which royal dogma had to resort in order to deal with her position as female Horus.

Yet most Egyptologists believe that the queen held a peculiarly important position in regard to inheritance. A queen could not rule, but she alone could transmit the right to rule. Legally, her husband held the throne only by virtue of his marriage to her, and her son had a prior claim—not on the crown, but on the next queen, who would normally be his sister, the daughter of his mother. The mystical sanctity descended from mother to daughter; her son had no part in it. If the heiress-queen had only daughters, it was all the more incumbent on the next king—who might be her husband's child by a lesser wife—to marry her eldest daughter, the heiress-princess.

This theory of inheritance is a good deal more complex than the good old European procedure, in which sanctity and crown were the possessions of a single individual. What makes the Egyptian version of the problem even more complicated is the fact that no one had ever pointed out the virtues of monogamy to the ancient Egyptians. If we are going to postulate a theoretical personage called an "heiress-queen," our first problem is to pick her out of the crowded harem. I once wrote a dissertation on this problem, so I can state with some confidence that there is no queen's title which distinguishes a royal heiress. If the job was that important, you would think it would have its own proper title. Some deductions can be made. For instance, if the heiress is the offspring of a queen, she must be a king's daughter. "King's daughter" is a common title in ancient Egypt; too common. It does not distinguish one princess from another, if there is any distinction to be made. To go one step further—if an heiress-wife was so vital to a reigning monarch, we would expect that she would be honored by the position of chief wife. Now we know that not all chief wives were heiress-princesses, or even king's daughters. It is possible that in these cases the king had no sisters and so was able to choose his consort to suit himself. But there is no way of proving it, one way or the other.

The trouble is that the Egyptians did not have family Bibles with pages for Births and Deaths. Sometimes we have the feeling that kings only mentioned their sons or daughters when they happened to think about them; new ones are always turning up, on newly found reliefs and inscriptions. Once in a while a king shows us a collection of sons and daughters; sometimes they are named, sometimes not. But never, or almost never, are we given all the information we would like to have—ages, names, parentage. In view of these gaps in our knowledge it is almost impossible to construct a theory which will hold together; there is usually a jump from assumption A to assumption D, the blanks B and C being filled in by the bland remark that there is no "contradictory evidence."

To confuse the issue further, we might note that Egyptian statements of relationship are very vague. It was recognized early in the game that the words "brother" and "sister" need not indicate ties of blood. They are terms of endearment, equivalent to "sweetheart" or "darling," or even to "husband" or "wife." But it took Egyptologists a few years to arrive at the dismaying conclusion that "father" and "son" are equally misleading—"father" might be applied by a king to his grandfather, or to an even more remote ancestor; "son" seems to be used for grandson as well. We are still clinging to 'mother" and "daughter" as meaning what they seem to mean; but we can never be sure that a newly discovered inscription may not knock the sense out of those words too.

With these cheerful facts in mind, let us take a specific case— the marital situation of Thutmose IV. It presents some interesting problems—not to Thutmose, as far as we know, but to archaeologists. We suspect, to begin with, that Thutmose's mother was not of royal birth. The evidence for the suspicion is negative evidence: the lady is never called "king's daughter." So, until we find a text which states her parentage specifically, we can establish her social status only as a probability. Let us assume that she was a commoner. The next step, if we follow the "heiress" theory of legitimacy, is to look for a royal princess among the wives of Thutmose IV. If one existed, she would have been his half sister— the daughter of Thutmose's father, Amenhotep II, by a royal wife who was not Thutmose IV's mother, because she (we think) was a commoner.

One of Thutmose's wives was a princess of Mitanni, who could not have been an Egyptian heiress. Another wife was a woman with a peculiar, untranslatable name, which, in view of its uniqueness, may not be a name at all. (And if you find that sentence confusing, the situation it describes is equally so.) A third queen of Thutmose IV was a lady named Mutemwiya, who was the mother of his successor; we assume that she was of non-royal birth because she, like Thutmose's mother, does not have the title "king's daughter."

The ambiguity of the problem may seem complete at this point; but it gets worse. For there may not be three queens involved at all; by the mental dexterity with which all true historians are endowed, we can reduce the three to one. The Mitannian princess could have taken an Egyptian name—Mutemwiya, for example. The lady with the unpronounceable name may be the Mitannian princess in disguise, and/or Mutemwiya. The titles of these ladies (however many they may be) add to the confusion. Asiatic princesses are not called "king's daughter." Mutemwiya is not called "king's daughter." The weirdly named queen is called "king's daughter," which makes her identification with either or both of the other two somewhat dubious. In fact, the whole business is extremely dubious, and I see no way out of it. The only point which can reasonably be made is that there is no proof which bears on the question of the heiress-princess, one way or the other; there is not even any proof as to Who was Who. It can, of course, be claimed that Thutmose IV had still another queen, unknown to us, who was an heiress-princess, but this is pretty weak logically. You can prove anything if you are allowed to make up the necessary evidence.

Actually, this theory of the royal heiress is one about which I have strong feelings. I do not maintain that the theory is wrong (although that's what I secretly believe), but I will maintain that there is not enough information available at the moment to construct a theory.

Let us forget about those ambiguous wives of Thutmose IV and go on to his son and successor, Amenhotep III. The period from the reign of this third Amenhotep to the end of the Eighteenth Dynasty constitutes a separate, interdynastic unit. Archaeologists call it the "Amarna Age." In formal terms, the Amarna period starts with the reign of Amenhotep III's son, Amenhotep IV, who is better known as Akhenaton; but the trends which culminated in the innovations of the Amarna period began under Amenhotep III, and so I would like to discuss his reign in connection with the period.

We cannot complain, as we did about Thutmose IV, that the rulers of the Amarna Age are colorless and lacking in individuality. Amenhotep III and his wife, Queen Ti, are extraordinary personalities, and their son, Amenhotep IV-Akhenaton, has aroused more controversy among Egyptologists than any other pharaoh. Yet the most famous king of the Amarna period was Akhenaton's son-in-law and the grandson of Amenhotep III. He is not remembered for his valiant deeds or for peculiarities of character. One might say that he is famous because he was *not* remembered—because he was forgotten by the world for over three thousand years.

VIII

The Great Heresy

Akhenaton

THE Arabs call it "Biban el Moluk"—the Gates of the Kings. A narrow cleft, deep in the western cliffs opposite modern Luxor, it is one of the most desolate spots on earth. Nothing grows there— no tree, nor shrub, nor blade of grass. The sun beats down from an eternally cloudless sky whose brilliant blue is the only color contrast to the monotonous, unrelieved dark gold of rock and sand, hills and valley floor. Yet this wilderness merits its name, so redolent of magnificence. It is literally honeycombed with tombs which, over the millennia, contained some of the richest treasures ever deposited by men to the honor of their dead. From its barren stones Howard Carter and Lord Carnarvon drew the fabulous funerary equipment of Tutankhamon.

Under the irreverent journalistic nickname of "King Tut," this young man is better known to the world at large than are any of the great rulers of ancient Egypt. Indeed, the discovery of the tomb created more publicity and sensationalism than the dignified world of archaeology has yet known. The story of the find has been told and retold; undoubtedly the best and most exciting account is that of Howard Carter himself.*

* See the Reading List at the end of the present volume.

The contents of Tutankhamon's tomb may be seen today in the Egyptian Museum of Cairo. Familiarity with the Egyptian collections of other museums, with their cases of cracked pottery and rows of garishly painted mummy cases, in no way prepares the tourist for what he will see in Cairo. It must literally be seen to be believed. Among the hundreds of objects from the tomb, my personal favorite is the canopic box with its four protective goddesses. This gilded shrine contained the four canopic jars which held the dead king's entrails. The four goddesses are distinguished only by their headdresses; they stand with arms outstretched, embracing and guarding the precious contents of the shrine. They are fragile guardians; the small figures are childishly slender and the delicate faces lack the awesome stamp of divinity. It has been suggested that the model for the figures was Tutankhamon's young queen, who was probably in her early teens at the time the shrine was made. The theory is plausible; the four statues are so much alike that each of the faces might be a copy of the others, and a portrait of the same individual. The faces are charming, and so are the little bodies, which are those of very young girls.

The most valuable objects are kept in the Jewel Room, which can be locked like a vault. The robber who could empty this one room would rank as a veritable king of thieves; but he would need a moving van and a regiment of assistants, and he might find it a trifle difficult to market his loot. Tutankhamon's innermost coffin is three hundred pounds of solid gold, with a portrait head which, in my opinion, is one of the most beautiful things ever to come out of Egypt. The portrait mask which covered the head of the mummy is also solid gold. Then there are bracelets and pectorals and rings, earrings, amulets and collars, all of gold and precious stones. The Egyptians did not work the true gem stones. They did know and use what we call the semiprecious gems—turquoise, amethyst, carnelian, lapis lazuli, onyx, jasper—and they used them with consummate skill. The blend of color in the inlay work of the coffin is truly masterful—blue-black, orange-red and turquoise, against the background of glittering gold.

Any one of the objects from this single tomb would be the prize of an average museum collection, and there are hundreds of

The goddess Selket, one of the four goddesses guarding the canopic shrine of Tutankhamon. *Photo by Dr. Josef Vogt.*

such objects. Intrinsically, the contents of the tomb are worth millions of dollars; as examples of the cultural and artistic life of a bygone era, they are literally beyond price. Yet the tomb of Tutankhamon was a disappointment in one sense.

Tutankhamon himself was a minor king who died at eighteen after an uneventful reign of only nine years. Nevertheless, when the discovery of the tomb was first announced, there were hopes that it would contain historical material which would shed light on one of the most intriguing figures the ancient world has ever produced—Tutankhamon's predecessor and father-in-law, the heretic king, Akhenaton.

If one were to collect the statues of Egyptian kings from earliest to latest times, and arrange them in chronological sequence, one might, at first glance, take them for portraits of the same individual. The artistic canon permitted few deviations, and its rules applied most rigorously to the depiction of the divine king. There are, to be sure, certain stylistic variations from period to period, and it is even possible to distinguish family types. Still, the long row of male figures would be superficially alike: stern, handsome faces and stalwart, muscular bodies, broad of shoulder and slim of hip, with never a hint of sagging paunch or double chin. All, that is, except one; and it would stand out from the rest with almost shocking singularity. The long, haggard face, with deep-set eyes and hollow cheeks, the strangely deformed, almost feminine body—this is Akhenaton, whom James Henry Breasted called "the first individual in history."

Breasted gave Akhenaton the distinction of being the founder of the world's first monotheistic religion. Breasted has been accused of overenthusiasm; some scholars loathe Akhenaton as much as Breasted admired him. Whatever one's bias, it cannot be denied that Akhenaton was a personality, unique and fantastic. The history of his times may legitimately be told in terms of the man himself rather than in terms of general historical trends; for whatever the processes, economic, political or cultural, they were certainly colored and shaped by the ideas of one man. We know far less about Akhenaton than we would like to know. Archaeology, which can never answer all questions, is particularly helpless in matters of motive. Again and again we find ourselves asking "Why?" And history gives no final answer.

We do know that Akhenaton was born about 1370 B.C., and was given the name of his father—Amenhotep—Amon is satisfied.

Amon had reason to be satisfied. The old provincial god of Thebes was now Amon-Re, king of the gods, and his priests controlled what was probably the richest ecclesiastical establishment in all of Egypt. To the temple of Amon, with its ever-growing circle of administrative and financial offices, came a goodly proportion of the foreign tribute. The memory of Thutmose III was still fresh in the minds of Egyptian vassal princes in Syria and Palestine; the military campaigns of his son and grandson reinforced Egyptian prestige in those areas and kept Asiatic tribute pouring south into Egypt. From Nubia, and from the mines in the eastern desert, gold continued to flow into the coffers of the king and the god. And to the king, besides gold and tribute, came letters from the rulers of the great powers of the ancient Near East—Hatti, Mitanni, Babylon, Cyprus—humbly requesting gold and offering their daughters for the harem of Horus.

As the head of this luxurious and wealthy society, Akhenaton's father deserved the epithet "the Magnificent," which has been given him by modern historians. In his youth, Amenhotep III showed signs of the athletic ability which had been the boast of his grandfather, Amenhotep II; an inscription claims that he killed over one hundred lions between his first and tenth years of reign. But it may be significant that the third Amenhotep carried out no important military campaigns, not even the customary punitive expedition into Syria at the beginning of his reign. He built widely, enriching the great temple of Amon at Karnak as well as other shrines. Of his imposing mortuary temple on the western bank of the Nile, only the two gigantic statues known as the Colossi of Memnon still stand. Weathered and battered as they are, they have an air of melancholy dignity as they stare sightlessly across the river at the ruins of Egypt's mightiest capital city.

Akhenaton's mother was a more remarkable figure. Her entrance into the royal family was treated in a manner which is unique in ancient Egypt. Amenhotep the Magnificent announced his marriage in a series of commemorative scarabs, the same shape as the well-known beetle amulets which modern tourists have carried away from Egypt by the thousands, but large enough to contain a short inscription on the flattened base. This inscription read:

> May he live, Amenhotep III, given life, and the King's Great Wife Ti, who lives. The name of her father is Yuya, the name of her mother is Tuya; she is the wife of a mighty king whose southern boundary is as far as Karoy, and northern as far as Naharin!

The challenge in the words is clear. Ti was a commoner, perhaps not even of noble birth; the tomb of her parents has been found, and their titles suggest a relatively humble origin. Amenhotep not only married this daughter of the people but made her his consort, and the inscription on the scarab makes it clear, with a conciseness that borders on arrogance, that the queen is above criticism or comment.

One cannot help but speculate about the personality of this Queen Ti, who rose from obscurity to be First Lady of the Land. She was Chief Wife in the fullest sense, appearing more conspicuously upon the monuments of her husband than had any Egyptian queen before her, and receiving letters from foreign monarchs which imply that she had a voice in political decisions. There is a striking head in the Berlin Museum which may be a portrait of the lady; it shows a hard little face with full, arrogant mouth and knowing eyes—not a beautiful face, but not all the great charmers of history have been beauties, and Ti certainly rates a place among them, with Cleopatra and Madame de Montespan, and the other women whose words have moved kingdoms.

Ti's son came to the throne bearing the traditional name of his house, which honored the great god of his city. At first the young Amenhotep IV may have ruled alongside his father, but after a few years Amenhotep III died, or became too feeble to carry on the affairs of state. There is evidence that even as Amenhotep IV the young king had set in motion certain of the trends which are associated with his heresy, but in his sixth year of rule he brought matters to a crisis.

The crux of the crisis was a new god. To honor him, the king changed his name from Amenhotep to Akhenaton, which means "it is well with the Aton." To further particularize the change of allegiance, Akhenaton moved his capital. Thebes was the home of Amon; the Aton should have a city upon soil which had never been dedicated to another god. He moved the court, bag and baggage, to a site three hundred miles north of Thebes; it is known today as Tell el Amarna, and the term "Amarna" is used to characterize Akhenaton's revolutionary ideas in religion, art and thought. On this site, where the cliffs along the Nile curve back to form a wide bay of land, Akhenaton built a new city called Akhetaton, "The Horizon of Aton." He set up formal boundary markers dedicating the spot to Aton forever, and vow ing never to change its borders.

This was radical enough, but Akhenaton went still further. He forbade the worship of the old gods of Egypt—that proliferous pantheon whose complexities must have baffled the ancient Egyptians themselves. In particular, he abominated the greatest of gods, Amon-Re. His agents were sent throughout the land, to temples and tombs and monuments, to cut the hated name from the rock walls even when it appeared in the name of his own father, Amenhotep. The other gods were not spared, and in some cases even the plural word "gods" has been scratched out.

Who was this Aton, for whom a king of Egypt committed such monumental offenses against tradition? He was not Akhenaton's own invention; the word *aton* was used in earlier times to refer to the orb of the sun, and by the time of Akhenaton's grandfather, Aton had become a proper noun, a god who received worship. Amenhotep III paid him trifling honors now and then. But at best he was a minor godling until Akhenaton discovered him.

The earliest representations of Aton show him as a hawk-headed human figure. This was in keeping with the conventional Egyptian treatment of the gods in art—the animal or bird head on the human body. Akhenaton soon abandoned this tradition too. He showed Aton as a solar orb, a sun-globe with rays which end in tiny human hands holding the hieroglyphic sign for "life"—the looped cross, or *crux ansata*. Not all the god's human characteristics were abandoned. He had the titles and cartouches of a king and wore, even as a sun-globe, the royal uraeus serpent; his jubilee, the anniversary of the coronation, was celebrated with that of

The old, conventional depiction of Aton
as an anthropomorphic hawk-headed god

Akhenaton himself. Just what was it then that Akhenaton worshiped? The theories vary. My own feeling is that it was the spirit
of animation and creation implicit in the heat- and light-produc-
ing sun which was the object of Akhenaton's adoration. That this
spirit implied more than physical well-being is suggested by the
king's insistence upon *ma'at*.

   We translate *ma'at* as "truth." Abstractions are hard to translate, and the English word "truth" means many things to many
people. In Egyptian, *ma'at* certainly could mean something like
our concept of "justice"; the word was personified by a goddess
who stood at the side of Re at the time of the judging of the soul.
The hieroglyph for *ma'at* is the feather, which was weighed
against the heart of the dead man—the heart must be empty of evil
to balance the feather weight on the other pan of the scales. But

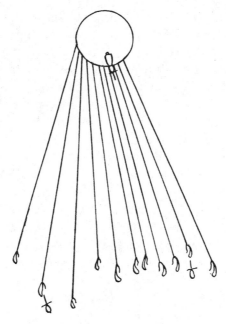

The Aton orb

ma'at went beyond justice; it has been defined as the universal order, the divine system of correctness—the *right* way to do things. Akhenaton's insistence upon his love of *ma'at* is too striking to be accidental, but there has been much discussion as to just what he meant by it. We do not see any conspicuous insistence on social justice, or any ethical content in the Aton creed as we know it— which is not to say that it did not exist. However, it is safer to interpret Akhenaton's *ma'at* as "sincerity," or "candor." This notion is readily apparent in the new art forms of the period, which Akhenaton encouraged.

We have already mentioned the features of this art form in royal portraiture, where its innovations are most noticeable. Akhenaton swept away the old canon of artistic taste; it was, per- haps, inevitable that the original freedom of expression which he may have meant to promote developed into a new canon, with its own set of rules. The strange bodily malformations of the king were copied in the portraits of his wife and children and, to a lesser degree, in those of the courtiers—the elongated skull and slender throat, the narrow, sloping shoulders and heavy hips. There are stages of development in Amarna art, signs of a growing maturity and skill even in the brief years of its efflorescence. The most exaggerated art forms—some of which verge dangerously upon caricature—appear at the beginning of Akhenaton's reign, even before he left Thebes. But when German archaeologists excavated at Tell el Amarna before the First World War, they found the ruins of the studio of a sculptor named Thutmose which contained some portrait busts of fantastic beauty—Amarna art at its latest, and highest, point of achievement. The most famous of these heads, the lovely painted bust of Nefertiti, is world-famous— an idealization of exotic feminine beauty as well as a living, breathing picture of an individual woman. It is hard to describe Amarna art objectively. Scholars speak of the increased sense of motion, and of the greater use of curved lines, but none of these criteria explains why the Amarna portraits, particularly the head of Nefertiti, catch at the imagination as they do. Heinrich Schaefer, one of the German specialists on this period, sees an "increased emotional content" in the new art. There is certainly a heightened sense of the individual; Khafre is a divinity, and Senusert III is a man of sorrows, but Nefertiti is Nefertiti, and we feel that we would recognize her anywhere and anytime.

Not only did Akhenaton encourage "Truth" in artistic technique, even the subject matter of the art becomes more candid and more natural. Intimate family relations are shown with amazing freedom and charm. The king's devotion to his beautiful wife is a favorite theme. He is shown with his arm around her, kissing her, leaning casually against her shoulder. To appreciate how daring this choice of subject really was, one must study the long series of stiff, formal representations of earlier kings and queens.

Akhenaton's six little daughters were, one suspects, badly spoiled by their doting parents. They accompanied the king and queen on drives and excursions, sat on their laps and ate from their tables at banquets. In one scene a small princess is shown slyly tickling the flanks of the horses her father is driving. The picture is one of family affection and peace which strikes the viewer with pleasure in spite of the exaggerated artistic techniques.

Akhenaton (?). *The Cairo Museum.*

Innovations in art, religion, and language—for it is at this time that the dialect known as Late Egyptian is first used in official texts—all these and other changes add up to a genuinely revolutionary spirit. But was the worship of Aton true monotheism, as Breasted believed? Some scholars deny this claim. They prefer to call Atonism "henotheism"—the worship of one god without denying the existence of others. They point out that Akhenaton never relinquished the traditional claim of the Egyptian king to divinity; that his followers worshiped not only Aton, but Akhenaton. They say also that Aton's titulary included the names of other gods—all sun-gods, to be sure, but separate gods nonetheless. And to crown their argument, they maintain that Akhenaton's savage attack upon the name of Aton's archenemy, Amon-Re, was in itself a tacit admission of Amon's reality. A man cannot fight an enemy who does not exist.

Religious dogma is a labyrinth of subtleties, even to the initiate, and it is certainly dangerous to try to impose modern concepts upon an ancient people. But some modern parallels may be illuminating. Akhenaton called himself the son of Aton, and claimed to be the only one who really knew his god; he may have been the first, but he was certainly not the last prophet to make these claims. The Aton titulary does equate the god with Shu and Re and Atum, all ancient solar gods; but this, to Akhenaton, may have had no more effect upon Aton's uniqueness than the concept of the Trinity has upon the monotheism of Christianity. As for the last argument, Akhenaton's attack on the old gods—this too has historic parallels. When Cortez flung the Aztec idols down from before their bloody altars, he was trying to destroy their supremacy in the hearts of their followers, not admitting their reality to him. Proscription of the old gods is a standard practice for prophets of a new faith, monotheistic or not; it is a notable, and comprehensible, fact that monotheism is, by its very nature, intolerant. Polytheistic religions are usually able, and willing, to identify gods of other regions with their own, or to add a few new ones. The Romans did not throw the Christians to the lions because they were heretics, but because they were guilty of a kind of treason. Hence Akhenaton's persecution of the gods of Egypt can,

I believe, be taken as an argument for the monotheistic character of his faith, rather than the reverse.

There can be little doubt that Akhenaton's personal faith was monotheism, in the most literal sense of the word. He believed in his new religion, and gave to his god the single-minded devotion of his entire being. The particular bitterness of his attack upon Amon may have been conditioned by a very practical fear of the threat posed against the throne by the wealth and power of the Amon priesthood; but Akhenaton did not limit his attack to Amon. And the great Aton hymn, which expresses Akhenaton's devotion, does not sound like the work of a politician who cloaks pragmatic deeds in eloquent but empty words.

This hymn has been found inscribed in the tombs of several of Akhenaton's courtiers at Amarna, and it is supposed to have been composed by the king himself. Its striking parallels with the 104th Psalm were first pointed out by Breasted:

ATON HYMN

When thou settest in the western horizon of heaven
The world is in darkness like the dead. . . .
Every lion cometh forth from his den,
The serpents they sting. Darkness reigns. . . .
Bright is the earth when thou risest in the horizon. . . .
The two lands are in daily festival,
Awake and standing upon their feet . . .
Then in all the world they do their work
How manifold are all thy works!
They are hidden from before us.
Oh thou sole god, whose powers no other possesseth.
Thou didst create the earth according to thy desire, being
    alone:
Men, all cattle, large and small;
All that are upon the earth.

PSALM 104

Thou makest darkness and it is night,
Wherein all the beasts of the forest do creep forth;
The young lions roar after their prey; they seek
    their meat from God. . . .

The sun ariseth, they get them away
And lay them down in their dens.
Man goeth forth unto his work
And to his labour until the evening. . . .
Oh Lord, how manifold are thy works!
In wisdom hast thou made them all;
The earth is full of thy creatures.

These similarities do not mean that there is a direct connection between Atonism and Hebrew monotheism, or that Moses learned about God at the court of Amarna. Rather, the Aton hymn and the psalm represent two examples of a literary tradition which flourished throughout the Near East over a vast span of time. Certain of the concepts, and even of the phrases, of the Amarna hymn occur in earlier Eighteenth Dynasty Egyptian hymns and persist after the heresy of Akhenaton had disappeared from Egypt. Still, it is interesting to see, in so familiar a volume as the Bible, echoes of the beliefs of an Egyptian pharaoh of the second millennium before Christ.

These beliefs, as we know them, were beautiful and kind—the love of the creator of all things for his creatures, and their jubilant adoration of him. "Thy dawning is beautiful in the horizon of heaven, Oh living Aton, beginning of life!" All creatures, even the humblest, hail the god's rising:

All cattle rest upon their herbage,
All trees and plants flourish;
The birds flutter in their marshes,
Their wings uplifted in adoration to thee.
All the sheep dance upon their feet, all winged things fly;
They live when thou hast shone upon them.

Aton is the god of Syria and of Nubia also:

Their tongues are diverse in speech, and their forms and their
    skins likewise;
For thou, Divider, hast divided the peoples.

In cloudless Egypt the phenomenon of rain may be viewed as an example of the creator's ingenuity in caring for his non-Egyptian subjects: "Thou hast set a Nile in heaven, that it may fall for them!"

A spirit of joyousness and of sunlit, open space, and an appreciation of the manifold beauties of nature breathe in the liturgy of the Aton faith and are found in other elements of the worship. No longer was the god adored, as was Amon, within a windowless, darkened shrine by a small band of initiates. The temples of the Aton were illumined by the rays of the god himself, their great altars being set in open courts. According to the tomb reliefs, which often show this scene, the offerings Aton loves to receive are those of fruit and flowers rather than bloody sacrifices.

In its prime, the city of Akhetaton must have been a fitting capital for a pristine new god. The handsome villas of the nobles were surrounded by gardens filled with pools and with flowers, surrounded by high walls for privacy. The workmen's houses were small and monotonously alike, but they compare favorably with some of the twentieth-century fellahin's dwellings. The king himself built several palaces. Like most Egyptian domestic dwellings they survive only as floor plans—the tombs were the Houses of Eternity, but a house was only designed for one lifetime. The palaces were handsome structures, filled with luxurious furniture and ornaments. From the objects found in Tutankhamon's tomb, some of which were doubtless made in Akhetaton, we know that domestic furnishings were designed with an eye to beauty as well as utility.

Akhenaton's palaces had lovely painted floors and walls with scenes of animals, flowering plants, and gracefully flying birds. Here he lived in peace with his exquisite wife and his six little daughters. In the great temple enclosure he worshiped Aton at the appointed hours; and in the cliffs behind the city he prepared his tomb. This tomb, together with those of his chief courtiers, has been excavated. All were empty; they had been robbed and defaced in antiquity. But from the scenes carved and painted upon the chamber walls, archaeologists have learned much about Akhenaton and his times; perhaps the most valuable inscription is the copy of the great Aton hymn. And from the walls of the royal tomb we learn that the king's life had its tragedies. The first person to occupy the rock-cut sepulcher was not Akhenaton, but his small daughter, the princess Meketaton. The scenes of her funeral still cover the walls of one chamber, and the grief of the royal parents is poignantly portrayed.

The loss of his daughter was a shattering blow, but it was only the first of Akhenaton's troubles. Potential sources of danger, centering in the displaced priests of the old gods, were gaining strength. And outside Egypt other clouds were gathering. We know of these foreign problems in some detail, thanks to an archeological discovery that far surpassed the tomb of Tutankhamon in historical value, though it was composed of no more valuable material than common clay.

In 1887, peasants tilling their fields near Tell el Amarna turned up some curious objects—broken squares of dried clay which could hardly be distinguished from the brown earth that hid them. An ordinary cultivator would have thrown them away, but the Egyptian fellah had become sophisticated. He knew that the black soil of Egypt yielded riches other than crops, and that even the most unlikely-looking object might have value. The peasants scraped off the disfiguring earth and found that the bricks were covered with strange scratches, too regular to be accidental.

Eventually the objects found their way to Cairo. They created little stir at first; unprepossessing in appearance and humble in material, they did not attract tourist or scholar. Many of the bricks were broken to begin with, and others were deliberately smashed in order to increase the find in numbers if in nothing else. But finally they came to the attention of specialists, and the queer scratches were recognized as cuneiform writing. Cuneiform, pressed into damp clay tablets by wedge-shaped styluses, was the script of ancient Babylonia; during the fourteenth century B.C., the Akkadian language, written in this script, was the language of international diplomatic communication, much as French was in the last century. The ruins of Akhetaton and the antique shops were combed, and some three hundred of the baked clay tablets were found. They are the ancient equivalent of the Foreign Office, or State Department Archives of our day, covering the reigns of Akhenaton and his father, and including letters from foreign monarchs as well as reports and dispatches from Egyptian emissaries abroad. They give a vivid picture of the international situation in 1350 B.C.; and the picture is not a bright one for Egypt.

Two of the great powers of this age which are mentioned in the diplomatic correspondence with Egypt were Hatti—the kingdom of the Hittites—and Mitanni, or Naharin. Both kingdoms lay north of the narrow coastal plain of Syria-Palestine, Mitanni on the Upper Euphrates and Hatti in Anatolia. Egyptian-Mitannian relations had changed since Thutmose III crossed the Euphrates with his army. Mitanni was now on friendly terms with the Two Lands and several Egyptian kings, including Akhenaton, had married daughters of the royal house of that nation. But the Hittites were a horse of a different color.

Like Sumer, Mitanni, and the ancient Indian civilization represented by Harappa and Mohenjodaro, the Hittite kingdom had vanished from human memory until it was resurrected by archaeologists. The fate of such cultures, once brilliant and flourishing and powerful, may be regarded as an object lesson in the brevity of human vanity. Archaeologists also view them as banners, bearing the word EXCELSIOR! If the last one hundred years have brought such discoveries into the light of day, what buried civilizations may yet lie hidden beneath the soil of the several continents?

The existence of the Hittites did not come as a complete surprise to scholars, for there were hints in the Bible and in other sources that such a people had once lived in the Near East; but it was not until after 1906, when the excavation of the Hittite capital at Boghazkoi in Anatolia began, that the full splendor of Hittite culture was really appreciated. The most astounding result of the excavations arose out of the study of the Hittite language; to the surprise of practically everybody, it turned out to be an Indo-European tongue related to Latin and the Germanic languages. To speak of the speech of Boghazkoi as one language is an oversimplification, for there were half a dozen different languages and two scripts—cuneiform, and the strange Hittite hieroglyphs. Still, the fact remains that Anatolia was, before the second millennium B.C., invaded by a group of warriors who spoke an Indo-European tongue, and who conquered the indigenous, non-Indo-European speakers who lived in the area. The grammatical awkwardness in the preceding sentence is intentional; "Indo-European" does not apply to peoples, only to the language they spoke, and I want to avoid even the faintest hint of Aryans or other racial wonders. We still do not know for sure who the Hittite conquerors were, where they came from, or when they arrived; but thanks to the excavations, and the decipherment of the many tablets found in Hittite cities, we know a good deal about Hittite culture as it developed in Asia Minor.

By the period we are considering, the Hittites were in good shape. The credit for their flourishing condition, internal and external, seems to belong to one man—Shubilulliuma, the king. The possessor of this mellifluous name must have been a dynamic personality, but we know him only from his deeds—which were admittedly considerable. One of his major achievements was the overthrow of Mitanni, which was too close, and too powerful, for Hittite tastes. He was then able to turn his attention to Syria, formerly part of the Mitannian sphere of influence. That nation was out of the running now. Babylon was fading fast, Assyria was virile but still young. There was only one remaining check to Hittite ambitions—Egypt, whose control over Palestine and part of the Syrian coast had been tacitly recognized by the other great powers.

Syria-Palestine has long been a focus of strife, no less so in Akhenaton's day than in our own. In spite of the military exploits of Thutmose III and his successors, the small city-states in the area never completely abandoned their dreams of independence. There were frequent "rebellions," as the scandalized Egyptians called them, particularly at the death of a pharaoh, when the internal confusion incumbent upon the accession of a young and inexperienced ruler might have kept Egyptian forces at home. But the great conquerors such as Thutmose I and III had been energetic men, conscious of empire. The rebellions were promptly subdued, and were followed by frequent tours of inspection and saber-rattling. By the time of Amenhotep III, the Egyptian provinces in Syria had settled down to enjoy the prosperity of the *Pax Aegyptiaca*. Or so it seemed.

From his perch high in the hills of Asia Minor, Shubilulliuma looked south, and plotted. There is little doubt that the Hittite king's machinations in Syria began while Amenhotep III was still alive. When Mitanni fell at last, there was no audible comment from Egypt. Then a new pharaoh ascended the throne; and while the youthful Akhenaton dreamed about truth at home, the old king of Hatti was playing the game of power politics in Asia. He would not risk direct military attack, not on Egypt, even if she was ruled by a fool. There were easier ways. So he wove his web, casting the strands into the city-states tributary to Egypt even while he was writing flattering letters, couched in the polished terms of diplomatic usage, to his unwitting "brother" of Egypt.

Shubilulliuma soon found the tools he wanted—Abdu-Ashirta, prince of the small state of Amor on the upper Orontes, and his son Aziru. Upon the death of his father, Aziru took over the rule of Amor as a vassal of Egypt; he also inherited the job of cat's-paw for Shubilulliuma. Aziru too wrote fulsome letters to Akhenaton protesting his loyalty and describing his valiant battles against traitors in other cities.

Aziru's first moves against these "traitors"—the loyal coastal cities of north Syria—were successful, and unopposed. Yet even the cities which had not felt the weight of the Amorite prince's hand were under no illusions as to his intentions. The elders of the wealthy city of Tunip sent to Pharaoh a plea for help, written with the eloquence of fear and despair:

> Who formerly could have plundered Tunip without being plundered by Thutmose III? When Aziru enters Simyra, Aziru will do to us as he pleases, in the territory of our lord the king; and on account of these things our lord will have to lament. And now Tunip, thy city, weeps, and her tears are flowing, and there is no help for us. For twenty years we have been sending to our lord the king, the king of Egypt; but there has not come to us a word—no, not one!

The trouble had begun under Amenhotep III, but Akhenaton took no steps to repair his father's errors. Simyra fell, as the elders of Tunip had feared; the city of Sidon, seeing no help forthcoming from Egypt, made terms with Aziru and assisted him in attacking Tyre. Before long all the coastal cities loyal to Egypt had fallen except Byblos.

By this time the prince of Byblos, and elderly nobleman named Ribaddi, was badly worried. He had been writing to his lord, Akhenaton, for some time concerning the doings of Aziru, and he knew that Byblos would be next. After the fall of Simyra his letters become absolutely impassioned, and one cannot but marvel at the old gentleman's tenacity, loyalty, and stubborn courage.

Evidently these qualities did not come through to Akhenaton. Aziru had a friend at court and this man, in the useful position of chief steward, somehow managed to conceal the truth of what was going on in Syria. His name was Tutu, or Dudu—a name which ought to be written in blood, beside the names of General Arnold and M. Quisling. Aziru himself was no mean persuader; he even convinced the Egyptian army officer stationed in Galilee that Ribaddi was a traitor, and talked him into sending Egyptian mercenaries to attack Byblos! After this unprovoked stab in the back, the city quite understandably rose in revolt against Egypt and ousted Ribaddi, delivering his scepter and his family into the hands of his bitter foe, Aziru. The valiant Ribaddi actually succeeded in regaining Byblos, but his situation was hopeless. Aziru still flourished as the wicked proverbially do, in spite of being summoned to Egypt to explain himself to a belatedly suspicious king; the ships of Ribaddi's enemies blockaded Byblos and cut off his supplies; even the old man's wife urged him to forsake the broken reed of Egypt and submit to Aziru. Still he held out, asking for only *three hundred* men to help him hold the city. To this letter, as to the others, there was no reply. Byblos fell; and Ribaddi's voice was no longer heard in the archives of Egypt.

In the south the situation was equally desperate, although the attackers were different—fierce desert raiders called the Habiru. These people have interested historians because of the etymological similarity between their name and that of the Hebrews. Probably the Habiru were a loose amalgamation of various ethnic groups rather than a distinct tribal entity, but they may well have included people of Hebrew speech and customs. They were not a civilized people, as Egypt and Hatti were civilized; but they were mighty men of war, and the fortresses of Palestine, weakened by years of neglect under Amenhotep III, fell to them like wheat under the sickle. And again—there was no help from Akhenaton!

"If no troops come in this year," wrote Abdu-Heba, Egyptian deputy in Jerusalem, "the whole territory of my lord the king will perish. If there are no troops in this year, let the king send his officer to fetch me and my brothers, that we may die with my lord the king."

We do not know whether Abdu-Heba gained the safety of Egypt or died in the ruins of his city; but Jerusalem fell, and Megiddo fell, and the southern half of Egypt's Asiatic empire collapsed as the northern half had done under the hammering of Aziru.

The historian cannot help but ask, at this point: What sort of man was Akhenaton, that he could see his empire crumbling into sand without lifting a finger to save it? If he was the idealist and pacifist that some Egyptologists believe him to have been—how could he watch unmoved the slaughter of his subjects and the betrayal of those faithful to him?

There is no certain answer, just as there is none to the basic problem of Akhenaton's character and motives. The true facts about the warfare in Syria may never have reached him. The workings of a complex bureaucracy such as Akhenaton's Bureau of Foreign Affairs are in themselves an excellent screen for truth, and there seem to have been traitors in the home office itself. Akhenaton may have sent aid to some of his vassals. The sequence of events I have narrated is not accepted by all scholars; since most of the letters can be dated only by internal evidence, there is still disagreement as to who was doing what to whom, and when. Even so—allowing for poor communication, for deception, and for any amount of official red tape—Akhenaton failed to take decisive action on evidence which would have sent his ancestor Thutmose III dashing into the field with an army at his back.

Trouble abroad, discontent at home; the underground rumblings of potential disaster must have reached Akhenaton's ears at last, deafened as they were to all sounds save the hymn to his god. What particular event, or combination of events, roused him to a realization of his peril, we can only guess; but during his twelfth year of reign we see signs of change. The dream had lasted a bare six years.

In his twelfth year Akhenaton's mother, Queen Ti, paid a visit of state to Tell el Amarna. Perhaps that shrewd lady spoke the necessary words of warning to her unconscious son. She had been living in Thebes, and was too intelligent to miss the signs of disaffection. Thebes was the cult center of Amon, and his home-less, discredited priests would be the most dangerous enemies of the new god and his royal devotee. The inarticulate mass of the people, uneasy and confused by the strange dogmas which had replaced the old, time-tested protective forces of life and death, may have found a voice. A third source of disharmony was the former aristocracy of Thebes, replaced by parvenus who paid lip service to Aton. If it sounds cynical to speak of lip service, we must note that some of Akhenaton's most favored courtiers sur-vived and flourished after his death, under the resurgence of Amon. His favorite, the elderly noble Ay, actually succeeded Tutankhamon as Horus, Lord of the Two Lands. And Ay's suc-cessor was a General Harmhab, who may have seen service under Akhenaton.

At any rate, Akhenaton began to look about him and realize that all was not well. One of his most pressing problems was that of a successor. He had begotten six daughters, but a woman could not hold the throne of Horus alone. He must seek successors by selecting husbands for his daughters.

The eldest daughter, Meritaton, married a young nobleman named Smenkhkare, whose exact parentage is never stated. Smenkhkare joined his father-in-law on the throne, as coregent; it is probable that he never reigned alone. The boy is one of the most ephemeral kings of Egypt, but we do know that he estab-lished a temple to Amon in Thebes. It is a small fact, but a significant one, for it meant—compromise. Akhenaton, who had attacked the age-old gods of Egypt for the love of Aton, sent his son and daughter to the stronghold of Amon to arrange a recon-ciliation. The specific threat, if any, that moved Akhenaton to the reversal of his vows is unknown. Perhaps practicality replaced idealism as he grew older; perhaps his withdrawal from the political centers of Egypt had permitted the growth of lawlessness and disorder, which came belatedly to his attention. We can only guess. But I find it hard to believe that Akhenaton's views had changed. Fanaticism, or idealism, of the degree that inspired the profound uprooting of the ageless religion of Egypt does not mellow in old age—quite the reverse, as a rule.

The king's bitterness at this forced decision, so antithetical to all his beliefs, may be imagined. Some scholars believe it was increased by the ending of the romantic idyll with his queen, Nefertiti.

Her name means, appropriately, "The beautiful woman has come." In the early days of their marriage Akhenaton spared no pains to show his love for her. Although she was probably a commoner, like her mother-in-law Ti, her husband composed a royal titulary for her and gave her the additional name Neferneferuaton, "Beautiful are the beauties of Aton." Her titles are phrases of endearment and tenderness: "Fair of hands, lady of grace, she at whose voice the king rejoices." Her exquisite portrait head is one of the all-time masterpieces of sculpture.

Nefertiti shared her husband's beliefs and worshiped Aton at his side. The reliefs of the Aton temple at Thebes, which are being reconstructed by means of a unique new computer process, show her prominence in the cult. The royal couple must have been united in their faith as they were united in their mutual affection and their love for their children. But something went wrong. The evidence is found at Amarna, where, in certain places, Nefertiti's name and titles were cut out and replaced by those of Smenkhkare and his wife Meritaton. Akhenaton showered attentions on his young coregent, giving him the name which had been Nefertiti's—Neferneferuaton. From this period may come another portrait head tentatively identified as Nefertiti's. It has the same slender throat and proudly poised head, the same delicate features as the more famous painted sculpture; but time has taken its toll. The almost imperceptible loosening of the muscles of throat and jaw, the tightness of the once gracious mouth, speak of disappointment or sorrow with a subtle skill that makes this head another Amarna masterpiece.

Perhaps Nefertiti's death explains why her name was given to another person. However, some Egyptologists believe that there was a break between her and her royal husband, and that she packed up and left him, taking with her her third daughter, Ankhesenpaaton and the girl's husband, Tutankhaton.

This brings us to the interesting question: who precisely was this boy, the most widely known king of ancient Egypt, whose treasures still draw crowds of tourists fifty years after his tomb was first discovered?

Surprisingly enough, despite the thousands of words that have been written about him, all we really know for sure was that he was Akhenaton's son-in-law. A recently discovered inscription makes it fairly certain that he was a king's son; but which king was his father?

The obvious answer would seem to be Akhenaton. However, Tutankhamon was related in some fashion to Amenhotep III, and a vociferous party of Egyptologists want to make that gentleman Tutankhamon's sire. In order to do this, it is necessary to postulate a long coregency between Akhenaton and his father, and I refuse to go into that debate, which has been the subject of several long, complicated articles. I have, of course, no objection to stating my own opinion; I think Tutankhaton was Akhenaton's son, by a lesser wife (he had them), and that Smenkhkare was also his son, the elder brother of Tutankhaton. This theory would explain the lavish affection showered on Smenkhkare by Akhenaton, which some archaeologists interpret as a homosexual relationship. Unlike the Greeks, the Egyptians didn't approve of love between men. Akhenaton was an iconoclast in many ways, but I find it hard to believe that he would have violated this particular taboo. It seemes more reasonable to me that the affectionate poses in which the two are often shown demonstrate a father's love for his son; some are strikingly reminiscent of similar scenes of Akhenaton and his daughters, of whom he was also extremely fond. Ah, well; some day an inscription may turn up which will solve the problem. In the meantime, life would be very dull without these arguments about Akhenaton's sex life.

Tutankhaton was the heretic king's successor. Akhenaton died in his seventeenth year of rule, under circumstances which are unknown. There is no record of his death, or burial, or mummification. Smenkhkare and his young wife Meritaton disappeared

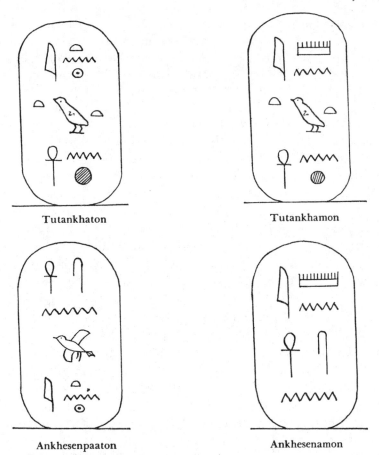

| Tutankhaton | Tutankhamon |
| Ankhesenpaaton | Ankhesenamon |

Cartouches of Tutankhamon and his Queen

from the stage of history at about the same time, in the same deadly silence; and the little king, Tutankhaton, ascended the throne. He was about nine years old. His wife was only a few years older—eleven or twelve.

For three years Tutankhaton remained at the city of Akhetaton. Then, suddenly, he moved the court back to Thebes, changed his name to Tutankhamon, and began restoring the temples which Akhenaton had desecrated.

The temples of the gods and goddesses had gone to pieces. The land was upside down, and the gods turned their backs upon this

land. Their hearts were hurt, so that they destroyed what had been
made. But I deliberated plans with my heart, seeking out acts of
service to my father Amon. All the property of the temples has been
doubled—tripled—quadrupled; their work is charged against the
palace, and against the estate of the Lord of the Two Lands.

So reads Tutankhamon's restoration inscription. In other
words, Pharaoh makes good, fourfold, what Pharaoh tried to destroy. The triumph of Amon was complete.

One wonders at the emotions of the two small rulers at this
capitulation, particularly at those of Ankhesenamon—for she too
had taken the name of the god her father had anathematized.
Were they in accord with the surrender to Amon or, being mere
children, were they helpless pawns in the hands of older players?
Tutankhamon had little time to assert his own personality, even if
he had wished to do so. He died violently at eighteen and was
buried in his small tomb in the Valley of the Kings opposite
Thebes. Robbers made two attempts to enter the tomb shortly
after the burial, but they were apprehended before they reached
the burial chamber, and the passageway was resealed. In the
Twentieth Dynasty, Ramses VI excavated his tomb just above and
to the left of Tutankhamon's, and the rubble from the digging
was flung over the lower entrance, hiding it from sight and from
memory until Carter's moment of triumph in 1922. In the tomb
were found two other mummies—those of infant girls, born pre-
maturely. So ended the hopes of the Amarna family for a permanent dynasty; but Tutankhamon's young widow made one last
desperate bid for power.

This incredible story is known, not from Egyptian archaeology, but from the excavation of the Hittite capital in Anatolia. In
the royal archives was a cuneiform text of the Hittite king,
Mursilis III, telling of a message sent by an Egyptian queen to his
father, our old friend Shubilulliuma.

"My husband is dead," she wrote, "and I have no son. People
say that you have many sons. If you were to send me one of your
sons he might become my husband. I am loath to take a servant of
mine and make him my husband."

If Shubilulliuma had acted promptly, he might have changed

history. But he was too sly to recognize candor when he met it, and there was reason for his skepticism. "Since of old such a thing has never happened," he exclaimed. So he sent his chamberlain to Egypt to investigate before making a decision. "Perhaps they have a prince; they may try to deceive me and do not really want one of my sons to take over the kingship."

In the columned and painted rooms of the royal palace at Thebes, Queen Ankhesenamon mourned her young husband and waited for word. No one had consulted her on the succession; she was only a woman, the daughter of a hated royal house. She had to act quickly, and in secret, for she was only a pawn in the current game of politics, to be disposed of as the winner decreed. It is pitifully clear that she could expect no help from any of her father's former friends; Hatti was a last resort.

But the slow days dragged on without an answer from the North, and Ankhesenamon must have found her mask of indifference harder and harder to maintain. Then, at last, came a message. We do not know how it was delivered, nor by whom, but its import is plain from the letter Ankhesenamon wrote in reply. I know of no more eloquent text from ancient times.

> Why do you say, "They may try to deceive me"? If I had a son, would I write to a foreign country in a manner which is humiliating to me and to my country? He who was my husband died, and I have no sons. Shall I perhaps take a servant of mine, and make him my husband? I have not written to any other country, I have written only to you. People say that you have many sons. Give me one of your sons, and he shall be my husband and king in the land of Egypt.

Bearing this message the courier set out again on the long journey, beset with many dangers. And this time Shubilulliuma was convinced. It was, in modern parlance, too good a chance to pass up. He sent his son, but too late. According to the Hittite records, the prince and his escort were attacked and murdered on the way "by the men and horses of Egypt." The conspiracy had been discovered.

And what of Queen Ankhesenamon? She was a true granddaughter of the shrewd little commoner Ti, who had fought for a crown in her own way; but alas, her husband was not "a mighty king whose borders reach from Karu to the Euphrates." Her husband was dead, and in his place stood the ex-vizier Ay, who had just had himself painted on the wall of Tutankhamon's tomb as the boy's successor. Excavators have found a gold ring whose bezel bears the joined cartouches of Ay and Ankhesenamon, side by side, as the name of royal consorts are written. This may indicate an attempt of Ay's to justify his seizure of the throne by marriage to Tutankhamon's royal widow. Since he was an elderly man, and a man who could shift allegiance from Aton to Amon without visible twinges of conscience, such a marriage would have been distasteful to the young queen from every point of view. She was never Ay's consort. The queen who stands beside him in his reliefs is the same woman who was his wife in his humbler days at Amarna, and Ankhesenamon, like her parents, vanishes from history.

Some scholars deny the clue of the ring and believe that Ay never had any plans to marry his youthful queen. I personally cannot produce any other explanation for the joined cartouches, which are never so paired unless the relationship is very close— parent and child, husband and wife, predecessor and successor. But for me the "clincher" is the queen's poignant letter to Shubilulliuma: "Shall I marry a *servant* of mine and make him king?" she asks, with furious contempt. Feminine intuition is as aggravating in historical study as it is in family discussions; yet I venture to suggest that this is precisely the comment a woman would make if she had been offended, as a woman and as a queen, by advances from a man of Ay's menial position and treacherous character. I suspect that Ay did not actually marry her—she is not shown as his wife. But he may well have planned to do so and been prevented, at the last moment, by Ankhesenamon's death. We have no positive evidence that she died; but, as in the case of Hatshepsut, the setting and the circumstances surrounding her disappearance do not allow any less dramatic end. It is usually assumed that she was murdered after the discovery of her attempt to deliver Egypt over to the Hittites, but another explanation is possible. Perhaps Ay was actually a "fate worse than death" to the proud daughter of the heretic king.

Many of the major actors in the drama of Amarna vanish from the scene as mysteriously and as inconclusively as does Ankhesenamon. Her husband's tomb is, of course, the most famous archeological discovery of all time, but there is one other burial from this period which must be mentioned. The contrast between this tomb and Tutankhamon's is theatrically sharp.

In 1907 Theodore Davis, a wealthy American archaeological amateur, came upon a burial in a remote corner of the Valley of the Kings. Within a small unadorned chamber in the rock was a mummiform coffin and a scanty, hastily assembled collection of funerary objects. The coffin was in sad condition; moisture within the chamber had rotted the wooden trestles which supported it, and its fall, as well as the damp, had damaged it greatly. The mummy had been reduced to a skeleton; thieves had ripped away the gold mask from the face of the coffin, and the name of the dead man had been cut away from the coffin and from the golden strips which wrapped the body. But enough remained to enable Davis to identify the coffin as belonging to a royal personage, and as dating from the Amarna period. Who but Akhenaton, he asked himself, would be so persecuted even in death that his name would be obliterated and his body hastily hidden in a grave that even a courtier would have considered inadequate? So word spread, among interested Egyptologists, that the mummy of the heretic king had been found.

Sober consideration, and a good deal of careful scholarly work, cast doubt upon Davis's initial contention. Physical anthropologists performed their detective work on the bones and pronounced them to be those of a young man, fifteen years or more younger than Akhenaton must have been at his death. Smenkhkare, the first of Akhenaton's sons-in-law, fits the age requirements, and for many years this burial was believed to be his.

Recently the whole question of the mummy and the burial arose again, and it may be worthwhile to treat the arguments in some detail, since they illustrate the specialized knowledge and the close attention to minutiae which modern archaeology requires. It is a far cry indeed from the early days of excavation, when battering rams and dynamite, and a bag of gold for greasing palms, were indispensable aids to excavators.

The inscriptions on the coffin, which are the obvious means of identifying the owner, are unhappily defaced. They consist of two main sections: a prayer, on the footboard, and a series of titles on golden bands which ran down and around the wrapped mummy. In all cases the name of the king has been completely cut away. Certain epithets remain, and they are epithets associated with Akhenaton. Originally, the names in the missing cartouches must have been his, but they could have stood as genitives after another name, as follows: "The king's daughter, Meritaton, daughter of Akhenaton," etc.

Most authorities agree that the coffin was first made for a woman. Later it was altered in order to serve for the burial of a man. In Egyptian the first person pronouns differ according to gender, the feminine being a small seated woman and the masculine a seated man. Kings and gods have separate pronouns, which in shape actually bear more resemblance to the seated woman of the feminine than the seated man of the commoner masculine. The pronouns on the coffin have been changed from feminine to royal masculine by the addition of kingly beard and a uraeus serpent on the forehead; beard and uraeus were also added to the face of the coffin. However, it is impossible to tell which royal male person came into possession of the coffin designed for a princess.

It would seem that definitive evidence could be found in the bones themselves. The deductive miracles of physical anthropologists, some of whom have worked with the police forces of various countries, are well known. It is now possible to tell sex, age, medical history, and other facts from a skeleton. Archaeology calls upon the talents of many specialists; why, then, does not a physician or anthropologist examine these bones and resolve the problem?

Such examinations were carried out. But the first of them was performed fifty years ago, when techniques were less advanced, and the experts, as often happens, did not agree on all points.

| Masculine | Feminine | Royal Masculine |

The first person pronouns in hieroglyphs

They did agree on two basic matters: the bones are those of a man; he was not more than twenty-eight years of age at the time of his death.

This would seem to eliminate Akhenaton, who must have lived to be about forty. But here we reach the crowning complexity of all. Judging from his statues, Akhenaton may well have suffered from some sort of disease. The archaeologists who wanted these bones to be his asked: Could the king have been the victim of an ailment which would alter the parts of the bone structure which determine age?

One of the major criteria used in aging bones (determining the age of their owner, that is) is the evidence of epiphyseal union. The chief center of bone formation in the shaft of a bone is called the diaphysis. The epiphyses are secondary bone masses at the head of the shaft, connected with the diaphysis by intermediate links of cartilage. Bone itself does not grow; changes in the stature of an individual take place by means of growth in the connecting cartilage, which eventually ossifies, thus binding together diaphysis and epiphyses.

The pieces of cartilage connecting diaphysis and epiphyses are clearly visible in a young bone, and do not complete their union until approximately the age of twenty-eight. Thus an expert can tell, from the condition of this cartilage, approximately how old the individual was at the time of his death. Epiphyseal union is only one of the criteria used in determining age, but in the case of the presumed skeleton of Akhenaton it seems to have been the chief criterion.

Now for the rub. There is a form of pituitary malfunction known as Froelich's syndrome, which can delay the union of the epiphyses. It would be possible for a man suffering from this disease to have, at the age of forty, bones which are in the state normally found in a twenty-three-year-old. What fascinated Egyptologists is the fact that a sufferer from Froelich's syndrome might also have certain of the physical deformities which are seen in the statues of Akhenaton—heavy thighs and thin calves, overdeveloped breasts and abdomen. The pituitary lesion affects the secretion of the sexual glands, producing feminine characteristics in a male.

A neat case, surely. There is only one difficulty. The victim of Froelich's syndrome is necessarily, totally, and unequivocally sterile.

What then do we do with Akhenaton's six daughters?

Some Egyptologists were quite willing to sweep the girls away rather than revise their theory, that the miserably buried skeleton was Akhenaton's. We can take it for granted that the children were born of Nefertiti, as the inscriptions specifically state; even the Egyptians could hardly have been mistaken about that. We might deliver ourselves from the manufactured dilemma by blackening Nefertiti's reputation; this would not be chivalrous, but then chivalry cannot stand in the way of scholarship. However, the aspersion is not only unkind, it is rather ridiculous. Who was Akhenaton trying to fool? Or was Nefertiti trying to fool him? If the king had to hire a substitute to father his daughters, the gentleman overdid it, rather. If I had not been trained to be polite to those who are my elders and betters in the field of Egyptology, I would say that this is one of the sillier theories to come out of a field which, unfortunately, abounds in silly theories.

I hope I may be excused for crowing just a little—since I seldom get that opportunity—because the latest medical investigation of the remains substantiates the belief I have always held— that they are indeed those of Smenkhkare. In 1963 a thorough anatomical investigation was carried out by Professor R. G. Harrison, of the University of Liverpool. He concluded that the bones were those of a man who was less than twenty-five years old at the time of his death, with twenty years being the probable age. There was no sign of gross abnormality, or of a pathological condition remotely related to Froelich's Syndrome. Harrison stated that the individual might have had an "ectomorphic constitution"—in other words, that he was slightly built—but that he was definitely a normal male.

The skeleton can't be Akhenaton. He is ruled out on the grounds of age alone. We can't prove that the remains are those of Smenkhkare, but the circumstantial evidence certainly points to him. He seems to have resided in Thebes, at least for a time, and to have died after a reign so short that there would not have been time to prepare his full funerary regalia. Hence the necessity of remaking a coffin intended for someone else. Smenkhkare's wife, who probably owned the coffin originally, would have a complete set of funerary equipment as a princess; she might own another set, or part of one, as queen, which would make it logical for her husband to have the coffin she no longer needed. The fact that he used it suggests that he died before she did, but this can't be proved. The funerary equipment in Tomb 55 is a motley enough collection; it implies a hasty, perhaps secret, burial. Some of Smenkhkare's burial furniture, such as the canopic cofinettes, was taken by Tutankhamon, who was probably his younger brother. The anatomical similarities between the body of Tutankhamon and the skeleton in Tomb 55 are quite close, confirming the identification of the latter with Smenkhkare; for it is unlikely that he would have taken precedence over Tutankhamon in the kingship unless he had had a stronger claim.

Despite the almost certain identification of the mysterious skeleton as that of Smenkhkare, the theorists have not abandoned their theories about Akhenaton's physical peculiarities, basing them now solely on the abnormalities depicted in the sculptures, which are admittedly odd enough. I still cling stubbornly to the belief that one cannot give a statue a physical examination, and the existence of Akhenaton's daughters—and perhaps his sons— seems clear evidence to me that he was not exactly impotent, whatever his other problems may have been. However, people will undoubtedly go on arguing until, and if, his mummy is found.

Will it ever be found? I must admit the possibility seems unlikely. Akhenaton probably died at Amarna and was buried there. His tomb had been prepared for him, and fragments of a sarcophagus found therein belonged to him. However, a shattered canopic chest from the same spot does not seem to have been used. It is possible that when Tutankhamon left the city of the Horizon of Aton, he moved the bodies of his royal relatives to Thebes for safekeeping. The royal tombs were happy hunting grounds for thieves, and the king had enough trouble guarding the necropoli of Thebes without having to worry about certain isolated burials three hundred miles away. But if this is what happened, then what became of Akhenaton's own coffin and golden ornaments, which must have surpassed those of Tutankhamon in splendor? He had seventeen or eighteen years in which to prepare them, in comparison with Tutankhamon's nine years of rule, and he was not, as his critics have pointed out, a humble man. The godson of the sole universal god deserved the best that imperial grandeur could supply; and the empire was in better shape at Akhenaton's accession that it was when Tutankhamon took over.

Lest the reader accuse me of going into inordinate detail over Smenkhkare's (!) mummy, let me assure him that I have not even touched upon many of the problems which are connected with this reign. More verbiage has been produced on Akhenaton and his times than on almost any other era of Egyptian history, and the work of scholars is remarkable for its heated tone. It is hard to be dispassionate about Akhenaton; you may loathe him or admire him, but you cannot ignore him. He has been described as a sexual degenerate and as a pure spiritual leader; as a destructive fanatic and as a great idealist. Psychiatrists have written about his psychoses, and doctors have diagnosed his diseases. And Egyptologists—well, they have theories, and passionate ones, about every aspect of Akhenaton's life except what he ate for breakfast. There is the co-regency school, which holds that Akhenaton ruled jointly with his father for some years, and the anti-co-regency school. The first has two sub-categories, the Long versus the Short co-regencyites. The inspiration for the Aton faith has been found in everybody from Queen Ti to Nefertiti, with a majority giving the credit (or blame) to Akhenaton himself. The break between Akhenaton and Nefertiti may not have been a break at all; there are other explanations for the erased cartouches of the queen, including the fascinating suggestion that Nefertiti was Smenkhkare!

Then there is the peculiar inscription which leads some scholars to believe that Akhenaton married his daughter, that same Ankhesenamon who was Tutankhamon's queen. If all the theories are correct, the poor girl was one of the most married of all Egyptian princesses; Akhenaton, Smenkhkare, Tutankhamon, and Ay have been mentioned as possible husbands of hers. I know of no better illustration of the subjectivity of some types of historical research than the widely varying approaches to the character and exploits of Akhenaton; and the bias extends to the minor characters. Some people, for instance, even persist in viewing that old scoundrel Ay as a dedicated servant of his country, and Ankhesenamon as a traitor to Egypt! I, of course, am completely dispassionate on this subject, as on everything that has to do with Akhenaton.

The city of the Horizon of Aton struggled on for a few years after Tutankhamon deserted it for Thebes, but it soon died, as cities will when the spirit that animated them is gone. The houses were razed, the beautiful palaces destroyed, and the tombs in the cliff were abandoned or robbed. The site has been methodically excavated in modern times, most recently by the Egypt Exploration Society of England, whose publication is the definitive work on the city. It yielded its treasures; the painted head of Nefertiti is perhaps the greatest, but there were other pieces of sculpture, some so naturalistic that they have been taken to be death masks. Fragments of the brightly painted floors of the palaces survived, to find their way into museums and collections. The plans of the villas and the workmen's village have been reconstructed; certain of the massive boundary stelae still stand, sadly ravaged by time and human destructiveness; but there is little left at Tell el Amarna to interest the non-specialist. At Thebes, blocks and statues have been found which came from Akhenaton's first temple to his god. They had been torn from their setting and used as filler for the work of later kings in the great Amon temple of Karnak. The mummy of Akhenaton's father, Amenhotep the Magnificent, was found in the cache of royal mummies in the tomb of Amenhotep II. At least, most scholars think it is his. I have my doubts. The mummies secreted in this hiding place had been badly battered before they were gathered up by the devout priests of a later period; the so-called mummy of Amenhotep III had been smashed to pieces by tomb robbers. It is possible, therefore, that the pious priests didn't always identify the ancient bones correctly. And Amenhotep III's remains show an embalming technique which was not practiced before the Twenty-First Dynasty; Elliot Smith, the authority on the royal mummies, claimed that this was the only known instance of it before that time. Yes, I am very skeptical about Amenhotep III, and the sad thing is that a lot of neat theories have been based on this mummy, its apparent age, and its abscessed teeth. The only mummies of the period that we definitely do possess are those of Tutankhamon and Smenkhkare.

When Howard Carter began what was to have been his last season of work in the Valley of the Kings, skeptics warned him that the site had been combed and recombed, and that he would find nothing there. Carter confounded the skeptics; nevertheless, there is more truth in the warning today. It is unlikely that anything new will be found in this particular area. However, the full archaeological story of the Amarna Age is yet to be told. The tomb of the great Queen Ti has never been found. It is possible that she was buried in the tomb of her husband, but her mummy ought to have turned up, somewhere, if only in fragments. The harsh, convoluted cliffs on the west bank of the Nile hold many secrets even yet.

Also missing are the mummies of Queens Meritaton and Ankhesenamon, the ill-fated daughters of Akhenaton, and their sisters, including Meketaton, who died in childhood and was almost certainly buried in the royal tomb at Amarna. Nefertiti intended to lay her bones within the royal tomb, but the empty, desecrated rooms contain no traces of her presence. A cache of jewelry, some of which bore her name, was found in 1882 by the fellahin who first discovered the royal tomb. Was it hidden away by frustrated tomb robbers of an early epoch, or mislaid when the royal mummies of Amarna were moved to Thebes? Speculation is fruitless, but entertaining.

And what of the heretic king himself? There is a melancholy possibility that his mummy no longer exists. Akhenaton aroused great hatred, and a fitting revenge for his heresies would be the total destruction of his body—and with it, his soul, according to Egyptian doctrine. However, active persecution of Akhenaton's memory did not begin immediately after Tutankhamon went over to the enemy. Six years later the boy-king could still place in his tomb many of the cherished objects he had owned while he was still Tutankhaton, "Living Image of Aton," including the throne which still bears the name and shape of the solar orb. We are safe in assuming that Akhenaton was laid to rest with all the pomp and reverence due a divine king of a mighty empire. What befell his body afterwards must be left to the imagination. Perhaps his enemies arose in their wrath and destroyed it utterly. More prosaically, perhaps it was desecrated by tomb robbers of ancient times, as were the mummies and the treasures of other pharaohs. A third possibility—that a small band of the faithful read the portents in time to remove the body of their leader and conceal it from the hatred of Amon—is really too romantic to merit acceptance. But how it kindles the imagination, to fancy that the mummy of the first great heretic still lies undisturbed in some remote valley near the desolate ruins of the city of the Horizon of Aton!

In later times Akhenaton's name, and that of his god, were cut from the inscriptions even as he had destroyed the name of Amon. His opponents tried to conceal the very fact of his existence, re-writing history in a manner reminiscent of *1984*. General Harmhab, who succeeded the vizier Ay as pharaoh, named himself the successor of Amenhotep III, ignoring Akhenaton and his sons-in-law, and claiming for himself all their years of rule. When it was necessary to refer to Akhenaton he was called, not by name, but by the epithet "that Criminal of Akhenaton." Never again did the solar orb of Aton appear on the walls of tomb or temple. The line of stiff, formal portrait sculptures resumes where it left off, before Akhenaton violated the artistic canon. Amon-Re resumed his place as king of the gods, and took back all the ground he had lost—and more. His devotees had good reason to write, after Akhenaton's death:

> Woe to him who assails thee!
> Thy city endures, but he who assails thee is overthrown;

The sun of him who knew thee not has set, but he who knows
    thee shines;
The sanctuary of him who assailed thee is overwhelmed in
    darkness,
But the whole earth is in light.

The shout of triumph rings hollow, however, after two thousand years. The attempt to obliterate Akhenaton's name failed,
thanks to the patient skill of historians, philologists, and archaeologists; he still exists in memory, to stir the imaginations of all who
know of him. Even the great god Amon-Re did not live forever.
He is as dead today as his old enemy Akhenaton; the sand drifts
over his altars, and his sanctuaries are laid open to the stares of the
curious.

IX
The Phoenix Enfeebled

Ramses III

THE grand sweep of history—as someone has probably called it—has a semihypnotic effect. A chronological treatment has its advantages for a writer, since his plot comes ready-made; he need not strain his wits to arrange the sequence of events. The disadvantage is that there are some subjects which cannot be readily fitted into this framework. Carried away by the general flow of things, I have neglected to touch upon one small matter, which deserves attention because it is both important and interesting—the Egyptian language and writing. We have now reached the end of the Eighteenth Dynasty. For various reasons, this is a good point at which to stop the relentless surge of history for a page or three, and I propose now to repair my omission.

Birds, Bees, and Flowers

Egyptian pictorial writing is one of the most attractive systems of writing ever devised. Incidentally, the correct noun form for the little images is "hieroglyphs"; popular writers occasionally call them hieroglyphics, and this small error scratches at the sensitivi-

ties of Egyptologists like a fingernail on a blackboard. The
hieroglyphic (adjective) script is of course quite distinct from the
Egyptian language. A particular script may be used to write a
number of languages, and a given language may be written in
more than one script. The hieroglyphs were never used to write
any language other than Egyptian, but Egyptian was written in
several scripts.

When I first began my study of Egyptian I was, like many
students, primarily fascinated by the hieroglyphic script. The little birds and flowers and people were such fun to copy that there
was a deplorable tendency to spend one's study hours reproducing
yards of small pictures instead of memorizing tedious grammatical
rules. Now it is sometimes necessary for the advanced student to
copy texts, since some of the material he wants to translate occurs
only in books which are out of print or hideously expensive; but
copying is not an end in itself. It takes up time which should be
spent on less decorative but more profitable pursuits, and it involves, initially, a decision as to precisely what to copy. Ordinarily

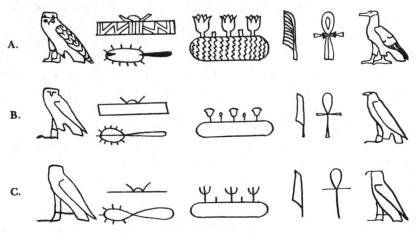

Types of hieroglyphic scripts

(A) is derived from ancient painted and carved hieroglyphs
in their more elaborate forms; (B) is taken from modern
printed versions of the hieroglyphs; (C) is a modern handwritten simplification.

the hieroglyphic texts which appear in books are reproduced by means of a photographic process rather than by printing. Only a few presses have hieroglyphic type fonts. The type faces are quite lovely; they come close to reproducing the pictures as the Egyptians carved them, and they are finely detailed. The student soon learns that he cannot duplicate the dainty, detailed typographical versions of hieroglyphs. Even if he has the necessary artistic skill, he has not the time. He must learn to write, not to draw.

Usually one of his professors steps in at this point and suggests a convention of simplification, which reduces the individual pictures to just enough detail for easy identification. The convention gets a bit tricky with certain types of signs; there are several dozen different birds used in hieroglyphic writing, all with different meanings, and all very much alike except for the curve of a tail or the appearance of crests and tufts in strategic spots. One interesting fact which emerges from the simplification techniques is that the hieroglyphic handwriting of two different people is as distinctive as their English hands; we students could always tell who had copied a particular text even when it was not signed.

Once the student has gotten over his initial preoccupation with the pretty pictures, and learned to write a few hundred signs, he comes up against a rather awful fact—namely, that he is not only learning a script, but a language. This comes home to him, if it has not already done so, when he begins to use the standard textbook, Gardiner's *Egyptian Grammar*. This book, which has over 600 pages, is now in its third edition. Although it is arranged like a typical grammar, with exercises and vocabulary after each lesson, it is also a standard reference work for advanced scholars.

The student sails along bravely through the beginning chapters of the monumental *Grammar*. Egyptian lacks declension endings and has only two genders, which facts make the noun and adjective in Egyptian fairly simple. But then the student gets to the second semester and hits the Egyptian verb, and the casualties begin. I do not intend to discuss the Egyptian verb. The proper study of the phenomenon requires a lifetime. Suffice it to say that there are dozens of different verb forms in the language, written almost identically and differing widely in meaning.

However, let us assume that the student has survived the first

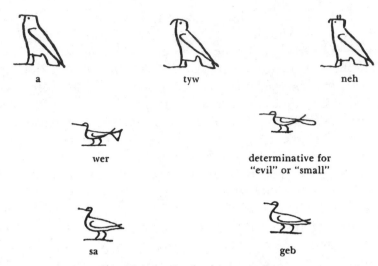

Bird hieroglyphs in a modern
handwritten convention

year of Egyptian. What he has learned—not too well—is only one
form of the language, and not the earliest form. The "classical"
dialect of Egyptian is what we call Middle Egyptian—although its
use is not restricted to the Middle Kingdom—and it is this which
the student tackles first. During the earlier Old Kingdom another
form of the language was written, and Old Egyptian is not exactly
identical with the dialect which we find in the Pyramid Texts.
Under Akhenaton the form known as Late Egyptian begins to be
used for written texts. Probably it had been a spoken language
earlier than that time; it is not unusual for the written language
to be slow in reflecting the changes which have taken place in
spoken idiom; the example of Italian and Latin is a typical one.

So far, we have been talking about various forms of the Egyptian language, all of which are written in hieroglyphic script.
They were written in another script as well—the "shorthand"
form known as *hieratic*. The hieroglyphs looked handsome on the
walls of tombs and temples, but they were just as unwieldy for a
busy Egyptian scribe as they are for us. Just as we simplify the
hieroglyphic pictures, in order to write them more quickly, the ancient scribes began to use cursive forms. Over the years—and the

process began very early, almost as soon as writing itself appeared —the forms became more and more cursive, until eventually the hieratic signs bore only a distant resemblance to their hiero-glyphic ancestors. The hieratic was written with a pen, on papyrus or potsherds, but even this script was too tedious for the over-worked scribes of the later bureaucracy. About 700 B.C. they developed another script, called *demotic*. Hieratic writing is child's play compared to demotic; at its worst, demotic consists of row upon row of agitated commas, each of which represents a totally different sign. It is perfectly dreadful stuff to read. Take a look at the right-hand column on page 254, and picture yourself trying to decipher a page of that—not on clean white paper, but on yellowed, faded, crumbling, rotten papyrus.

Stoop-shouldered and myopic, suffering from headaches and pains in the lumbar region, our hypothetical student has now, we may assume, mastered all the forms of the Egyptian language and script mentioned so far. But he is not finished. The last form of Egyptian, Coptic, was not written in hieroglyphs or demotic or hieratic, but in the Greek alphabet, eked out with a few signs derived from demotic to express sounds which did not occur in Greek. Coptic was replaced by Arabic as the national language of Egypt after the Moslem Conquest, but it survived in the liturgy of the Coptic (Egyptian Christian) church. There are no longer men in Egypt who speak the tongue of Thutmose III, but there were certainly small Coptic-speaking groups in remote regions of the country as late as the 1930's.

Coptic employs the Greek script, but it is an Egyptian lan-guage, although there are numerous Greek words added to the vocabulary. The literature is not too exciting to an Egyptologist, who usuallly closes his book at the Persian Conquest. But it is one of the subjects in which a candidate for the doctorate is supposed to show proficiency—laughable word—along with demotic, hiera-tic, Middle and Late and Old Egyptian, archaeology, art, history, and the archaeology and history and languages of related areas which he has also studied.

Coptic has one great gift to offer the Egyptologist who is primarily a linguist, rather than an archaeologist or historian. Since it used the Greek alphabet, it reproduced the vowels. Thus

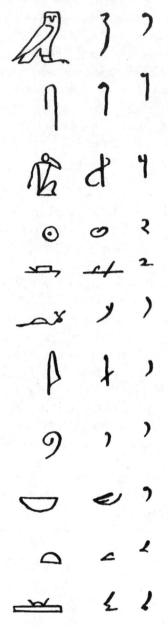

Hieroglyphic   Hieratic Demotic

Examples of hieroglyphic,
hieratic and demotic signs

we know how this form of the language was pronounced, which is not true of any other form of Egyptian. Hieroglyphic writing expresses only the consonants—and since hieratic and demotic are derived from hieroglyphs, the same is true of them. Therefore, when Egyptologists *transliterate* Egyptian, they write a word with only the consonants: *nfr*, or *bn*. When students read the texts aloud in class, they follow a convention which inserts an "e" between consonants to facilitate articulation: *nefer, ben*. But if you listen to someone reading Egyptian aloud, following this convention, you will not be hearing Egyptian "as she was spoke" in 1750 B.C. The convention is allowed only because the true vocalization is still in doubt. Indeed, it is wonderful that we have attained a state of doubt rather than one of pure ignorance, in view of the fact that we have only the consonants. We have the Coptic, yes; but it was not written down until almost three thousand years after the first texts in Old Egyptian were composed. A language can change quite a lot in three thousand years. By various tedious and complicated techniques, such as the cautious extrapolation of Coptic examples backwards in time, we now have a vague idea of how the ancient language may have been vocalized. Another useful, but limited clue comes from the examples of Egyptian words written in other ancient languages; the names of the kings and officials mentioned in the Amarna letters are rendered in cuneiform script, whose syllabic signs consisted of a consonant plus a vowel.

When we come to the problem of rendering Egyptian names into English, we run into another field of controversy. Among themselves Egyptologists transliterate, reproducing only the consonants which are given by the hieroglyphic signs. But you cannot call Thutmose the Great *Dhwty-nht* and expect anybody but an Egyptologist to recognize him. The name "Thutmose" is one of the more deplorable conventions. The element "Thut" comes from the Greek word for the god of wisdom, Thoth, whose Egyptian name was *Dhwty*; "mose" means "son of" in Egyptian. So we have a bastardized form, half Greek and half Egyptian, which is unaesthetic and inaccurate, but so well known that it is inexpedient to attempt to change it. I have taken the easy way out in this book by using the versions which comes most easily to me, even when I know better. Sir Alan Gardiner, of the aforementioned *Grammar*, says that Hatshepsut's name should be written Hatshepsowe; and if he says so, that's the way it must be. But I was not able to bring myself to do it. I have tried to avoid such "dated" forms as Ikhnaton, which is what Breasted called the Great Heretic; the initial sound was probably pronounced "akh" rather than "ikh." (The "kh" is a guttural, like German or Scotch "ch.") But when it comes to Amon vs. Amen, the reader can take his choice.

The said reader being intelligent and well-educated, I will not insult him by mentioning that hieroglyphs are not an alphabetic script. The first steps in the process of writing were probably based on whole words. The picture of a bee meant "bee," and the picture of an arrowhead meant "arrowhead." But the utility of writing could be greatly expanded by the application of what we call the rebus principle. The word for brother had the same consonants as the word for arrowhead—"s" and "n." The Egyptians could then use an arrowhead to write the word "brother." But there was an ambiguity in writing which did not occur in speech. The two words may have been pronounced differently, but since the vowels were not written, they looked exactly alike in script. The Egyptian solution to this problem was typically ingenious—and typically complex. When they wanted to write "brother," they added a second sign to the arrowhead—a seated man, which designated the class "human." By the use of the class signs, or determinatives, as we call them, the Egyptians could distinguish many words which, in their consonants, were otherwise identical.

The consonantal signs, as opposed to the determinatives, represented sounds—one or two or more consonants. A single consonantal sign might represent an entire word, or it might be combined with other signs to make up a word. Let's look at a few examples.

The sign which is transliterated *nfr*, and read "nefer," depicts the heart and windpipe of an animal, but for some reason it means "good," or "beautiful." Nefer is a triliteral sign, expressing three consonants all by itself, without any help from anybody. (Page 257, a) But when the Egyptians wrote the word beautiful, they usually added the signs for "f" and "r" (b). The word was

Various uses of the hieroglyphic signs

not read "neferefer," but "nefer"; the additional signs merely "firmed up" the reading. However, the nefer sign could be used alone, in a compound word such as "nefer-hat" (c), "diadem"; the second sign in this group is the forequarters of a lion and it means, as you might expect, "front." Now when "nefer" was used as a noun, a determinative was added to the sign—a papyrus roll tied with a bow, which indicated the class of abstractions (d). "Neferet" could also be a woman's name—the additional "t" is the feminine ending—and in this case the determinative for the class "woman" is added (e). Logically enough, this determinative is the tiny figure of a seated woman. As this example shows, the hieroglyphs were not the mysterious, esoteric signs that earlier scholars believed them to be. At times they are almost too concrete for refined tastes. The determinative for the verb "to give birth"—to take a comparatively genteel example—is self-explanatory (f). It is a pity that other words are not so obvious.

Incidentally, the plural in Egyptian is indicated by three strokes, or by a threefold repetition of the word signs, and it adds a "w" to the reading of the singular. "Neferew," "beauties," is written with three windpipes (g)—a particularly unfelicitous choice, I admit. Some years ago a novel on ancient Egypt contained a heroine with the melodious name "nefer-nefer-nefer."

After reading the preceding paragraphs, you can see that no Egyptian lady, even a courtesan, would have had such a name, and you can also understand the misinterpretation which led the author into his little error.

You have no doubt noticed another point worth pursuing, though I slid over it very slyly. If "nefer" can be written with separate signs for "f" and "r"—did the Egyptians have an alphabet after all?

Curiously enough, they had the makings of one. There are about two dozen signs which represent single sounds. With a little ingenuity, these could have been used to write the entire Egyptian vocabulary. You could use them to inscribe your name, or any other English word, in hieroglyphs, if you ever felt an urgent need to do so. The Egyptians never took the seemingly simple, but tremendous step of eliminating all but single-sound signs. Don't ask me why, because I don't know. Yet the birds and bees of the ancient Egyptian script may have a more direct relationship to our own alphabet than we realize.

Back in 1905, the ubiquitous Flinders Petrie was working in the wilds of the Sinai peninsula, disregarding its hellish climate with his usual equanimity. There were plenty of Egyptian inscriptions to copy, for the Egyptians had mined the beautiful blue-green turquoise of Sinai since earliest times. But among the material Petrie found were tablets carved in a curious script, some of whose signs were clearly derived from hieroglyphs, while others were of unknown origin. Petrie copied the texts, although he could not read them, in the same spirit which had led him to preserve his ugly scraps of pottery. A decade later, the material came to the attention of Professors T. E. Peet and Alan H. Gardiner, who were working over the entire body of Sinai inscriptions. Gardiner took up the copies of the strange unknown script reluctantly, for he had little hope of eliciting anything useful from them. The first sign he noticed was an ox-head, and all at once he remembered an old theory, that the letters of the Hebrew alphabet had been based on the acrophonic principle. Let not the reader be dismayed by this word; he has been acquainted with the principle from a tender age, unless he is young enough to have been subjected to a "progressive" education; the old first-grade readers used acrophony in their "A is for apple, B is for ball" routines. In regard to the Hebrew alphabet, the original simple picture sign came to stand for the initial letter of the word depicted, and the name of the letter was the same as the object. "Aleph," which in Hebrew corresponds to our A as the first letter of the alphabet, meant "ox-head."

Could the strange script be an alphabetic one, Gardiner asked himself, with the ox-head standing for aleph? The examples from Sinai have been dated to the Middle Kingdom, which seems far too early for such a development; yet there were Semites in Egypt and in Sinai at that time, and they might have spoken a language distantly related to Hebrew. It seemed too simple to be true; but when Gardiner looked further he found other correspondences. His moment of triumph came when he was able to read the word "Baalat," by using the Semitic meanings he had assigned to various signs. This is the name of the feminine counterpart of the despised Baal of the Old Testament, and would logically appear on tablets dedicated by Semitic workers to a goddess whose Egyptian form was Hathor, goddess of love and beauty—and Hathor was the protective divinity of this mining community, where she was known as "lady of the turquoise."

The process by which these unsung Semitic geniuses derived a system of alphabetic writing might have been as follows: they knew the shapes of the hieroglyphic signs, which covered the rocky cliffs where they worked, although they could not give them their Egyptian names. So they took the water sign, which is Egyptian for "n," and read it as their word for water—"mem," or something of the sort. Application of the acrophonic principle gave them the meaning "m" for the sign. Using Egyptian signs, and their own words for the objects they represented, the Semitic miners worked out a genuinely alphabetic script—one of the oldest yet discovered—which spread to Phoenicia and heaven knows where else, and eventually became the ancestor of our own alphabet.

Unfortunately, "Baalat" was Gardiner's high point; other attempts to apply the principle to additional groups of signs did not work so well, and there is still some scholarly debate about his theory. I like it, for no good reason except that it is interesting—and because Sir Alan said so—and so I am passing it on to you.

Look on My Works!

There is no apparent reason why Egypt should not have arisen refulgent from the minor brush fires set by the Amarna heresy, as it had been reborn out of the conflagrations of the two Intermediate Periods. To the men and women who lived out their lives under the first kings of the Nineteenth Dynasty, this resurgence was probably taken for granted. Yet to me—I think it would be unfair to drag anyone else in on this opinion—the greatness of Egypt is gone. "Greatness" is a hard word to define. But—whether Egyptian achievements are defined in terms of the rampantly successful imperialism of Thutmose III or the defiant spiritual challenges of the First Intermediate Period; the fable-making iconoclasm of Akhenaton or the more than oriental splendor of his father's court—in almost every sense, Egyptian culture has passed its prime. This interpretation is faintly radical, and more than faintly subjective. It can be "proved" most easily in the realm of political activity. Except for short periods of domestic calm under a strong pharaoh, the internal picture is one of slow but unmistakable decay. Abroad, the attempts of the Nineteenth Dynasty kings to regain the lost empire of Egypt fell far short of Thutmose III's activities, and their descendants were unable to hold even the little they had gained. The intangibles involve the personal taste of the beholder, yet few would deny that sculpture and painting have seen their best days, and that literature, though often good, is not as fine as the products of the past. It is a melancholy task to view the decline of a culture so bright and attractive as that of Egypt, but it would be futile to try to paint the dying organism in the colors of life. So let us take up the story where we left it after the tragedy of Amarna was ended.

Ay, the old councilor who disposed of Tutankhamon's crown and—I suspect—his widow as well, did not live to enjoy his dubiously acquired gains. After his death there was no man in Egypt who could put forth even a faintly legitimate claim to the throne of the Two Lands. Contemporary inscriptions tell us that the internal affairs of Egypt were not flourishing. Egypt needed a strong hand to put down domestic disorder and civil strife, and a strong hand was just what she got. Ay's successor was a military man named Harmhab, who had served under Tutankhamon. It is rather pitiful to see how few genuine converts the charming, if shallow, creed of Aton could claim. It was in truth the personal faith of the king and his family; many of Akhenaton's leading adherents turned their coats with shameful haste after he died.

Harmhab gives himself the credit for cleaning up the mess in Thebes. Tutankhamon had claimed the honor of reestablishing orthodoxy and repairing the temples ravaged by Akhenaton's decrees, and Ay had been an eager servant of Amon's; but neither of them was as zealous as Harmhab. He added greatly to the Amon temple at Karnak, using the pieces of Akhenaton's temple to Aton to fill up his pylons.

By what specious right Harmhab claimed the throne of Horus we may never know. Amon, of course, hailed him as his son, and some scholars think he established his legitimacy by marrying a sister of Nefertiti's who had survived the anti-Amarna reaction. It is difficult to see what good this could have done the general. Nefertiti was only a member of the royal house by marriage, and her sister could not by any stretch of the imagination be considered a royal heiress. If such a lady had been available, and if our theories of the heiress are correct, Ay would have married her. One wonders what had happened to Akhenaton's daughters. The three oldest were probably dead by the time Harmhab claimed the throne, but what about the younger girls? Were they disregarded, as members of a tainted family, or did they too die before their time? Harmhab may be an example of a man who claimed the throne *de iure belli,* like many a dynasty before and after him.

Though a military man, Harmhab had little opportunity for warfare. The confusion within Egypt occupied him throughout much of his reign, and he seems to have dealt with it ably. He had no son, so when he died he passed the kingdom on to an old friend, another general, named Ramses. With this king the Nineteenth Dynasty properly begins.

Ramses I was an old man when he came to the throne, and he only held it for a year or two. His son, Seti I, was a man in the prime of life and a vigorous, energetic ruler. He must be given the credit for a number of more or less laudable deeds: he built largely and with taste, he kept internal affairs under control, and he made the first serious attempt to reconquer the lost Asiatic empire of Egypt. His campaigns were successful, but limited; he seems to have realized that it would take more than Egypt had then to offer to regain all the territory Thutmose III had held. He commemorated his victories by a series of very handsome, delicately carved reliefs on the walls of the great temple of Karnak. As they stand today, the fine lines of the relief set off by the brilliant sunlight and sharp shadows of the Egyptian climate, they are among the most decorative of all ancient reliefs. However, to many of us, Seti is chiefly memorable for a somewhat dubious ‑attribute: he possesses (or should one say possessed?) the handsomest mummy ever to come out of an Egyptian tomb.

Egyptian mummies in general are not precisely beautiful, so to call Seti's the best may seem a doubtful compliment. But it is more than the best of a bad lot; it is a positively good-looking mummy, the features being those of a man of truly kingly appearance and noble looks, with the relaxed aspect of a man asleep.

Seti's elegant mummy was not found in his tomb; like so many other royal mummies, it had to undergo repeated transfers for the sake of safety. But the tomb was worthy of its occupant. It is today one of the three or four royal tombs in the Valley of the Kings which are always shown to the tourist, and it is certainly the most impressive of them all. Its total length is over 300 feet, and the walls of corridors and chambers are adorned with attractive paintings of the king and the gods, many of which still retain their original color. These traces of paint have always given me a queer sense of the insubstantiality of time. Three thousand years have passed since the hands of the artist completed the laying on of orange and white, blue and gold; yet still the colors remain, frail shells of actuality.

Head of the mummy of Seti I, now in the Cairo Museum. *Photo from The Metropolitan Museum of Art.*

Seti was responsible for another tourist attraction, this one at Abydos, which is well worth a visit. The Abydos temple is a beauty, with reliefs of very fine quality. Being in Abydos, it could only be dedicated to Osiris, which suggests a pleasing irony: the sanctuary to the murdered god built and dedicated by the namesake of his murderer! Seti was named after Set, the Enemy, and he paid his tutelary deity cautious honor. Whether he remembered the ill-fated Set movement of the remote Second Dynasty, or had any desire to imitate it, is highly doubtful; it was as much ancient history for him as it is for us. But if he did know about the event, it would have warned him against any attempt to give Set more than his due. At Abydos where, of all places on earth, Set's name would be *de trop*, the king substituted the hieroglyphic image of Osiris for the figure of Set which formed part of his own name. This is a solution which only a theologian or an Egyptian could regard as sensible.

I used to wonder, when I listened to the tales of my acquaintances who had been fortunate enough to travel in Egypt, at the animosity they displayed to Ramses II. I knew nothing particularly favorable about the gentleman then, but I was unaware of any deed of his which might have prompted the snarl of contempt with which his name was mentioned. Now that I have visited Egypt myself, I can understand the reaction; I, too, snarl. One gets so *tired* of Ramses; his face, his figure, and/or his name are plastered over half the wall surfaces still standing in Egypt—at least it seems that way. He was probably the most monumental egotist of all time. Egyptian sculpture during his reign was on the decline, and the statues of Ramses which so often weary the eye are usually stubby and unattractive. But worst of all is the sheer number of them, which is surpassed only by the number of his cartouches.

He was the son of Seti I, and he was the pharaoh who made the name of Ramses almost a synonym for kingship. He had some help in this from a later Ramses, the third in number; but the chief responsibility rests with him. If the average man knows the name of only one Egyptian king, that name is almost sure to be Ramses; and Ramses II's fame was created by the liberal use of a

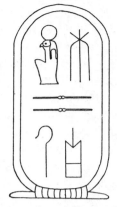

Cartouche of Ramses II

well-known principle of modern advertising—repetition. How little he deserved the reputation he built for himself may be seen by one striking incident of his career, and the expert use he made of it in order to build the desired image.

His father Seti had begun the reconquest of Egypt's Asiatic empire. Just how far the older man got we do not know, but he had evidently regained Palestine and parts of southern Syria. Ramses burned to surpass his father; he wanted to be a warrior. His first campaign was a tentative push into Palestine, in his fourth year. In the following year he was ready for a more ambitious project.

His goal was a famous city indeed. Thutmose III had captured it twice, though not without difficulty. It had been the home of Thutmose's most trying adversary, and it was still an important city; its name was Kadesh. Part of the city's strategic strength lay in its position, near the mouth of the valley between the Lebanons through which a north-bound army would normally pass. And Kadesh was a mighty fortress, and it was defended by a mighty army, for Ramses' opponents were none other than the Hittites. Shubilulliuma, who had outfoxed himself only once in the matter of Tutankhamon's widow, was long dead, but his grandson, Muwatallis, still felt that the Hittites had a claim on the city-states of north Syria. Conflict with the Hittites was inevitable to any Egyptian army bent on expansion during these years, just as a collision with Mitanni had been inevitable for Thutmose III. Hatti had replaced Mitanni as the most important power of the area; of the two powers, the Hittites were probably far more formidable.

At this period the Egyptian army was an impressive institution, professional in character, well trained and well equipped. In one important particular it had altered since the heyday of Thutmose III; more and more of the troops were non-Egyptians, mercenaries or conquered enemies forced to serve under the banners of Egypt. Ramses' army was divided into four sections, each named after one of the great gods of Egypt—Amon and Re, Ptah of Memphis, and Sutekh, who was a Semitic deity related to—of all people—Set.

A month after the army left Egypt, Ramses found himself standing on a hill about fifteen miles from Kadesh. No doubt he stood dramatically on the top and shaded his eyes with his hand, straining to see the grim towers and formidable walls in the distance. The strength of the army at his back, and his own stunning self-confidence, left him in no doubt of the eventual outcome. He set out for Kadesh early the next morning, hoping to get the business settled before dark.

Ramses personally commanded the division of Amon, which he led down the steep slopes to the ford of the Orontes, the first spot at which an army might cross that river. As he was preparing for the crossing, a pair of wandering Bedouins was scooped up by Egyptian scouts and brought to the king. They proclaimed themselves Hittite deserters who were anxious to fight on the right side—the Egyptian side—and they volunteered the welcome news that the Hittites were not at Kadesh at all; they were in Aleppo, far to the north. Ramses' reception of this cheering information was no doubt conditioned by the fact that it was just what he wanted to hear. He pushed on toward the city, leaving the three divisions of Ptah, Sutekh and Re far behind and, in his zeal, even outstripping the division of Amon. When he set up his camp on the west of the city he was accompanied only by his bodyguard.

Then it happened that two more Asiatics were captured by the Egyptians; and the story they told did not exactly jibe with the

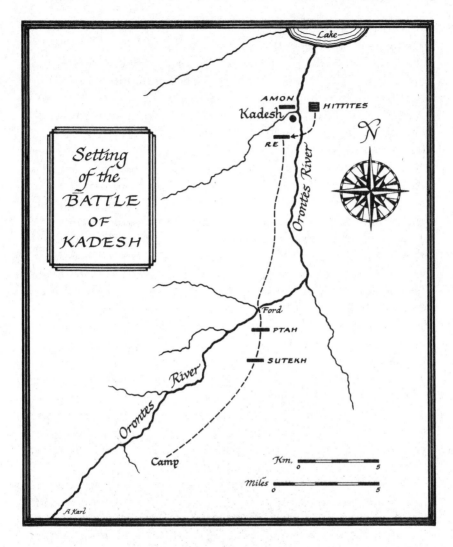

first report of the two Bedouins. The Hittites, as a matter of fact, were not in Aleppo. They were on the other side of the city of Kadesh, and they had not been idle while Ramses was trying to outrun his army.

Even Ramses the Imperturbable must have lost his breath for a few minutes when he heard that news. His reaction was typical; he called his commanders in and told them what fools they were.

He then did something practical, but a little too late, sending messengers speeding south to summon the division of Ptah. The division of Amon had caught up with its complacent leader, and Ramses knew that the division of Re was not far behind. This latter division was actually closer than he knew.

Back at the Hittite camp, matters had been progressing well— from the Hittite point of view. Muwatallis, the Hittite king, was a strategist so superior to Ramses that his talents are obvious even in the Egyptian version of the story, which was not designed to glorify the enemy. He had, to begin with, completely fooled Ramses with his carefully planted Bedouin "deserters" and their implausible story. (The nameless Bedouins were patriots of a high caliber; they were risking their necks, in case the Egyptians did not believe their story, and I personally hope they slipped away from their guards in the confusion which was to come.) Then, as Ramses proceeded blithely along the plain on the west side of Kadesh, Muwatallis led his army south on the east side of the city, unseen by the Egyptians; crossed the ford; and smashed into the division of Re before its commanders so much as dreamed that there was a Hittite within fifty miles of the place.

Ramses, stamping and swearing, was not aware of this latest disaster until the fugitives from the broken and demoralized division of Re burst into his camp and on through it, carrying with them the bewildered division of Amon. The pursuing Hittites were not far behind. They surrounded the camp; and there was Ramses, all alone except for the Hittites.

He says he was all alone, and even allowing for poetic license the statement is probably not too inaccurate. A few officers, the remains of the household troops—not much against 2,500 chariots filled with ferocious Hittite soldiers. According to Ramses, however, he had no support at all. "There was no captain with me, no charioteer, no soldier of the army, no shield-bearer; my infantry and chariotry melted away before them, not one of them stood firm to fight."

So the king addressed himself to Amon:

"Have I done anything without thee, do I not walk and halt at thy bidding? What careth thy heart, O Amon, for these Asiatics, so vile and so ignorant of god?"

After working himself up to the proper pitch of religious fervor, Ramses hurled himself upon the enemy. He routed them single-handed, driving them into the river. It seems that we must credit Ramses II with one virtue: he did not lack courage. He was also a magnificent liar, but then that was expected of him; even if the king had ordered his scribes to write down a tale of stupidity and defeat, his horrified courtiers would have carried him quietly away and then made sure the conventional eulogy was carved on the walls of his temple. We know that Ramses survived the battle, got back to Egypt, and ruled for many more years. What saved him was the arrival of aid. The divisions of Re and Amon were in headlong flight to the north; the division of Sutekh was far in the rear, near the ford, and in fact, it never saw fighting at all. The division of Ptah was his best hope, but with the scanty resources at his command in the camp he could not expect to hold out until that division came up. But there were other troops, not part of the regular army, on the way. We do not know exactly where they came from, for they are called only "the boys from the land of Amurru." The boys fell upon the Hittites from the rear, and with their help the king managed to hold the field until the rays of the declining sun caught the tips of the golden standards of the division of Ptah, toiling along the dusty road toward the succor of its king.

Nightfall ended the fighting, but brought no decision as to victory. The enemy withdrew to the city, leaving Ramses in possession of the bloody field; the straggling soldiers of the divisions of Amon and Re crept shamefacedly back to the king they had deserted. Ramses says the Hittites then sued for peace, which he magnanimously granted.

At this point we are faced with a major problem in historiography. In other words, how much of this nonsense can we reasonably swallow? We have seen how varied and how remarkable are the sources from which a student of history may derive the information he uses to make up a consistent story of what happened in the past. When written records are few the historian uses other materials, which require complicated analyses. But even when an event is well documented, even when we have a written, pseudohistorical account—we must still evaluate the reliability of the source. Many questions must be asked. Is the tale written by an eyewitness, or does the author rely on secondhand information? If the former, was he a good observer? If the latter, has he examined his witnesses and tried to test their eyesight and credibility? What is the bias of the author—is he for or against the people he is writing about? Even if he professes to be moved solely by a desire to record the "truth," is he sufficiently detached from the scene and the players of the drama to write about them dispassionately? Does he have a conscious or unconscious purpose—vilification or glorification of a man or a belief, self-aggrandizement, propaganda? In some cases we must pry into the entire life history of a chronicler or writer of history in order to discover his prejudices and the bearing they may have on his interpretation of the events of his time.

Our task of evaluating the written records of ancient Egypt is relatively easy, since we can start with the assumption that every scribe had an ax or two to grind. The annals of the various kings are not a dispassionate record of events; they are intended to glorify the kings, on earth and in the Hereafter. Hence we can, and must, take every statement made in such annals with a good-sized chunk of salt. We cannot even be sure that Thutmose III was all that good. We think he—and when I say "he," I mean, of course, the scribe who composed the inscriptions under the king's watchful eye—we think Thutmose III was fairly accurate. We can check some of his accounts through other sources, and his story has a certain indefinable, but significant, air of verisimilitude. Ramses II's version of the Battle of Kadesh is transparently, naïvely eulogistic, and what actually happened was so bad that even the Egyptian scribe could not conceal all the disasters nor all his king's stupidity.

Since we know that the purpose of the narrative was the glorification of the king, we can assume with some confidence that any anti-Ramses or anti-Egyptian remarks are probably correct. Thus, when interpreting the battle inscription, we state that Ramses outstripped the rest of his army; he credulously accepted the story of the two patriotic Bedouins; the division of Re was caught unawares and was annihilated; the majority of the forces encamped with the king were swept away in the rout. We can also state that

Ramses, by some miracle, survived the battle and got home. Egyptologists generally concede Ramses' personal valor, while condemning him as a poor strategist and a poorer general; but we cannot even be sure about that. Ramses might have spent the battle hours hiding under a baggage cart while some unnamed (and short-lived) hero of Egypt rallied the meager forces in the camp and held them firm until help arrived. Let no one believe that I am misled by personal animus against a man who has been a mummy for several thousand years. I am perfectly willing to concede that Ramses may have been an Achilles in battle. Achilles was none too bright either. All I am saying is that we will never know whether Ramses was brave or not.

We do know that the Battle of Kadesh did not have the results which the Egyptians claimed—results which would be hard to believe in any case, just on the basis of the situation that prevailed at the end of the first day of battle. The Egyptian army had been badly demoralized, one quarter of its strength annihilated at the very beginning of hostilities. The Hittites had certainly suffered severely during the afternoon, but they withdrew to the city in good order and their leader was not killed (the Egyptians would have gloated over his demise if it had occurred, and given Ramses the credit). It is inconceivable that they would have tamely surrendered after such an inconclusive "defeat" as the Egyptian records claim was inflicted.

Fortunately we do not have to rely on logic to prove that the Egyptians lost that fight. By one of those almost miraculous coincidences which do occur, we have at our disposal the Hittite version of the same battle, from the royal archives of the capital of Boghazkoi. According to it, Ramses was defeated and had to retreat, losing much of the territory his father had held.

Of course the same criteria apply to the Hittite records as to the Egyptian; the kings of Hatti were no more averse to flattery than were their royal counterparts to the south. But while Ramses' annals tell of further victories in Asia in later years, the final conclusion to the rivalry of Hittites and Egyptians was not a resounding defeat for either side. In year 21 of Ramses II a treaty of peace was concluded between the two powers—the first international treaty of which we have record. And, to make the wonder more complete, we have both versions, Hittite and Egyptian. The Egyptian copy of the treaty survives from the walls of Karnak and the Ramesseum, and the Hittite copy on two clay tablets from Boghazkoi. The latter was probably an archival version of the original, which was supposed to have been inscribed on plates of silver.

In their essential provisions the two texts are strikingly similar, which indicates that they were really parallel versions of the same agreement. They begin with a reference to former treaties, none of which is definitely known. Then the two monarchs mutually renounce any attempts at future invasion, and swear perpetual peace. The treaty establishes a defensive alliance, which holds both in case of external invasion or internal rebellion. It also provides for the mutual extradition of refugees. The Egyptian version reads as follows:

> If a man flee from the land of Egypt—or two, or three—and they come to the Great Prince of Hatti, the Great Prince of Hatti shall lay hold of them, and he shall cause that they be brought back to Ramses, the great ruler of Egypt. But, as for the man who shall be brought to the great ruler of Egypt, do not cause that his crime be raised against him; do not cause that his house or his wives or his children be destroyed; do not cause that he be slain, do not cause that injury be done to his eyes, to his ears, to his mouth, or to his legs.

The same provisions hold in the case of fugitives from Hatti who escape to Egypt. The striking aspect of this section is not the notion of extradition, nor the unmistakable ring of the lawyer's phraseology, but the humanitarianism enjoined upon the two kings. It seems quite inexplicable unless we assume some mutually accepted moral or legal code of—not so much justice as mercy, for the malefactor's crime is to be forgiven him.

The two treaties are almost exact parallels—but not quite exact. The Egyptians felt it incumbent upon them to add a Prologue explaining that the treaty was granted by merciful Ramses after the Hittite king came crawling and begging for peace. No comment.

Some years later, the alliance was cemented by a royal marriage, and Ramses' version of this diplomatic stroke is equally—I almost said characteristically—egomaniacal. The Hittites are described as coming "with fearful steps, bearing all their possessions as tribute to the fame of his Majesty. His eldest daughter comes before, in order to satisfy the heart of the Lord of the Two Lands."

Ramses evidently could not recognize an inconsistency if it walked up and bit him. He implies that the poor Hittite princess was thrust into the ravening jaws of the dragon Ramses by her trembling father; but elsewhere he exchanges the role of dragon for that of a chivalrous prince, who rushes out at the head of a well-equipped escort to meet his promised bride with all honor. The tale concludes in the second, fairy-tale strain: "She was beautiful in the eyes of his Majesty, and he loved her more than anything!"

It is a shame to dim the glow of this pretty story, which would make a standard diplomatic marriage into a case of love at first sight; but, of course, the version we have is another of the standard court fictions. The Hittite princess—poor girl—was raised to the rank of chief royal wife, but her throne was uncomfortably crowded. The women's quarters were a standard architectural element of all Egyptian palaces; but it is probable that few kings of Egypt had harem quarters covering as many acres as did Ramses. We do not know exactly how many wives he had. Most of them were not wives, strictly speaking, but occupied a position analogous to that of legal concubine. A higher rank in the harem was held by the "king's wives," who were not so numerous as the concubines. We usually translate "king's wife" as "queen," but the woman who really held the place of royal consort was the "king's great wife," or "chief royal wife." Sometimes this lady was a lowly commoner; sometimes she was the king's half sister or his full sister. Brother-sister marriages were common in the royal house of Egypt, although we cannot be sure that they were indulged in by humbler folk. The king was a law unto himself, in marriage as in other matters, and we have a few cases of father-daughter marriages; at least the evidence is hard to interpret in any other way.

Ramses II was one of the kings who apparently married one of his own children. It is possible that he had forgotten momentarily that he was related to her; the total sum of his offspring exceeded one hundred and fifty, and no man can be expected to keep that many little faces clearly in mind. Because of paternal pride—or some other reason—Ramses liked to show off his children, and if you visit the temple of Luxor at Thebes, you can see a hundred or more of them carved on the wall, all in a row like so many sardines.

The Luxor temple, begun by Amenhotep III, was only one of the many monuments dedicated by Ramses to the greater glory of Ramses. In order to achieve this noble end, he spared none of the works of his ancestors, razing the temples and pyramids of past ages in order to obtain handy pre-cut building blocks. At this time the royal capital was in the Delta region, which has not been so methodically excavated as has Upper Egypt; hence Ramses' most famous temples are in the southern part of Egypt, and they include some of the standard tourist attractions. He was responsible for finishing the great Hypostyle Hall of Karnak, the most spectacular section of that crowded and complex temple. The vast, trunklike columns are staggering in their size and number, and no traveler comes away from Egypt without a photograph of a row of them, with a handy Arab posed against one to give some idea of relative dimensions. Ramses' mortuary temple, across the river from Karnak, is called the Ramesseum and it too is on the list of Things to See in Thebes. The best known of all his monuments is the rock-cut temple of Abu Simbel, in Nubia. This temple, with its four colossal seated statues of the king, was the most conspicuous of the Egyptian antiquities threatened by the dam at Aswan. A second, smaller temple at the same site was dedicated to Nefertari, one of Ramses' queens. A special UNESCO committee collected funds to save these temples from a watery grave. The problem was certainly one of the most fantastically difficult ever faced by a team of archaeologists, and some of the solutions proposed were even more fantastic. The simplest suggestion was to build a dam around the temples, and install a pumping station to take care of seepage and overflow. But if the pumps had failed, for any reason, the temples would have been flooded in no time. So this scheme had to be abandoned.

The most intriguing suggestion was one proposed by Italian engineers—to cut both temples free of the cliff into which they had been carved, and lift them up above the water level by means of hydraulic jacks. Concrete blocks would be inserted underneath as the temples slowly rose. Impossible as this plan sounds, it was approved by an international committee of experienced engineers, but it, too, had to be given up because of the prohibitive cost. The estimate was eighty-five million dollars.

The plan which was eventually carried out was to carve the temples up into thirty-ton blocks and move them. They stand today atop the cliffs, two hundred feet above their original location, where they attract as many tourists as they always did. The blocks were stuck back together with one of the new synthetic glues.

Undoubtedly this was a monumental achievement and a magnificent testimonial to international cooperation, but there

The temples of Ramses II (left) and Nefertari (right) at Abu Simbel, in their new locations atop the cliffs. *Photo from the Egyptian Tourist Bureau, New York.*

were a few cynics who wondered whether it was worth the effort. Abu Simbel is not one of the world's most beautiful temples. The Hypostyle Hall, the Ramesseum, and Abu Simbel are representative of the architectural efforts of this age and, honestly, none of them really satisfies one's finest aesthetic yearnings. They are imposing . . . impressive . . . stately . . . what you will—but not beautiful. Compared with Hatshepsut's gem at Deir el Bahri, Ramses' temples come in a poor second in everything but size. The same criticism may be made of his statues, whose appalling numbers would not be so offensive if the sculpture itself were better. No doubt Ramses was perfectly delighted with temples and statues both; size and quantity would have been his major criteria of artistic effectiveness. If he had been able to line the Nile with colossi of himself, from Elephantine to Memphis, he would have died happy.

Though this ambition (which is admittedly my own invention) was never attained, Ramses probably gave up the ghost with the satisfying feeling that he had done the best he could. In matters of less consuming importance he was no less diligent. There would be no dangerous uncertainty about a male heir to the throne; Ramses had supplied Egypt almost as abundantly with sons as with statues. He reigned for 67 years and must have been about eighty when he died; a ripe old age indeed, considering the state of ancient medical knowledge, but then Egypt has a notoriously healthy climate, and clean living tells in the end. A goodly number of crown princes abandoned hope and died while Ramses flourished. He was succeeded by his thirteenth son, Merneptah, who was himself middle-aged when he finally gained the long-awaited crown. The poor man deserved a peaceful reign after waiting so long for it; but it was his unhappy fate to meet the greatest challenge Egypt had had to face since the days of the Hyksos.

Peoples of the Sea

The man who climbed the steps to the throne of Horus was no muscular warrior-king. The elaborate Double Crown hid his balding pate, but his prominent paunch was pitilessly betrayed by the sheer linen robes—no corsets in ancient Egypt. He had occupied his throne only five years when he received word which hastened the loss of his few remaining hairs.

For almost two hundred years, the military ambitions of Egypt had been directed toward Syria and the east. Since Ahmose's fury pursued the fleeting Hyksos invaders into Palestine, this area had provided the greatest challenges, and the most pressing dangers, to Egypt. There were always battles in Nubia to the south, and with the Libyans, west of the Delta; but these were minor affrays compared with the great confederations of Syrian princes and the eastern empires of Mitanni and Hatti.

Now the status quo was changing, and drastically. A new wind was blowing against the isolated green island of Egypt, a wind cold and sharp with northern ferocity. The immediate threat to Egypt, the news of which reached the elderly king in March of his fifth year, came from the desert regions west of the Delta, which were occupied by various Libyan tribes. Maraye, king of the Libyans, was driven by need; he led not only his fighting men but all the peoples of his tribe, women and children, with their cattle and household equipment, in a vast migration. Yet the threat of the Libyans was not new. What was new, and disturbing, was the presence of alien peoples among the military allies of Maraye. They have strange names: the Akawasha and the Luca, the Tursha and the Sheklesh. Perhaps the names will not sound so strange if we give the now commonly accepted equivalents: the Achaeans and the Lycians, the Tyrsenoi and the Sicilians.

The Egyptian records call these tribes "peoples of the sea." We know them from Greece and also from Italy, if the Tyrsenoi are in actuality the ancestors of the Etruscans. How they came to be allies of a Libyan chieftain is a mystery, but it seems that there was ferment and unrest, and a great movement of peoples, throughout Asia Minor. The ancient empire of the Hittites was rocking on its foundations; Merneptah had sent grain to that country in order to relieve a severe famine. With a little ingenuity, we can trace most of the "peoples of the sea" to homelands in Asia Minor. The Tyrsenoi had lived in Lydia before they emigrated, and the Achaeans may have inhabited the Mycenaean colony at Miletus just south of Lydia.

If the famine and the general brouhaha which can be read in the Hittite records of this period affected the whole area of Asia Minor, the "peoples of the sea" may have been forced to migrate by hunger, or by pressure from other tribes to their rear. Whatever their motive, they and the Libyans posed a formidable threat to Egypt, and Merneptah, in his extremity, sought advice from the gods.

They were reassuring. Ptah himself appeared to the king in a dream, and offered him a sword. Merneptah, on this symbolic advice, sent out the army. We cannot condemn him for not taking part himself, for he was probably too old and too fat for such exercise. But victory, in the orthodox view, was a gift of the gods who employed men and weapons as their tools, so Merneptah's "pull" with divinity very properly received credit for the Egyptian success. Over 6,000 of the enemy were slain, and 9,000 were taken prisoner.

Merneptah commemorated "his" victory in writing, upon a wall at Karnak. He also caused a stela to be carved—on the back of a stela of Amenhotep III's, but he was not about to apologize for a minor usurpation of that sort after the great example his father had given him. The inscription on this stela is one of the best-known texts in Egyptology, and for a rather peculiar reason. It gives the standard shouts of praises for the warrior-king, ending with a long list of conquered towns; perhaps the word conquered should be in quotes, for there is not much evidence that Merneptah ever fought in the regions which he was supposed to have conquered. The style of this hymn of victory is reminiscent of modern football reporting, which seems to have an unwritten rule against the use of the word "defeated." Southern Cal smashes or flattens, or walks over, or edges an opponent; Merneptah plundered, and laid waste, and destroyed. Among the variegated verb forms we find the following phrase:

"Israel is desolated, and has no seed."

Naturally, this stela is called the "Israel stela," and the reader can understand why it is so widely known. This is the first, and only, mention of the country of the Israelites in all the Egyptian inscriptions we possess. And, of course, it provides a terminal point to the vexed question of the Exodus, which we glanced at in the chapter on the Second Intermediate Period and then put off for future consideration.

The wicked pharaoh of the Exodus has long been sought by Biblical scholars, and formerly Merneptah was a leading contender for the job. Proponents of the theory were confounded when Merneptah's mummy was found, resting in peace though in poverty, in 1898; they had expected that it would long since have dissolved in the waters of the Red Sea. The mummy is irrelevant to the problem, really; the thing that eliminates Merneptah as the pharaoh of the Exodus is this very stela, which demonstrates that Israel was an integrated nation or people by the time of Ramses' son.

Who then was the pharaoh of the Exodus? Or was there a pharaoh of the Exodus? Was there, in fact—let us be daring—an Exodus at all?

A popular compromise answer holds that there was no single, massive exodus as described in the Old Testament. Asiatic peoples were continually wandering in and out of Egypt, as visitors or as conquered slaves, according to the vicissitudes of the Egyptian empire in Asia. A group of the people whose descendants formed part of the kingdom of Israel may have entered Egypt with the Hyksos; another group may have been led in chains behind the victorious chariot of Thutmose III; one group was active in the deserts of Palestine during the reign of Akhenaton, if the Habiru who devastated the southern half of Egypt's empire at that time have any connection with the Hebrews. The Biblical narrative specifically mentions the treasure cities of Pithom and Ramses, which implies that some of the Hebrews dragged stones under Merneptah's father. There is the possibility that the cities were added by a later compiler of the original tale, for the name of Ramses early came to loom large in the minds of men who thought of Egypt. Or perhaps an active minority of the leaders of Israel did slave for Ramses. As you can see, the problem is not simple. But we can admit a bondage and an exodus—giving both nouns small letters—without wondering why the Egyptians never mentioned either event. To the complacent egocentric people of

the Nile valley, the Asiatics were all one, wretched and insignificant, and their doings bulked very small in the universal order. The small group of Asiatics who called themselves, or came to call themselves, Hebrews, understandably viewed the matter in a different light.

Gallant—or lucky—old Merneptah, who was not the pharaoh of the Exodus, had a few years left to him after the battle with the Libyans and the Sea Peoples, and he spent them emulating his father; he tore down as many monuments as he could get at, and built himself some memorials. Since he did not reign as long as Ramses II, he was unable to wreak so much havoc. When he died, a time of anarchy ensued, as Egyptologists like to say. It ensues, henceforth, with alarming frequency. During this particular ensual, a certain pattern is visible which gives us a shock of *déja vu*. A woman occupied the throne, taking the titles of a king; the succession is uncertain, some cartouches being erased and others written over them. Yes, the outlines are familiar—but they are only outlines. Queen Tausert is only a name to us, not a personality like Hatshepsut; the other players are equally two-dimensional, stick figures sketched on the wall of a tomb. Probably this impression stems from the fact that we know less about these people than we do about Hatshepsut and her friends and enemies, yet it is somehow symptomatic of Egypt in her decline. Now and again we find repetitions of early situations, attempts to regain the glories of the past; but, as Tausert is only a shadow of Hatshepsut, the later history of Egypt is the hollow simulacrum of what had been.

The Last of the Ramessids

The genealogical confusion ended with the beginning of a new dynasty, the Twentieth. The founder, Setnakht, was a man of unknown antecedents, but if he was not royal in ancestry, he was in accomplishment. He established order, and the succession, and his son was the last of Egypt's native-born "great" kings.

The "Israel" stela of Merneptah, now in the Cairo Museum. *Photo from The Oriental Institute, University of Chicago.*

Ramses III and friend

This son took the name of Ramses (we call him the Third) and he strove in every way to emulate his namesake. The name had already become one to reckon with, and Ramses III's aping of his predecessor was certainly deliberate; it is too exact and too consistent to be otherwise. We have been somewhat disparaging about Ramses II—unfairly so, probably, since the difference between him and his fellow monarchs was one of degree rather than kind—but if he was not much, Ramses III was even less. Once again an effort to recreate the past could only produce something less than the original. Ramses III built grandly and without undue modesty. His most famous monument is his mortuary temple, which today bulks large upon the west bank of the Nile across from Karnak, not far from the mortuary temple of his idol, Ramses II. Medinet Habu is the name given to the temple of the third Ramses; it has been studied with more intense concentration than has any other Egyptian temple. The Oriental Institute has been copying texts and excavating in and around the temple for more than thirty years. The results fill several immense volumes, each about half as tall as I am, and they may truthfully be said to be as precise and accurate as any product of modern archaeological methods can be. If you visit Medinet Habu—which you certainly will do if you go to Thebes, since it is part of the standard tour—you will be struck by the yards and yards of in-scriptions. I have a personal interest in these texts because I spent one semester translating some of them in a seminar, and I con-templated the inscribed walls with loathing. The laudatory texts are as turgid and repetitive and pompous as the architecture. Once again—compare it with Deir el Bahri.

Medinet Habu was more than a temple. The king had a palace here, one of a number that he maintained, with the usual offices and servants' quarters. Ramses kept his harem in the gatehouse, and the reliefs that survive here are chastely indicative of the purpose of the structure. In defense of the adverb, let me add that the Egyptians saw nothing shocking about nudity; climate and common sense alike decreed relatively few garments in informal situations.

The Medinet Habu reliefs and inscriptions tell of more seri-ous matters than dalliance with the girls of the harem. When Merneptah crushed the Sea Peoples and the Libyans, he may have believed that he had settled one problem for good and all. But he had only encountered the first wave of the great migrations, or *Völkerwanderungen*, which marked the first millennium before the Christian Era, and revamped the political map of much of the Near East. The Sea Peoples and the Libyans were on the march once more; the old tribes who had harassed Merneptah had ac-quired fresh allies. Some of the new names may be identified; the Danu are possibly the Danaoi of the *Iliad*, and the Peleset are surely the Philistines, who settled along the coast of Palestine and irritated the Israelites in succeeding years. These people were not so much an army as a swarm of army ants, a vast column of war-riors, oxen, children, wagons and baggage carts which swept like a scourge through the eastern lands. They dealt the Hittites their death blow and came down on Egypt by sea and by land.

Ramses III defeated them, in ferocious fighting on land and water. In three separate engagements he took care of the Libyans and the Sea Peoples, which makes his military accomplishments much more impressive than those of Ramses II. But there was one important difference. Ramses II, for all his ineptitude, was fight-ing at Kadesh, in what might be called a war of aggression, hundreds of miles from Egypt. The men who fought under

Ramses III had their backs to the wall, and they fought with the knowledge that defeat meant slavery or annihilation. The Egyptian empire was dead. Later there would be attempts to resurrect it, just as there would be weak imitations of other elements of past glory. But the *ka* of Thutmose III, ruling the Land of the Westerners, was not re-embodied in Egypt.

The end of the Twentieth Dynasty is a frightful spectacle. Almost every document that survives from this time, beginning with the last years of Ramses III, tells the same tale of corruption and abuse, a deadly rot which invaded every cell of the body politic. The death of Ramses III is an example; it does not seem appropriate to call it a "good" example. He was probably murdered by members of his own household in a case involving the blackest treachery, witchcraft, and subornation. The conspirators were headed by a queen named Ti, who wanted to see her son upon the throne of Egypt. The true heir, Ramses IV to be, did not succeed in saving his father's life—was it, one wonders cynically, his primary aim?—but he defended his own rights with a vigor which he displayed in no other activity during his brief reign. The queen, her son the pretender, and certain harem officials were seized and condemned to trial.

During the hearings the ghastly tale of black magic emerged. One of the criminals "began to make humans of wax, inscribed, so that they might be taken in by the inspector of the harem." To what purpose? one wonders. Were the waxen images used as they have been used in European witchcraft? Such a doll could be identified with a particular individual by means of fingernail clippings, hair, or the like kneaded into the wax; torments worked upon the image inflicted corresponding injuries upon the victim's body. The use of these "humans of wax"—or clay—is very, very old, but it is impossible to be sure that this is how they were used by the Egyptians. There is a suggestion that one of the figures may have been that of Ramses III, animated by means of a magical roll and thus a puppet in the hands of the conspirators. Though we do not fully understand the means, the deadly purpose of the magic is clear enough. To make matters worse, some of the judges fell under the influence of two of the accused criminals, consorting and carousing with them while the trial was underway. All the criminals died. The lesser were executed, but those of higher rank were accorded the privilege of supervised suicide.

The last kings of the Twentieth Dynasty are a dreary roll of Ramses—eight of them. The events of their reigns are equally dreary. Asia, as a field of conquest, was closed to Egypt, and Ramses VI was the last king to work the mines in Sinai. At home, the sad stain of decay spread and deepened. The necropolis workers of Thebes, the men who built and maintained the tombs on the west bank, went on strike on numerous occasions, demanding the pay which was overdue them. Each time the responsible officials met them with soothing words and promises which were never, or inadequately, fulfilled. Tomb robberies, which had never been completely suppressed, increased and went unpunished. We can sympathize with the thieves, who must have worked with the connivance or the assistance of the necropolis workers whose duty it was to protect the tombs. They were starving for lack of grain which they had honestly earned, while behind the cliffs the silent dead glittered with gold and jewels. Several documents give clear evidence of graft and outright theft by the officials of the treasury and the court.

The priests were no less venal than their counterparts in the civil bureaucracy. Indeed, the distinction between civil and religious functions was far from sharp, and a man might hold offices in the temple and in the court simultaneously. But if he had to choose between the two, the service of the gods was preferable. While the power and wealth of the kingship steadily decreased, the temple properties grew ever greater. A document called the Papyrus Harris, written at the end of the reign of Ramses III, lists the extent of the temple property. We are not sure whether the fantastic figures indicated only the gifts of Ramses to the gods, or the total amounts including his donations; but in either case the holdings of the ecclesiastical foundations must have been enormous. Estimates range from two percent of the people of Egypt and fifteen percent of the land, to twenty percent of the people and almost one-third of the total acreage. The figures would not be so formidable if the wealth had been equally divided; Egypt had so many gods and so many temples that the grand total would have been safely fragmented. But the great gods of Egypt held the lion's share of the wealth, and the greatest of them all, Amon-Re of Thebes, was mightiest in temporal terms as well. One scholar has estimated that Amon alone owned one-fifteenth of the population and one-eleventh of the land.

As far back as the Eighteenth Dynasty the convenient omniscience of historians allowed us to utter dire predictions of the danger of the trend which Papyrus Harris illustrates so vividly. We were able to view the generosity of Thutmose III and his successors to their patron god as a portent because we knew what was going to happen. It has been suggested that there was an element of political expediency in Akhenaton's religious experiment, if not in Akhenaton himself. However, this interpretation necessitates the assumption that someone possessed a remarkable degree of insight into a situation which had not, at that time, taken on the shape it was to assume later, and which was probably never defined in such clear-cut terms. The conception of church and state as separate, rival entities was antithetical to the Egyptian world view.

Whatever the causes of the heresy, the results did not weaken Amon, but gave him renewed strength. With the progressive debility of the state, and the succession of feeble pharaohs clinging to the name of Ramses as to a talisman, the power of Amon continued to wax. Under Ramses XI we have evidence of a revolt against the high priest of the god; perhaps the saintly man had been premature in an attempt to extend his authority to its logical conclusion.

By this time the office of High Priest of Amon had become hereditary, like the kingship; the haughty prelate who was overthrown had inherited the office from his father and had shown signs of increasing presumption by having himself carved on a temple wall the same size as the pharaoh whom he faced. This would have been inconceivable in earlier times, and the offender met a well-deserved fate—though whether for this or for some other enormity we do not know.

His successor in the high office was a figure of some stature. Here the envisaged conflict between church and state is reduced to its proper proportions, for Herihor, who eventually became

Church and State in person, was a partisan of neither camp to begin with. He was a soldier, and when he rose to the rank of Viceroy of Nubia he commanded a large and effective army. The High Priesthood was a prize of his progress rather than a source of it. When he added the titles of High Priest to those of his military rank, he had more prestige than any man in Egypt except the pharaoh, and more real power than any man, including the pharaoh. It was only a matter of time before he would adjust the fiction to fit the fact and climb into the throne—from behind it.

The reliefs on the walls of the Khonsu temple at Karnak tell the tale with an ironic clarity that needs no words. In the outer courts the High Priest usurps the functions of the king and makes offerings in his own person; in the inner courts, the latest to be built, he usurps the crown and the cartouche. So pass the Ramessids—unwept and unhonored, no doubt, but not unsung, thanks to the strenuous efforts of the second and third bearers of that now diminished name.

X

The Long Dying

Psamtik

Adventures of a Man of No Consequence

IN the spring of a year some thirty centuries ago, an Egyptian official set out from Thebes on a long and tedious business trip. His destination was Byblos; his mission, the acquisition of cedar wood for the divine boat of Amon-Re. The name of Amon's messenger was Wenamon, and his adventures are told in one of the most famous papyri of ancient Egypt. The story may be the ancestor of all historical novels, a felicitous blending of fact and fiction. True or not, it is a wonderful tale, a tragicomedy of adventure and misadventure; and it incidentally tells us a great deal about the state of affairs in and around Egypt in the twelfth century before Christ.

Wenamon's overlord was the High Priest of Amon, Herihor, who was obviously master of Upper Egypt, in fact if not in name. But when Wenamon left Thebes he soon entered the territory of still another man who claimed royal status—Nesubanebded, known to the Greeks as Smendes, of Tanis in the Delta. Wenamon had to secure the approval of the northern king of Upper and Lower Egypt before he could continue his journey. This was easily done, for Smendes and Herihor had an "understanding"; but it is one of the symptoms of breakdown which the story illustrates.

288

Wenamon took passage on a ship leaving for Palestine—another bad sign, for an emissary sent on such a mission by the god in better days would have had his own fleet. By the time the boat reached Dor, in Palestine, Wenamon's store of money—not too great at best—had been stolen by a member of the crew. Raging, Wenamon made his way into the presence of the prince of Dor and demanded justice or restitution, preferably the latter. The prince met his unreasonable demand with remarkable forbearance; indeed, he appears much more urbane than the Egyptian. We can almost see his eyebrows lifting as he inquires coolly, "Are you serious, or are you inventing? Indeed, I know nothing of this tale which you have told me." The prince pointed out that the thief was not one of his own subjects; if this had been the case he would have replaced the money—an offer which diminishes the amount to a bagatelle unbefitting an Egyptian envoy of Amon. But, since the thief belonged to Wenamon's own ship, the prince felt that he had no obligation. He did offer to institute a search. When this proved fruitless, poor Wenamon went on his way, his heart despairing and his eyes wide open.

Shortly after he reached Byblos, Wenamon had made good part of his loss. Although he is understandably vague about details, we are led to understand that he had "liberated" thirty deben of silver from certain subjects of the prince of Dor, blandly informing the victims that he was taking their money in compensation for that which was stolen by their fellow countrymen. This specious argument—if it can be called an argument—was accepted by the robbed with surprising meekness, which leads the reader to wonder whether Wenamon really waited around the scene of the crime long enough to discuss the problem. So Wenamon sat down by the shore in the harbor of Byblos and congratulated himself. His rejoicing was premature. For reasons which Wenamon does not mention, the prince of that city had taken a dislike to him. "I spent twenty-nine days in his harbor, and he sent to me daily, saying 'Get yourself out of my harbor!' " Wenamon remarks morosely.

After twenty-nine days of this, Wenamon took the hint. He was looking for a ship back to Egypt when a strange incident occurred. We would call it luck, or coincidence, but in the eyes of the Egyptian it was undoubtedly a miracle, produced by the direct divine intervention of Amon himself. During a ceremony in the temple, one of the prince's attendants was "seized by the god," and cried out, "Bring up the god, bring up the messenger who is carrying him; Amon is the one who sent him!"

It happened that Wenamon, in lieu of cash, brought along a portable statue of his god, which was called "Amon of the Ways." The frenzied youth's reference was too exact to be ignored. The prince of Byblos sent for Wenamon.

"I found him sitting in his upper room with his back to a window, so that the waves of the great Syrian sea broke behind his head," says Wenamon poetically. The two men got down to business, and with every word Wenamon was deeper in trouble. The prince spared the humiliated Egyptian no embarrassment. He admitted that Amon was supreme, that Egypt had once been the hub of the world, and that his own land owed much to the skill and learning it had acquired from Egypt. But this was in the past. Where was Wenamon's ship, the prince asked sarcastically—for surely a man on so important a mission would have been given an official vessel for his journey? Where were his credentials? Most important of all—where was his money? Byblos was not subject to the ruler of Egypt. Even in the past, when a king of that land ordered a shipment of the fine cedar wood, he had paid for it, and paid well. The prince brought out his account books to prove it.

Wenamon "was silent in that great moment." There really wasn't much he could say. But he hit the one argument he did have, and hit it hard—the power and might of Amon and the spiritual benefits he could bestow, benefits beside which mere gold and silver were trivial. His speech was masterful, fully worthy of the man who could talk his way around a robbery, and it had its effect. The prince of Byblos let him send back to Tanis for goods with which to trade, and he began to load the cedar.

Wenamon's troubles were not over. Once out of the spell of the Egyptian's eloquence, the prince began to get dubious about the enterprise to which he had committed himself. And to crown the climax, just as Wenamon was, finally, about to set sail for Egypt with the hard-won cedar, he saw ships speeding in to port. The ships belonged to the prince of Dor, who was hot in pursuit of the money Wenamon had liberated. Wenamon knew, as soon as he identified the ships, that he was in for it. Stiff upper lips and Anglo-Saxon phlegm were unknown to the ancients; when they suffered, they wanted everybody to know about it. Wenamon suffered all over the beach of Byblos, in a tone of voice that was clearly audible up at the palace. One can only marvel at Wenamon's oratorical talents. His character or personal habits apparently induced instant hatred in the people who met him, but when he started talking he had the situation under control. The prince of Byblos was as responsive as a hypnotized rabbit to the Egyptian's rhetoric. Although Wenamon's loud laments—before the boats had even landed!—were an open confession of guilt, the prince stood by him. He sent the woebegone Egyptian a message telling him not to worry, and reinforced the advice by a gift of food and the temporary loan of an Egyptian singing girl. The following day he got Wenamon onto a ship and out of Byblos —with, no doubt, a hearty sigh of relief. The Egyptian ended up in Cyprus, and the inhabitants naturally wanted to kill him; this seems to have been the instant reaction of most of the people Wenamon met. He forced his way through the enraged throng and appealed to the queen of Cyprus for protection. The papyrus unhappily breaks off at this point, but no doubt the eloquence of Wenamon once again saved his life. He got back to Egypt to tell his tale.

The most important historical fact about this picaresque story is what it tells us of Egyptian prestige in the areas which had once been controlled by swaggering Egyptian troops. The breakdown at home was reflected by the contempt in which the once powerful nation was held abroad. The dynasty which we, following Manetho, call the Twenty-First was actually composed of two ruling houses; the one founded by the High Priest of Amon, Herihor, held the southern area, and the descendants of Smendes ruled the Delta. There were good relations between the two, cemented by intermarriage.

The capital of the northern kingdom was at the city of Tanis. The kings of the Nineteenth Dynasty had moved their political center northward, first to Memphis, then to Tanis in the Delta, but had always returned to Thebes in death, to be buried in the holy cemetery on the west bank of the Nile. The Twenty-First

Dynasty gave up Thebes entirely; the royal tombs of this period were found by the French archaeologist, Pierre Montet, who worked at Tanis during the 1950's. He had the good fortune to run into one of the gilded caches which now and then reward the efforts of archaeologists. The tomb of Smendes' son, Psusennes I, somehow managed to escape the notice of the industrious tomb robbers. The king himself still rested in it, richly adorned, and in side chambers of the tomb were the mummies of two of his most favored courtiers, one of whom wore a distinctive and rather handsome gold mask. Later on, the burials of two other kings of the Twenty-First and Twenty-Second Dynasties were secreted in Psusennes' tomb. But these burials seem impressive only by contrast with the majority of excavated tombs, which are completely empty. Next to the gold and gilded coffins of Tutankhamon, the silver coffin of Psusennes is fairly poor. The workmanship of some pieces, vases and bowls of precious metals, is still good, but in sheer mass and in general skill, this funerary equipment does not compare with that of the Eighteenth Dynasty, and Psusennes' very sarcophagus was stolen from Merneptah of the Nineteenth Dynasty.

The Quick and the Dead

The official transfer of the royal residence to the north stripped Thebes of much of its glory. Long before this time, the city of Amon had, for all practical purposes, become a twin entity. On the east bank of the river were the great temples of Karnak and Luxor, the harbor and its attendant buildings, and a residential area inhabited mainly by civil servants and temple officials. Across the Nile, under the shadow of the western cliffs, lay the greater city, which belonged to the dead. For generations the tombs of kings and commoners had honeycombed the hills; a row of great mortuary temples lay along the edge of the narrow cultivated land; and some kings of the New Kingdom had built their palaces there as well. The dead were not the only inhabitants of western Thebes, for they required an army of workmen, priests, soldiers, and artists, to maintain their Houses of Eternity.

The royal necropoli on the west bank of the Nile had never been completely safe, but with the decline of the throne after the Nineteenth Dynasty, the grisly depredations of the tomb robbers multiplied and went, often, unpunished. We have a document, one of the most fascinating papyri ever discovered, which gives the details of a series of tomb robberies under Ramses IX, around 1120 B.C. The picture is one of depressing, widespread corruption. The accused are humble workers whose poverty might excuse their crimes, but the most casual reading between the lines makes it painfully clear that more important people were criminally involved. The only bright and shining figure of virtue is that of the accuser, Paser, mayor of eastern Thebes, the city of the living. Paser's counterpart in western Thebes was named Paweraa. He was not only mayor of the western city, but chief of the Necropolis police, and one of his primary responsibilities would be the safeguarding of the tombs, royal and otherwise. This was the man whom Paser accused—of negligence at the very least.

If we wanted to be cynical, we might speculate about Paser's motives; like his counterpart across the river, he was a politician and when politicians fall out the worldly-wise may reasonably look behind the noble speeches. But it is kinder to view Paser as the one little candle in a naughty world. He certainly sounds righteous. Having received information to the effect that tomb robbers had been flourishing in Thebes of the Dead, under Paweraa's control, he promptly filed charges with the vizier. His informant had been specific; Paser mentioned by name ten kings, four queens, and many nobles whose Houses of Eternity had been recently defiled.

The vizier appointed a commission to investigate—and what a discouragingly modern sound that has!—and put the mayor of western Thebes in charge. This was a perfectly logical appointment, considering Paweraa's position, although a Solomon of a vizier might have reasoned that Paweraa would not be strictly impartial on the matter in hand. The commission accordingly tramped out across the steaming sands—this was in August, when most people simply collapse between the hours of ten and four— and checked all the questioned tombs. They reported their results. Only one of the kings' and two of the queens' tombs mentioned by Paser had been robbed; in respect to the nobles' tombs, the mayor of eastern Thebes racked up an astonishing one hundred percent accuracy.

On the face of it, this report would seem to confirm the charges. Robbery was certainly progressing at a rapid rate; the exact proportion of tombs violated was really beside the point. But the mayor of western Thebes interpreted the findings of the commission differently. On the following night, he allowed—the verb may be rather weak—his people, the workers of western Thebes, to demonstrate in celebration of his "vindication." The mob made its way to the house of Paser, the accuser, and stood around jeering at him. Paser was vexed. He lowered himself so far as to come to the door and exchange insults with the crowd. During the flow of repartee, the infuriated Paser bellowed that he was not ready to give up; he had heard about other tombs which had been robbed.

His rival across the river promptly reported the latest doings to the vizier, taking a tone of injured innocence. A new commission of inquiry met next day in the temple of Amon, with Paser on the bench along with certain high nobles and the vizier himself. This gentleman—the highest appointed official in the land— then proceeded to render impotent the commission he had set up. He opened the hearings with a statement which implied that he had already checked the suspected tombs, and found nothing wrong! This took the wind out of Paser's sails. Imagine him, squirming on the bench and growing paler and paler as the suspects he had dragged in took their cues from the vizier, and denied everything.

That was the end of Paser; reformer or not, he was trying to swim against the tide. He sank. We never hear of him again, whereas his opponent, Paweraa, was still mayor and chief of police seventeen years later. The tomb robberies continued, and increased, under the latter's administration. Every now and then a petty carpenter or humble coppersmith was tried and executed, as a sop to the proprieties; but it is so obvious from the papyrus itself who the guilty parties really were, that we wonder how anyone reading the report could have missed the truth. The answer may lie in the fact that the highest official who dealt with the matter was the vizier; and I have my doubts about him.

Recorded confessions of tomb robbers make it clear that part of the normal business expense in the trade was the bribery of officials. The situation went from bad to worse; by the time of the Twenty-First Dynasty, the priest-kings of Thebes were ready for drastic measures. Most of the royal tombs were completely stripped of treasure, but the royal mummies were still intact. How long they would remain so was a question. If they were left in their tombs, whose location was almost a matter of public record, some disappointed thief might destroy the sacred remains—as was in fact done by one set of robbers whose trial records we possess. So the descendants of Herihor, who were in power at Thebes, concerted a plan. A royal commission met and took council on the problem of the dead. The solution they produced was a desperate last expedient. One by one the despoiled bodies of the ancient kings were gathered together, and one night—a moonless night, no doubt—a great cortege might have been seen winding furtively through the black canyons of the cliffs of western Thebes. In a small and insignificant rock-cut chamber near Hatshepsut's temple of Deir el Bahri the bodies of Egypt's greatest kings were secretly consigned to their last rest. There was little left to them of princely adornment, and the hurried priests had no time for ceremony. The coffins were simply shoved in, one on top of the other, until the small tomb was nearly filled. Then the weary officials retired, the entrance was concealed—and silence descended for almost three thousand years.

The Deir el Bahri cache was not the only one: the tomb of Amenhotep II in the Valley of the Kings was selected as the hiding place for other royal mummies, most of them coffinless and in poorer condition than the remains which had been hidden at Deir el Bahri. Later, another tomb was reserved for the high-ranking priests of Amon; no less than 153 of them were found, with their families, in another tomb near Deir el Bahri. By some means or other the secret of the large multiple burials was well kept; and, oddly enough, all three of them were rediscovered, in modern times, within a period of about twenty years.

There is a small village near Thebes called Gurneh whose inhabitants can claim a unique distinction. They are the inheritors of the oldest family business in the world; they and their ancestors have been robbing the tombs of Thebes for almost four thousand years. There is nothing surprising or supernatural about the long continuity of the trade, when one considers the overpowering temptations of the location; yet one cannot help but feel that the desire of the men of Gurneh to rob tombs is more than just a quest for wealth. It seems, at times, to amount to a hypnotic obsession—witness the robbery of the tomb of Amenhotep II in 1903, which was mentioned earlier; a case where the thieves must surely have known that the mummy had been stripped of all valuables.

The most famous—or the most notorious—of all the tomb robbers of Thebes was the Abd-er Rasul family. They are the only tomb robbers mentioned in "Who Was Who in Egyptology." One of the brothers, Mohammed, was in the service of Mustafa Agha, a consular agent at Thebes. Ahmed and Soliman, the other brothers, "dealt in antiquities." It was a setup too good to neglect when, in 1871 the brothers found the Deir el Bahri cache. Consular agents had a certain diplomatic immunity, and the brothers may have been under a false impression that their employees did also.

The brothers were too smart to flood the market; gradually they sold small objects, papyri and the like, and increased the family income considerably. Nevertheless, the fact that they had to market their finds, however cautiously, betrayed them in the end. Again the detective talents of an archaeologist were employed and in this case the methods were those of regular police investigation.

The world of archaeology is a small one, and collectors and scholars keep in touch with one another. Within a few years after the Abd-er Rasul brothers struck it rich, objects began to turn up in museums and private collections all over the world. They were important objects, and yet no new tomb discovery had been officially reported. The matter came to the attention of Gaston Maspero, the French Director of the Egyptian Antiquities Service. Maspero's methods infuriated Petrie, but he was a brilliant and enthusiastic scholar, and his integrity was beyond question. Maspero kept an alert eye on the antiquities market, and gradually a pattern began to emerge. The probable source of the new objects was narrowed down to Thebes; although they came from the burials of different persons, the fact that they had been put on the market more or less simultaneously indicated that they had been found together. What was sought, then, was not a single royal tomb, but a cache where many mummies were concealed. Maspero asked the police to look out for a man from Thebes who was spending too much money.

The Abd-er Rasul family soon came under suspicion, but nothing could make them divulge their secret, although the methods used by helpful local authorities were not always pretty. Then, in a fine moral fashion, the thieves fell out. Mohammed thought his brothers were getting the lion's share of the loot, nor could he give them the complete trust which brothers ought to feel for one another. In pure self-protection, fearing they were about to betray him, he betrayed them first.

Maspero was not in Egypt when Mohammed's revelation broke, but his assistant, brother of the German Egyptologist Karl Heinrich Brugsch, went at once to Thebes. He was led to the cache, which was entered by a long shaft leading from a small opening in a sheer rock wall. Emil Brugsch was stupefied by what he found—the coffins of the mightiest pharaohs of Egypt piled one atop the other like kindling wood. He had the mummies removed to Cairo by boat; and as the slow vessels moved downstream the villagers gathered on the shore, wailing and keening in a form of mourning millennia old. It was a touching sight; but one wonders whether they were mourning the loss of their ancient kings, or the removal of a sizable source of local employment.

The Deir el Bahri cache was, in sheer weight of numbers, the most dramatic discovery ever made in Egypt; it was outdistanced in historical value by other finds and outbedazzled by the Tutankhamon discovery, but it was still quite a thing. Here we have the actual physical remains of men who ruled one of the world's mightiest empires thousands of years ago, men whose names and reputations were as old as legend. Scholars found it a trifle disconcerting to recall that the momentous discovery was made by a pack of crooks, but these lucky intuitive moments do occur, even to the uneducated. They were willing to forgive and forget. In a burst of generosity, the Antiquities Department hired the stool pigeon, Mohammed. It was a good demonstration of the practical value of high moral gestures. In 1891, ten years after the Deir el Bahri find, Mohammed came to Grebaut, Maspero's successor, and ended what must have been a long and painful mental struggle—his new loyalty to the Antiquities Department against his instincts and family ties. The uneducated but inspired Abd-er Rasul boys had found another tomb, and had made good use of it while Mohammed was wrestling with his principles (the fight had lasted quite a long time). It was the third of the big multiple reburials, that of the High Priests of Amon-Re. The second, in the tomb of Amenhotep II, had been found in 1898 by Loret, a professional Egyptologist, who thus retrieved some of his colleagues' battered reputation for insight. With Amenhotep II's mummy were, among others, those of Thutmose IV, Amenhotep III and Seti II.

The royal remains found by Loret were brought to Cairo and united with those of their peers in the Cairo Museum, where they lie today. Tutankhamon's sadly decayed mummy, marred by the very unguents and ointments which were meant to increase its hopes of survival, still rests within its gilded and guarded coffin in the Valley of the Kings. The skeleton of his brother Smenkhkare is also in Cairo.

One might assume that after the bodies of the kings were found in modern times they could expect a final end to their wanderings, in whatever dignity the museum can afford. But such was not the case. The royal mummies had one more journey to make—a short trip but one which, unfortunately, had unavoidable touches of macabre comedy.

In the early 1930's, when the National Party came to power in Egypt, the prime minister, Nahas, erected a costly mausoleum to shelter the body of Zaghlul, the founder of the party. Later the Nationalist government fell and was replaced by a hostile coalition which wanted to lessen the propaganda impact of Zaghlul and his mausoleum. In order to diffuse public interest, the new prime minister ordered the royal mummies to be placed in the tomb alongside the Nationalist idol. Then the Nationalists got in again, and decided that too much admiration was being lavished on the mummies, and not enough upon their hero. They sent a curt message to the museum, ordering the authorities to come and get their old kings. Somewhat nonplussed, the museum people hired a couple of ambulances and in the dead of night entered the mausoleum. The last funeral cortege—to date—of the royal dead of ancient Egypt wound through the streets of the sleeping city into a court of the museum, and the bodies were reverently placed in an unused room. For some time thereafter it was necessary to secure permission to see them from the appropriate Egyptian Ministry, and only scholars and distinguished visitors were accorded the privilge. When I was last in Egypt the only criterion to which tourists were subjected was the payment of a fee amounting to about a dollar in American money; this was sizable compared to the admission charge for the museum itself, which was about one-tenth the sum, but it certainly did not limit the view to scholars and royalty. Today the mummies are all together in a single room, guarded by a man who collects the admission tickets. They lie in separate glass cases, each with a pall of purple velvet. The velvet is faded and dusty.

Perhaps the relatively exorbitant admission charge does deter the great majority of the irreverent. There is so much to see in the Cairo Museum that only necrophiles and archaeologists are apt to pay an additional sum for the privilege of gazing on the ghastly remnants of the long-dead. Certainly these tattered specimens deserve the courtesy of silence, at the least, and I am in complete sympathy with any edict which would exclude wisecrackers and comedians. We had a couple of mummies at the Oriental Institute when I was a student there—two little old ladies (they were certainly old) who were known to the students as Mert and Mabel. I found them just as interesting as anybody else did, but I used to cringe at those nicknames. I am not sure that I would recommend a visit to the royal mummies at Cairo as an enjoyable experience. Sekenenre is there, the holes of the battle ax piercing his skull and his mouth agape in the last horrid scream of anguish; Ramses II, the great warrior and womanizer, still has some nasty, rusty white hairs on his withered skull; even Seti I, who must have been a particularly stately and handsome man, is very *dry*. One comes away with a great thirst, and with a dim reluctance to eat or drink anything for a little time. The sunlight seems too bright, and the noises of the city streets strike strangely on the ear.

Miscellaneous Dynasties

The Twenty-First Dynasty at Tanis nominally controlled the country for a time, although Herihor's descendants at Thebes now and then turn up with the royal titles. The dynasty ended around 950 B.C.—the date seems almost recent compared to the hoary antiquity with which we began—and was succeeded by the first ruling family of non-Egyptian stock, if we do not count the Hyksos. These foreigners, kings of the Twenty-Second Dynasty, were Libyans; they called themselves "chiefs of the Meshwesh." The Meshwesh were one of the Libyan tribes whom Merneptah and Ramses III had defeated, but the particular Meshwesh who became kings of Egypt were thoroughly Egyptianized and had lived in Egypt for a long time. We have a neat family tree which takes their ancestry back into the Twentieth Dynasty, at which time their forebears had settled in Egypt. The stela comes from a well-known site—the fantastic Serapeum at Sakkara. This immense underground structure was the burial place of the sacred Apis bull, a form of the god Ptah; after the animal died, it became the Osiris-Apis, and in Ptolemaic times a hybrid deity, Serapis, evolved out of the dual nature of the dead god. Like the Catacombs, the Serapeum has a somber gloominess which reminds the visitor only too vividly of the transcience of mortality. Some of the big stone sarcophagi are big enough to hold a dinner party in.

The first king and founder of the Libyan or Twenty-Second Dynasty had the barbarous (from the Egyptian viewpoint) name of Sheshonk; as Shishak, he is well known to Biblical scholars, for it was he who sacked Jerusalem in the fifth year of King Rehoboam (1 Kings 14:25–26). Shishak did not consider Jerusalem worth mentioning in the great entrance portal he built at Karnak, but he gave a long list of other conquered towns in Palestine.

The Twenty-Third Dynasty is a hopeless confusion; the kings are obscure, and the whole dynasty was probably contemporaneous with the Twenty-Second. The kingdom was breaking up, back into the small states from which it had arisen. Judging from Egypt's past, the nation was ripe for invasion, which was just what it got. The Assyrians were coming down; and they were not the only ones. The Egyptians were not as adept in the "mysteries" as the Rosicrucians believed them to have been, and their varied contributions to civilization did not include the Ouija board. But if they had contacted the shade of Thutmose III he would probably have warned his remote successors to watch out for the Asiatics. Thutmose was too long dead; he would have been astounded at the direction from which the inevitable conquest finally came.

Horsemen from the Holy Mountain

Out of the level stretches of sand rise the pyramids, row on row. The gray smoke of incense ascends to heaven, and the voices of white-clad priests chant the old sacred hymns to the god. "O Amon-Re, Lord of the Holy Mountain . . ."

Wait a minute. Amon-Re—and pyramids? An anachronism has reared its ugly head. Pyramids were replaced by rock-cut tombs at about the time Amon began his spectacular rise to supremacy.

No, no anachronism. The pyramids and the great temples to Amon were contemporaneous, but not in Egypt. We must go back now in time, and south in space, to witness the flourishing of a strange hybrid which was to have a significant impact on the dying culture of ancient Egypt. Men of a distant clime and an alien race (I use the word poetically) once again carry weapons into the land of Horus; but they come as saviors, not as conquerors, and represent themselves as the true heirs of the son of Osiris against the degenerates who call themselves pharaohs.

We talked about Nubia when we were discussing the Middle Kingdom, but we have had to neglect the region since for want of space. Other developments of the New Kingdom deserved more attention, for Nubia was not a problem during that period. At the beginning of the Eighteenth Dynasty the kings of Egypt regained the Middle Kingdom heritage in the south without difficulty, re-occupying the old forts and building new ones. More than forts, they built towns and temples; the difference in architectural style indicates that there was, after a time, no longer any need for the strong defenses which Senusert III had erected. The New King-dom frontier in the south was eventually set at the Fourth Cat-aract. Trade flourished; Egyptian traders, priests, and craftsmen kept the river crowded. Even during the struggles of the post-Amarna period Nubia remained peaceful, and it may have been the uninterrupted flow of riches from this region which allowed the later kings to maintain their imperial courts and raise their expensive temples, even though their sources of income to the east were gradually abandoned. These kings built in Nubia as well as in Egypt, and some of the temples are quite splendid. All this activity had its effect on the Nubians. As early as the Second Intermediate Period there are signs that the native peoples of the area were getting interested in Egyptian wares and opening their minds to Egyptian ideas.

Politically, the land of Nubia must have been an increasingly important factor in internal Egyptian affairs. The office of the "king's son of Cush," who was viceroy of all the southern lands, was established during the Eighteenth Dynasty. During the Twentieth Dynasty, Nubian strong men had a hand in the harem conspiracy which ended the rambunctious career of Ramses III, and also in the establishment of Herihor, viceroy of Nubia and High Priest of Amon, in control at Thebes. This last event took place around 1085 B.C.

The collapse of Egyptian unity and prestige in the years that followed—remember poor Wenamon and his journey to Byblos—is reflected in Nubia by a failure of inscriptional and other mater-ial. We do not know exactly what was going on down there. The curtain next rises upon a blaze of activity, but what went on behind the scenes to prepare the way for the new refulgence is unknown.

When the curtain does rise, it is upon a scene which we have never observed before in our study of Nubia. The *locus* is neither town nor Egyptian fort, but a handsome city, with a royal palace and a temple to Amon crowning a high, flat-topped hill. The hill is now known as Gebel Barkal, and the ruins of the city of Napata are to be found near the Fourth Cataract, at the far end of the fertile Dongola Reach. To the north is the royal cemetery; the tumbledown pyramids once housed the bodies of the kings of Napata.

The kingdom of which this city was the capital is that which the Greeks later called Ethiopia. We usually apply this term to Abyssinia, but the Greeks evidently used "Ethiopians" to designate any dark-skinned people in remoter Africa. We will avoid confusion by referring to this Nubian nation by its Egyptian name Cush.

So much for the scenery and the program notes. Now let the play begin.

There is a Prologue, whose details are vague; it concerns a king of Cush called Kashta, whose mission it was to carry regeneration into Egypt. We have no inscription of his, so we do not know when, nor how far, nor even if, he invaded Egypt; but we think his authority extended over the Theban nome. The real protagonist of Act One is Kashta's son, Piankhi.

See him as he occupies the seat of Pharaoh—he claims those titles, and wears the full regalia of an Egyptian king. The great god Amon extends his protecting hand over Piankhi, his son; and Piankhi worships the god devoutly and purely. He has been ruling his lands for twenty-one years. His territory in Egypt is in good hands. The petty bickering of the local nobles far to the north keeps them occupied and allows them no time for transgression upon the realms held by Cush.

Then, in the first month of the twenty-first year, comes ominous news. One has arisen among the dynasts of the Delta, a man named Tefnakhte, of Sais. He has seized the whole west, coming southward with a numerous army, while the Two Lands are united behind him, and the princes of walled towns are as dogs at his heels. Herakleopolis is besieged; and Namlot, prince of Hermopolis, has submitted himself to Tefnakhte as his lord, forswearing his allegiance to Piankhi.

Piankhi received this news with a shout of laughter.

His loyal courtiers wondered if the old gentleman had lost his wits. But Piankhi was only expressing his nonchalance. He was so confident of the result that he did not even take the field himself. The troops he sent to Egypt received noteworthy instructions: they were to conquer, of course; but equally important was their conduct when they came to the sacred city of Thebes, the home of Amon-Re. "Bathe in the river, dress in fine linen, unstring the bow, loosen the arrow; let no chief boast of his might, for there is no strength without Amon."

After paying its respect to the god at Thebes, the army proceeded to Herakleopolis and lifted the siege. Among the besiegers were Namlot, the prince of Hermopolis who had cast his lot with his fellow countrymen against the Nubian Piankhi, and Osorkon III, the last king of the feeble Twenty-Third Dynasty; though he has the title of king he is obviously only one prince among a lot of princes.

Piankhi's army drove the Egyptians away; Tefnut headed for Sais, his home town, while Namlot escaped to Hermopolis, and shut himself in. The Cushites settled down around the latter city and sent word home to Piankhi.

Piankhi was not pleased at the news of victory. He had expected to hear of annihilation, and he must have known that he would have no peace to worship Amon while Tefnakhte and Namlot were still on the loose. He contemptuously ignored "Pharaoh" Osorkon, and with good reason. When Piankhi, deciding to take matters into his own hands, came north in person, Osorkon hurried to make his submission. Piankhi had stopped at Thebes on his way, of course, to take part in the great feast of Amon, and when he went out to battle, he was well fortified with the grace of the god. The big battle was at Hermopolis, where Namlot was still holding out, but in great discomfort: "Days passed, and Hermopolis was foul to the nose, without perfume." According to Piankhi's story, the citizens of the dying city came forth to plead for terms. Piankhi was stern until the ladies made their appearance. Namlot's wife and daughter sought out the womenfolk of Piankhi (what they were doing on a military campaign is never explained), and on their bellies begged the Cushite queens to intercede with their lord. Evidently chivalry was not dead; perhaps Piankhi was also moved to clemency by the rich gifts which Namlot sent him.

Piankhi's behavior, on entering the city in triumph, is so pious and austere as to be priggish. First of all he visited the temple—Thoth, the patron of scribes, was in charge at Hermopolis—and only then did he turn his attention to the loot. Among the booty was the harem of Namlot, whose members hopefully "saluted his majesty in the manner of women." Piankhi would have nothing to do with them. (This touch of chastity is all very well, but it does not jibe with the fact that Piankhi could not even fight a war without dragging his own women along.)

Namlot's horses aroused Piankhi's passions as Namlot's women had failed to do. When he visited the stables he found that the horses, naturally enough, had suffered from the siege. "It is more grievous in my heart," said Piankhi reproachfully to the humble Namlot, "that my horses have suffered hunger than any evil deed that thou hast done." This is a truly royal "my"; but Piankhi was being a little unreasonable. The horses were lucky to be there at all, if the city had reached the state of woeful hunger implied by the narrative. Perhaps Namlot tended them with anxious care, knowing of the Cushite king's major weak spot. Piankhi's love of horses is attested by other evidence, notably the fact that he began the custom of burying his favorite steeds honorably near the royal tomb. Whenever a penitent rebel wanted to get in Piankhi's good graces, he offered him a horse.

Despite Namlot's neglect of "his" horses Piankhi dealt mercifully with him and the other rebels he encountered on his northward march. Even the archenemy Tefnakhte was allowed to surrender, with solemn vows not to do it again.

Piankhi naïvely took his word for it. This was a mistake, but an attractive one. Piankhi was hopelessly old-fashioned in his piety, and perhaps he trusted in the oaths of others because he did not readily break his own word. There is no point in worrying about the moral rights involved in the conquest of Egypt. Piankhi was in one sense a foreigner and an invader; but the native Egyptians he fought had been squabbling unpleasantly among themselves for generations, and would squabble again as soon as he left the country. There has been a lot of debate about Piankhi's "race," or ethnic connections; some Egyptologists want to make him a Libyan, others claim he was a descendant of Egyptian emigrants to Nubia. But there is no reason not to take Piankhi for what he seemed to be, a Nubian—whatever that means. Judging from the most significant factor, that of cultural affinity, Piankhi was an Egyptian of the Egyptians and considered himself the heir of Egypt's long, rich past.

So Piankhi sailed happily home to Napata, leaving Tefnakhte, no doubt, rubbing his hands together and chortling like Iago. At Thebes, Piankhi took advantage of a custom which had been established some centuries earlier. Since the Twenty-First Dynasty, the power of the High Priest of Amon had been gradually transferred to—of all people—a woman. The lady was one of the princesses of the royal house and bore the title of "God's Wife." It was an old title of the queen whose precise import is difficult to ascertain, but in the late period it was primarily of religious significance and probably implied that the lady in question was reserved for the god. We know of no husbands or children of any of these Gods' Wives, but they came to hold political as well as religious power. Whenever a new dynasty took over, the ruling king had his daughter adopted by the reigning God's Wife, thus giving his family a powerful hold at Thebes. Piankhi requested the current God's Wife to take his daughter under her wing, which she did all the more readily because she herself was the daughter of Piankhi's father, who had installed her in the office as the successor to the daughter of the last king of the preceding dynasty.

As soon as Piankhi left, Tefnakhte was up to his old tricks. We do not know what Piankhi was doing while his enemy was breaking his solemn vows; he lived long enough to set up a handsome stela, written in good Egyptian, in the temple of Amon at Gebel Barkal. It is from this stela that we get the story of Piankhi's conquest. Certain it is, however, that Tefnakhte was successful enough to set up his son as pharaoh. This son, known to the Greeks as Bocchoris, is the sole king of Manetho's Twenty-Fourth Dynasty. The Nubians, beginning with Piankhi, are the Twenty-Fifth; a slight confusion chronologically, but that is the least of the confusion that attends upon the last years of Egypt.

Bocchoris did not last long; Manetho says he was burned alive by Shabaka, the successor of Piankhi. The burning may be apocryphal, but Shabaka did put a premature end to Bocchoris and his dynasty. The Cushite conquered all of Egypt, transferred his capital to Thebes, and ruled as "king of Egypt and Cush."

At this point we acquire some new sources of information. The most important comes from the kingdom of Assyria, which was fighting its way to world supremacy in a series of bloody battles in western Asia. From this time on we can also see Egypt and Assyria through the eyes of the Israelites. The books of *Kings* tell of the terror of Assyria and the broken reed of Egypt, upon which the small kings of Judah and Israel tried to lean in their struggle for independence against the fierce warriors of Sargon and Sennacherib. The Egyptians are typically silent on the subject of Assyria.

This is the time of Hosea, when Sargon II carried Israel away captive, and Egypt sent no help. The name given to the Egyptian pharaoh in the Biblical account cannot be identified with any of the men ruling in Egypt during this period; it may have been that of a viceroy or general. A few years later, perhaps under Shabaka, came the rebellion of Hezekiah, and the first meeting of the two powers—Assyria, young, arrogant, in the early morning of its strength, and Egypt, the tottering wreckage of the colossus which had for thirty centuries towered above the East. The event is described in *Kings II*, which is more to be commended for its literary style than for historical accuracy; the chronicler may have confused this Assyrian campaign with another one, twenty-five years later. At any rate, he says that Sennacherib of Assyria led his armies against the rebels in Jerusalem. When the soldiers of Egypt came to defend their temporary ally, the Assyrian king jeered at them, using the familiar analogy of the broken reed. But plague—or the visitation of God—decimated the Assyrian ranks, and the army had to retreat. The crucial meeting between Egypt and Assyria was yet to come.

Shabaka was succeeded by his brother, or perhaps his son, named Shabatka; and he in turn was succeeded by his cousin (?) Taharqa, the last of the strong Cushite kings. Taharqa has left a number of stelae at various places in Nubia, which is one reason why we know more about him than about some of his predecessors. One of the Greek historians accused him of murdering his predecessor, but this may be just a nasty rumor. His pyramid at Napata is the biggest of the lot, but it is pretty pathetic compared with even the Middle Kingdom royal tombs of Egypt. Despite their poor construction, the pyramids of Napata still stand upon the plain near the Holy Mountain, Gebel Barkal. They are in ruinous condition and look peculiar because of their slope, which is much steeper than the standard 52-degree angle of Egyptian pyramids. All of them were robbed in antiquity; in modern times they were excavated by Reisner, whose precise and painstaking methods allowed him to reconstruct the genealogy of many generations of Cushite kings.

Before Taharqa concerned himself with his pyramid, he had other problems to face. Thebes was too far south for his tastes; he resided most of the time at Tanis where, one supposes, he could better watch the activities of the threatening Assyrians. Sennacherib, the scourge of Jerusalem, was dead, but his son, Esarhaddon, was an even more formidable warrior. He had to deal with a number of rebellions among the vassal cities of Phoenicia, in some of which we may see Taharqa's fine Nubian hand. His attempts to distract the Assyrian only delayed the inevitable. In 671, Esarhaddon marched south, driving Taharqa's army before him, until at last he stood before the walls of the most ancient city of Memphis, Menes' capital. There is a ring of truth in the Assyrian king's grim record of the campaign; Egyptian records, needless to say, are conspicuously silent on the matter. Esarhaddon gives Taharqa his due; the battles he fought were bloody ones, and he claims to have inflicted no less than five wounds upon the person of the Cushite king. Taharqa's valor was in vain. Assyria took Memphis and leveled its legendary walls. Among the captives were the women of Taharqa's harem and his brother.

In succeeding years the fortunes of life and death turned the struggle between Egypt and Assyria into a deadly seesaw; Esarhaddon's departure enabled Taharqa to recover Memphis for a time, but after the death of the Assyrian king, his son Asshurbanipal returned to quell the stubborn Egyptians. Once again Taharqa fled from Memphis to Thebes and then to Napata, where he remained.

Up to this point the Assyrians had committed one important error which later conquerors did not repeat. They conquered—and departed. Taking heavy loads of booty with them, and extorting great oaths of fealty from the Egyptian vassals they established in office, they departed. And as soon as they left, the rumble of rebellion began again. Even in the final throes of degeneration and defeat, the Egyptians were hard to conquer. Like wheat before the storm they bent and were not broken.

When Asshurbanipal left Egypt, after chasing Taharqa home to Cush, he left a power vacuum. The various petty princes of the country started their aping of imperial dignity. Taharqa died soon afterward; his nephew, Tanutamon, stepped into his place. But Taharqa's sandals were too big for Tanutamon, and even Taharqa had not been able to stop the Assyrians. Again a Cushite king came north, besieged Memphis, and ruled Egypt—for a brief time. Asshurbanipal returned, and finished Tanutamon. He followed his uncle's example, retreating first to Thebes and then, when that city was threatened, to Napata. In the far regions of the south the Cushite kings were safe, for no Assyrian wanted to pursue them through the difficult regions of the cataracts. But Thebes, abandoned by its *soi-disant* king, met the full fury of Assyrian wrath. The sack of Thebes was an effective object lesson to rebels; for over fifty years its fall haunted the memories of men and found an echo in the words of the prophet Nahum when he threatened Nineveh with similar fate.

Asshurbanipal also left a description of the destruction of Amon's holy city. "Heavy booty, beyond counting, I took away from Thebes. Against Egypt and Cush I let my weapons rage and showed my might." The conquest ended the glory of Thebes, and the pretensions of the Cushite dynasty. If we want to think in terms of national psychoses, we might say that the Cushite kings had developed a trauma about Egypt. Up and down, back and forth; every time they had sallied forth to Memphis, the Assyrians had appeared and sent them packing. Enough was enough. They were safe and prosperous in their own kingdom, and there, from this time on, they stayed. The subsequent history of the kingdom of Cush, which turned its eyes away from Egypt and to the south, is fascinating, and I wish we had time to talk about it in detail. The capital was finally shifted even farther south, to Meroë, and here a bastardized version of Egyptian culture lingered for centuries, mixed with various native elements. The last pyramids in Africa were built in Cush, odd little red brick imitations of the towering monuments of Giza and Dahshur. A new language developed, called Meroitic; temples and palaces were built and maintained. Cush looked to Egypt as the font and origin of its culture, but never again did it contemplate the Two Lands as a field for conquest. The splendor of Egypt, which had dazzled the vision of Piankhi and Taharqa, had blinded Tanutamon.

Back to the Drawing Board

Sooner or later, most historians succumb to the urge to discover causes in history. We have had occasion to ponder causality once before when we talked about the genesis of civilization and hauled out the homely analogy of the wagon on the slope. I could belabor this figure of speech further. It lends itself, with an aptitude I had admittedly not foreseen, to the process of decline as well as to the process of growth. But I will assume that the reader is imaginative enough to invent his own images: wagons grinding to a halt, level and monotonous plains, etc. Let us, instead, go on to consider some of the factors which have been suggested as causes for the decline of Egyptian civilization: the rise of the priesthood, who not only controlled a paralyzing amount of the national wealth, but exercised a stagnating influence upon experimentation and new ideas; the power of the army and the military leader; the appearance of iron, which is not found in Egypt, as a material for weapons and tools; the pressure exerted by the great folk migrations; the corruption of the native Egyptian genius or ethos by poorly assimilated influences from without; the increasingly formalized social structure, with the rich getting richer and the poor getting poorer; the substitution of form for content and resignation for struggle in the intellectual and spiritual realms.

There you are; a nice representative sampling. None of the above is original with me, as far as I know. Perhaps I ought to invent a couple of my own: 1) that fatal something in the psychology of the Egyptian people, the desire for regimentation and blind obedience; 2) the will of God.

I doubt if I can persuade the reader to take my second cause seriously; even devout historians assume that the Deity works through certain ascertainable rules. The first of my suggestions may not sound so immediately implausible. Its absurdity should become apparent when I explain that I copied the sentence from a context which has nothing to do with ancient Egypt—a commentary on the events leading up to the Second World War. I changed only the names of the people referred to. An appeal to "the fatal something" in a nation's psychology is not an explanation of anything, only an admission of the inability of the commentator to produce an explanation. The only difference between God and innate racial characteristics, psychological or otherwise, as causes, is that one is no longer fashionable and the other—alas—is only too much *au courant*. Either may be valid—though I take leave to doubt it—but neither is particularly useful as a principle of historical study.

The fact that acceptable theories of causation fluctuate is a disturbing phenomenon if we would like to believe that real reasons really exist. A number of theories have come in and gone out in the past century, in addition to the will of God. Causality is a dangerous word for a historian to play with; if he presses it too far he finds himself, sooner or later, locked in a death-grapple with a philosopher. Historians—and who can blame them?—try to avoid such encounters. Their causes are not philosophical profundities, as a rule, but prosaic, matter-of-fact explanations which are comprehensible to any well-read person. But historical causes are inevitably affected by the intellectual climate of the times. We no longer accept supernatural explanations—God and the Devil are equally out of style—because our present world view does not include a belief in the direct intervention of such forces in man's affairs. Economic explanations are still respectable, despite the unfortunate use which has been made of poor Karl Marx, but most historians would not regard them as valid exclusive causes.

One very popular class of causes these days is the psychological, applied to nations or to individuals. It does not require much insight to identify the Egyptian who is most popular with the psychologists. Freud found Akhenaton perfectly fascinating,*

---

* *Moses and Monotheism*, by Sigmund Freud. Knopf, 1939.

even though his childhood memories are irretrievably lost. One psychologist has gone Freud one better: he not only supplied the missing details of Akhenaton's childhood, and pronounced him to be suffering from an Oedipus complex, but proposed the novel theory that Akhenaton was, in fact, Oedipus.

I am doing historians who employ psychological techniques a grave injustice by mentioning the Oedipus-Akhenaton theory, for it cannot be taken seriously, either as psychology or as history. It is representative of one of the lunatic schools which flourish around the fringes of many fields of scholarly discipline, and it differs from the outpourings of the Pyramidiots only in the air of verisimilitude it creates. You need not know anything about Egyptian archaeology to realize that the writings of the Pyramid mystics are nonsense; it is for this reason that Egyptologists seldom bother to refute them. Admittedly, Egyptologists do not often argue in public with people like the author of *Oedipus and Akhenaton* either; but they ought to do so. Certainly, the Oedipus-Akhenaton equation sounds ridiculous. It is ridiculous; but it should not be dismissed without investigation. We cannot afford to dismiss any theory just because it flatly contradicts all our pre-conceived notions of actuality. The Oedipus-Akhenaton theory is invalid, not because it is new and startling, but because it is based upon a series of misstatements and misinterpretations, presented with considerable skill and with a respectable imitation of schol-arly style, whose errors can only be perceived by a reader who knows a good deal about Egyptian culture. Yet its basic sin against true scholarship, the same sin that mars the books of the Pyramid mystics, is that the author is not working with an open mind. He is not using facts to construct a theory, but is selecting facts to support a preconceived and unshakable belief. Whatever the techniques a historian chooses to work with, he must use them without prejudice and be prepared to revise, or dismiss, his theory when he runs up against a fact his tools cannot handle.

An excellent example of the whimsy of historical fashion is given by the rise and fall of the Great Man theory. Simply stated, this is the biographical approach to history. The plot of the past is produced by the players; Great Men (and Women), by virtue of their personalities or their positions, not only influence the shape of events but bring them into being. After a period of relative respectability, this attitude was to some extent replaced by its converse, which has been called the Cultural Process. Men do not make events; events make men. Hitler did not "cause" the Second World War; the circumstances in Germany and the rest of Europe would have produced this fatal misery even if Hitler had never been born, and some other leader would have been coughed up by body politic to assume the role which the character of the times demanded. Akhenaton did not initiate a religious revolution; Egypt was ripe for an attempt at reform, and the general sentiment of the time would have forced such a move with or without Akhenaton.

You may feel that the Cultural Process is a rather extreme way of looking at history. I think it is; and I am happy to tell you that the Great Man is coming back into fashion. Some sort of middle ground is probably necessary; any man is the product of his culture, in the broadest sense, but to deny the particularity of Hitler or Akhenaton is rationally impossible.

It seems, then, that we are still a long way from final causes. Not only do we find that categories of explanations change their status with alarming frequency, but we have always with us certain more elementary problems. We can isolate discrete cultural or political phenomena—the advent of iron, the wealth of the priesthoods—but what is a cause and what is an effect? The effect of one cause may be the cause of another effect—or it may be neither or both, but simply a—thing. Sometimes you can't tell one from the other without a scorecard, and the scorecard has not yet been written. The situation is trying enough for the modest scholar who is only attempting to explain an isolated phenomenon in a single culture. When a historian tries to extend explanations into the world at large, and compose a universal theory of history, he is really in trouble.

This has been a very superficial, limited probing of some of the types of problems we encounter when we talk about causes in history. We have not even settled the important question of whether there *are* causes. Yet we will probably go right on looking for them, and talking about them. The intellectual climate of our own era asks for explanations. We would like, if we could, to reduce all phenomena to systems of logical sequence. In part this is the effect of the prestige of the physical sciences, and this effect is not always for the good. History may be "scientific" in its approach, and the social studies may be "social sciences" in the sense that they apply dispassionate, critical, and rigorously logical analyses to the subjects of their discourse. But the disciplines which deal with man and his peculiar affairs cannot expect to use the methods, or anticipate the results, of the physical sciences. The human experiment will not reproduce itself under laboratory conditions; we can never control our specimens to such a degree that we can isolate a pertinent stimulus or determine a specific conclusion. My personal antipathy toward the use of the term "scientific" in the humanistic disciplines is that the very application of the word sometimes suggests to the user that such isolation and such determination are possible. Sometimes I wish they were.

We have a more personal need, in our time, to dissect the past in search of its pathology, for according to some historians our own culture is showing disturbing signs of disease. However you define the developmental stages of civilization, and upon whatever step you put us here, in this twentieth century of the Christian Era, it seems unlikely that we are at the beginning of any process. This leaves us with the dismal possibility that we may be nearing the end. If so, it behooves us to discover, insofar as we are able, where we are, and why. If there are universal causes, and if we are able to see them plainly, we may learn how to avoid their more disastrous consequences.

That is one of the reasons why we look for reasons. Whether we have any grounds for supposing that we will find them is another question. At the moment, it appears that our only recourse, if we are about to fall, is to go down gracefully.

The Final Humiliation

Let us leave this depressing subject and proceed to view, with comfortable detachment, the decline and fall of somebody else. The Assyrians had ended the power of Cush, but they had not yet done with Egypt. Assyrian strength was extended to its uttermost; the vast, dissatisfied empire required constant sorties in force to keep the vassal areas under control. Asshurbanipal could not spare enough troops for a military occupation of Egypt. He had to rely on the loyalty of the vassals he selected. And Egyptian oaths of fealty were written on water. Whether one commends the Egyptians for their stubborn hatred of foreign domination, or damns them as oath-breakers, one must confess that they did not lie down until they were dead. Asshurbanipal left a man called Necho, of Sais, in charge of Egypt when he went home. Necho, of course, rebelled the first chance he got, and Necho's son Psamtik I was the founder of what Manetho calls the Twenty-Sixth, or Saite, Dynasty. Psamtik must have had some of the old spark. He succeeded in persuading his bickering fellow nobles to unite against the Assyrians, and got control of Thebes by ordering the God's Wife at that place to adopt his daughter.

Psamtik's success gave his subjects an illusion of rebirth. But it was no more than an illusion. A surge of real vitality produces new cultural features, which resemble the products of other Renaissances only in the strength and creativity of the impulse which gave them birth. But when the impetus and the vigor are lacking, a backward-looking society may strive to emulate the past by imitating its external symbols. That is what happened in the Saitic revival of the Twenty-Sixth Dynasty.

Copying is the most striking manifestation of the revival of painting—a copying so anxious and so exact that the men of this time reproduce, line for line, the paintings of the old tombs of the Old and Middle Kingdoms. Not all art was slavish imitation; beginning in the preceding dynasty, perhaps under the influence of the energetic Cushite rulers, we see a new style in sculpture. It is found, at its best, in certain heads of kings and nobles. They are hard—hard in surface and in style, formalized, and yet giving an impression of realism. These two seemingly contradictory impressions, naturalism and formalism, are found at the same time and in the same work of art, and the result is extremely curious. But works of this original type are rare.

The altered mood of the literary texts is even more indicative of the change in national attitudes. There is a wistful charm in some of the late wisdom texts; in some ways the sentiments they express are more sympathetic to us than the rather cold-blooded practicality of earlier advice to the young. Take this section, from the "Instructions" of a father to his son:

> Double the food which thou givest thy mother, carry her as she carried thee. She had a heavy load in thee, but she did not leave it to me. After thou wert borne she was still burdened with thee; her breast was in thy mouth for three years, and though thy filth was disgusting, her heart was not disgusted. When thou takest a wife, remember how thy mother gave birth to thee, and her raising thee as well; do not let thy wife blame thee, nor cause that she raise her hands to the god.

There is plenty of sentiment in this passage, although the tone and the candid selection of details raise it above mere sentimentality. Now compare the words of Ptahhotep of the Fourth Dynasty on a similar subject:

> If thou are a man of standing, thou shouldst found a household and love thy wife at home, as is fitting. Fill her belly, and clothe her back; ointment is the prescription for her body. Make her heart glad, for she is a profitable field for her lord.

Tastes may differ as to the relative wisdom of these excerpts, but there is no doubt about the change in attitude. The dominating theme of the later texts is submission and patience; the key word, terrifyingly reiterated, is "silence." An Old Kingdom Egyptian would have laughed incredulously at such guides to success; what, sit silent like a fool while some glib talker shoves his way ahead? The self-assertion of the earlier dynasties is not unattractive; it is breezy, bouncy, a little naïve, and wholly sympathetic. In its greatest form, it dared to question the immortal gods as to the meaning of life. The spirit of ancient Egypt was indeed dead when men could boast of being silent.

The theme of silence is found in another "instruction," which has an unusual interest beyond the fact that it gives the attitudes of a particular age. The wisdom of Amenemopet may be as early as the Eighteenth Dynasty, or as late as the Twenty-first.

The reader may recall that we mentioned the parallels between Akhenaton's famous sun hymn and one of the Psalms, and then rejected a romantic story by claiming that the resemblance did not prove a direct connection between Egypt and Israel at that period. With the Amenemopet text, the dramatic conclusion is hard to avoid, for its parallels with the Biblical book of Proverbs are so close that only the dependence of one upon the other can satisfactorily explain the resemblance. It has been suggested that the Egyptians borrowed their text from the Hebrews, but most scholars incline toward the opposite interpretation. There is nothing "un-Egyptian" about the contents of Amenemopet; the text is perfectly consistent with the feeling of the age, as expressed in a variety of other cultural phenomena. If we compare Amenemopet with the Biblical text, especially with Proverbs 22:17 through 24:22, we find the same precepts repeated, often in almost the same words. But the final proof of relationship is a really beautiful bit of philological research, which enabled an Egyptologist to correct the Hebrew text.

The Egyptologist was Adolf Erman, the teacher of an entire generation of archaeologists, British and American as well as German. In looking over the passage in Proverbs, Erman noted the twentieth and twenty-first verses of Chapter 22, which, in the King James version, read as follows:

> Have I not written unto thee excellent things, in counsel and
>   knowledge,
> That I might make thee know the certainty of the words of
>   truth; that thou mightest answer the words of truth to
>   them that send unto thee?

The words "excellent things" were marked with a question. The Hebrew had *shilshon*, "formerly," which is obviously an error; the original editors had suggested *shalishim*, "officers," which is hardly an improvement. Now Hebrew, as it was originally written, resembled Egyptian—and other Semitic languages—in that it wrote only the consonants. Much later a system was developed which indicated vowels by means of "points," small marks written above or below the line. The reader will note that the Hebrew words which have been suggested for the disputed reading differ only in the pointing, their consonants being the same.

Erman, of course, was familiar with the Amenemopet text, and he had found a passage which in many ways seemed to resemble the two verses of Proverbs. But the Egyptian text reads: "See thou these thirty chapters; they entertain, they instruct. They are the foremost of all books; they make the ignorant man to know."

As Erman studied the text he was struck by the recollection that the Hebrew word for "thirty" is *sheloshim*—a word which involves only a small change in pointing and makes better sense of the Hebrew than do any of the suggested renderings. The Egyptian text contains precisely thirty chapters; the Hebrew passage is not so divided, but it does contain thirty different precepts. Erman's discovery not only settled the question of borrowing between the two sources, but made the direction of the borrowing pretty sure, for the use of the word "thirty" is more logical in the Egyptian. The applicability of the numeral to the Hebrew text is not so obvious, and it is easy to understand why later copyists misread the word or tried to substitute a—to them—more logical alternative.

After the transitory, shadowed reflection of greatness which appeared during the Twenty-Sixth Dynasty, the aging giant on the Nile stumbled ever faster down the ignominious path to annihilation. Assyria fell, but Babylon took its place as a conquering power; the last pharaohs of Egypt fought their hopeless battles with the aid of mercenaries, Greeks, who had settled in large numbers in the Delta. Toward the end of the dynasty the decline of Babylon left Egypt temporarily at peace, but Babylon had fallen to the conqueror Cyrus, the Achaemenid. Cyrus left a far-flung empire to his son Cambyses; it included most of the known world—except Egypt. Cambyses remedied this lack. In 525 B.C., at the Battle of Pelusium, he broke the back of Egyptian independence. The country became a province of the vast Persian empire, and Manetho's Twenty-Seventh Dynasty consists of Persian kings. The Twenty-Eighth through Thirtieth Dynasties were "native" again, feeble princes who took advantage of Persia's preoccupation with other areas to attain an illusory independence. In 343 B.C., the Persians found time to remember Egypt.

As a result we have a Thirty-First Dynasty, another Persian one, which was later combined with Manetho's Thirtieth—to make them symmetrical, I suppose.

Meanwhile, in the barbaric backwaters of Macedonia, a youth was dreaming strange dreams. Alexander scooped Egypt into his bulging sack in 332 B.C. Then followed Greeks, Romans, Arabs, Turks; an Albanian adventurer and a Corsican artillery captain; British administrators and French advisers. Egyptian history did not end in 332 B.C., but Egyptian culture was transformed out of all recognition. The old gods died and their temples were used as quarries by the devout of other faiths. The language passed from the knowledge of men, and the hieroglyphs became a source of wild speculation and mystical theorizing. The wisdom of Egypt would become a legend, but its learning was lost beneath the weight of twenty centuries of dust and ignorance. Yet still today the forested pillars of Karnak trumpet the name of Ramses to men and women from lands which the conqueror never knew existed, and until the last stone falls from the sides of the Great Pyramid of Giza, men will marvel at the might and the presumption of its builder.

A goodly number of books on archaeological subjects end with resounding sentences like that last one. There is a perfectly good reason for the popularity of the theme. The physical survival of the great Egyptian monuments is a noteworthy phenomenon in itself, when one considers that most of the other civilizations of comparable antiquity are visible to us only as mud-brick-foundation outlines, or as verbal reconstructions. Structures such as the Pyramids, the Karnak temple, and the temples of Philae, Abu Simbel, and Abydos, would be astonishing even if they were not so old; in size and magnificence they compare favorably with the ruins of almost any other past culture which is known to us.

Still, I have a prejudice against an emphasis of this type; or perhaps it would be more accurate to say that I have a predilection in favor of another sort of emphasis. The tombs, the temples, the golden coffins of Tutankhamon, are exciting and dramatic, yet they have not so much fascination for me as have other, less tangible, contacts with an antique and alien world. My interest in archaeology was stimulated initially by the lure of buried treasure; but eventually I found myself allured by the ideas of the past even more than by its artifacts. And this development led to another, very personal and perhaps subjective, discovery. People who read and write about history, particularly about ancient history, are wont to marvel at the "unexpectedly modern" sound of an ancient institution or expression. I do it myself, and I enjoy the small thrill of recognition which reults from such an encounter. Yet in a broader sense the works of the past to which our emotions respond are not "ancient" or "modern," not "Egyptian" or "American," but simply—human. The specific expression of a given motivation may be one which our society no longer uses or accepts; but it may be completely valid for the culture in which it operates, and as we come to understand other elements of that culture we will see, behind the unfamiliar facade of exotic custom, a human urge which should be as recognizable as our own features in a mirror.

This is not to disparage, nor to disregard, the uniqueness of history. The richness and variety of the attempted solutions to man's numerous problems are marvelous and appalling, and a lifetime is not long enough to begin to comprehend their manifold complexities. This unending diversity is one of the attractions of historical study, and the glamour of exotic custom is another. Egyptian mortuary practices—to take a single example— have quite understandably intrigued readers for generations: the process of mummification, the elaborate tomb, the magical rite, the rich equipment of the dead. As we read the descriptions of the fantastic tombs, we marvel at the ingenuity of their builders, who provided for every conceivable mishap that might befall the naked soul wandering through darkness toward immortality. How richly grotesque—how bizarre—was the spiritual world which these long-dead aliens envisaged!

And then we come upon a single sentence, or an isolated phrase, and the mask of ceremonial vanishes to expose the familiar poignancy of man's quest for immortality, with all its uncertainty and its aching desire. "No one has returned from thence to tell us how thy fare."

The lament for a dead child, the demand for justice, the lover's yearning for his beloved—before our recognition of the universality of human emotion, time and distance shrink, the barriers of language, color, and nationality go down; we look into the mind of a man three millennia dead and call him "brother."

Chronology

about 4500–3110 B.C. PREHISTORIC (*Neolithic to Dynasty I*)

3110–2686 PROTODYNASTIC (*Early Dynastic, Thinite*) PERIOD
Dynasty I; Menes
Dynasty II; Peribsen, Khasekhemui

2686–2181 OLD KINGDOM
Dynasty III; Djoser to Huni
Dynasty IV; Snefru, Khufu, Khafre, Menkaure
Dynasty V; Userkaf to Unis
Dynasty VI; Teti, Pepi I, Mernere, Pepi II

2181–2040 FIRST INTERMEDIATE PERIOD
Dynastis VII-VIII at Memphis
Dynasties IX-X at Herakleopolis (Achtoy and Merikare)

2134–1786 MIDDLE KINGDOM
Dynasty XI; Intefs and Mentuhoteps
Dynasty XII; Senuserts and Amenemhats

1786–1570	SECOND INTERMEDIATE KINGDOM
	Dynasty XIII at Thebes
	Dynasty XIV at Xois
	Dynasties XV, XVI(?), the Hyksos
	Dynasty XVII at Thebes (Sekenenre, Kamose)
1570–1085	NEW KINGDOM (EMPIRE)
	Dynasty XVIII; (Thutmoses, Amenhoteps; Hatshepsut, Akhenaton)
	Dynasty XIX; Seti I, Rames II, Merneptah
	Dynasty XX; Ramses III through XI
1085–525 B.C.	LATE DYNASTIC PERIOD
	Dynasty XXI, at Thebes and Tanis
	Dynasty XXII, the "Libyan," at Tanis
	Dynasty XXIII, at Thebes
	Dynasty XXIV, Tefnakhte and Bocchoris; contemporary with:
	Dynasty XXV, the "Ethiopian" or "Cushite" (Piankhi, Taharqa)
	Dynasty XXVI (Saite Period)
525 B.C.	PERSIAN CONQUEST
525–404 B.C.	Dynasty XXVII, Persian Dynasty
404–341	Dynasties XXVIII-XXX, ephemeral Egyptian
341–333	Dynasty XXXI—Second Persian Dynasty
332 B.C.	ALEXANDER'S CONQUEST
332–30 B.C.	GREEK PERIOD: ALEXANDER AND THE PTOLEMIES
30 B.C–A.D. 324	ROMAN PERIOD
A.D. 324–640	BYZANTINE OR COPTIC PERIOD
A.D. 640	ARAB CONQUEST

Additional Reading

Let the reader beware; his pleasure and edification were secondary motives in the following selection of books. My primary aim is to disprove the slander that scholars cannot write readable English prose. All the books in the following list are by specialists: Egyptologists, archaeologists, and historians. Luckily for the reader, he cannot lose by the exercise of this criterion. Most of the books listed are eminently readable; many are much more entertaining than the "popular" books on Egyptology. They are not only written well, but they are written by men who know what they are talking about. There is no substitute for this sort of expertise, the result of a lifetime of study, whereby the basic facts of the field of specialization become as much a part of the subconscious as the multiplication table.

Goodness knows, not all Egyptologists write respectably. The archaeological journals, like those of most professional fields, are filled with articles whose style is so turgid that it obscures the thought processes of the author to a point where the weary reader may wonder if they exist at all. Nevertheless, some Egyptologists have written some perfectly elegant books. They cannot be accused of illiteracy; they can, perhaps, be accused of hiding their light in professional journals and university presses. This particular evil has been mitigated in recent years; the popularity of books on archaeology has taught the professional archaeologist that he owes a duty to the reading public, and some books by scholars have been published by commercial presses. Another factor which has disseminated scholarly books is the marvelous phenomenon of the paperback. A surprising number of technical books are available in this form, and they may be found as close to home as the corner drugstore.

The best source of books, however, still remains the public library. The books which are starred in the following list can be obtained in local libraries of any small city or large town. The others are not always so easily available unless the reader lives in Manhattan; the New York Public Library has one of the finest collections of books on Egyptology in America. Another source which you might explore is the library of your local university or museum; in many cases the reading rooms are open to the public, and the librarians are more than happy to assist interested persons.

In this connection I cannot resist repeating a story told me by a friend in Munich, a distinguished Egyptologist who is connected with the Aegyptologisches Institut of that city. One day a respectable gentleman wandered into the reading room of the Institut and asked for a copy of a particular ancient text. Dr. von Beckerath had never seen him before, but he produced the volume requested. Watching the visitor bent studiously over the page of hieroglyphs, his curiosity got the better of him—unknown philologists do not walk into an Egyptologist's life every day—and he asked politely if the visitor could read the text. "Certainly," was the stiff reply. "I should be able to; I wrote it in the first place." After such encounters, scholars and librarians are more than happy to extend their services to *you*.

GENERAL WORKS
1. Arkell, A. J., *A History of the Sudan*. London: the Athlone Press, 1955. The best short history of the area, for the reader who is interested in archaeology.

*2. Breasted, James Henry, *The Development of Religion and Thought in Ancient Egypt*. New York: Harper Torchbooks, 1959. Now in paperback form, this classic work is written with Breasted's unmistakable elegance, though not all scholars subscribe to his conclusions.

*3. ——, *A History of Egypt*. 2nd ed. New York: Charles Scribner's Sons, 1948. Don't let the size scare you; this is a *must*. Superb historical writing, and still a basic work.

4. Brunton, Winifred, *Kings and Queens of Ancient Egypt* and *Great Ones of Ancient Egypt*. London: Hodder and Stoughton, 1925 and 1929. Brisk historical studies by various scholars; the charm of the volumes lies in the lovely portraits by Mrs. Brunton, the wife of one of Petrie's former students.

5. Emery, Walter B., *Lost Land Emerging*. New York: Charles Scribner's Sons, 1967. A good popular history by a distinguished excavator, with a record of the archaeological work carried out under the threat of the High Dam at Assuan.

*6. Gardiner, Sir Alan, *Egypt of the Pharaohs*. Oxford: Oxford University Press, 1961. A popular history by one of the most distinguished Egyptologists, including Sir Alan's superb translations of many important texts.

7. Säve-Söderbergh, Torgny, *Pharaohs and Mortals*. Transl. from Swedish. Indianapolis: Bobbs-Merrill, 1961. Chatty and episodic and entertaining; by an eminent Swedish Egyptologist.

*8. Steindorff, George, and Seele, K. C., *When Egypt Ruled the East*. Chicago: University of Chicago Press, 1957. A German and an American scholar collaborate to produce an authoritative, short history, concentrating on the New Kingdom period. Paperback.

*9. Wilson, John A., *The Burden of Egypt*. Chicago: University of Chicago Press, 1951. Also in University of Chicago paperbacks, under the title *The Culture of Ancient Egypt*. Thoughtful, urbanely written; an intellectual history and a fine one, by the former director of the Oriental Institute.

10. ——, *Signs and Wonders Upon Pharaoh: A History of American Egyptology*. Chicago and London: University of Chicago Press, 1964. This is an absolute joy.

THE TEXTS

1. Pritchard, J. B., editor, *Ancient Near Eastern Texts Relating to the Old Testament*. Princeton: Princeton University Press, 1950. Translations of most of the Egyptian texts quoted in this book, and others, by Dr. Wilson, whose talents as a historian were equalled only by his philological abilities; the other texts, by equally competent scholars, are also worth reading.

*2. Erman, Adolf, *The Ancient Egyptians: A Source Book of Their Writings*, translated by A. M. Blackman. New York: Harper Torchbooks, 1966. A classic, now in paperback.

*3. Simpson, W. K., editor, *The Literature of Ancient Egypt*. New Haven and London: Yale University Press, 1973. The latest, most authoritative, easily available, collection. Paperback.

CHRONOLOGY

*1. Aitken, M. J., *Physics and Archaeology*. New York: Interscience Publishers, 1961. The latest on Carbon-14 and the other dating and mapping techniques of the physical sciences; I couldn't understand more than half of it myself, but what I did understand was fascinating. If you are a physicist you'll do better.

2. Parker, Richard A., *The Calendars of Egypt*. Chicago: University of Chicago Press, 1950. Not for the easily distracted; but if you are really interested in Egyptian calendars, this is it.

ART AND ARCHITECTURE

1. Hayes, William, *The Sceptre of Egypt*. 2 vols. New York and Cambridge, 1953 and 1959. This started out to be a large-sized guidebook to the Metropolitan Museum's superb collection, and ended up as a fine history, leaning heavily, of course, on art—sculpture, household crafts, and so on.

*2. Smith, William S., *The Art and Architecture of Ancient Egypt*. Baltimore: Pelican Books, 1958. Not light reading, but written by an indubitable authority. Anything you want to know about Egyptian art is probably here.

PYRAMIDS

1. Edwards, I. E. S., *The Pyramids of Egypt.* 2nd ed. Penguin Books, 1961. A handy little paperback, full of meat.
*2. Fakhry, Ahmed, *The Pyramids.* Second edition. Chicago: University of Chicago Press, 1974. Brings the subject up to date, after Edwards; beautifully designed and very well written. The author is a well-known Egyptian archaeologist. Now in paperback.

THE EXCAVATOR SPEAKS

1. Carter, Howard, and Mace, A. C., *The Tomb of Tut-ankh-Amen.* 3 vols. New York: Cooper Square Publishers, 1963. Beg or borrow it, but do not steal it; it would be a crime to deprive someone else of the delight of reading this, the most exciting story of excavation ever told.
2. Emery, W. B., *Archaic Egypt.* Penguin Books, 1961. Wonderful paperbacks! A neat summary of what is known about the first two dynasties, on the basis of the new excavations at Sakkara; by the man who made them.
*3. Goneim, M. Zakaria, *The Lost Pyramid.* New York: Rinehart and Co., 1956. Light reading, by the Egyptian archaeologist who excavated the pyramid of Sekhemkhet.
4. Petrie, Sir William Flinders, *Seventy Years in Archaeology.* London: Sampson, Low, Marston and Co., 1931. The professional autobiography of the father of "scientific" archaeology, which, incidentally, reveals a lot about the character of the man.

INDEX

(Italicized names are those of Egyptian kings.)

Aamu, 134
Abu Simbel, 95, 274–76
Abydos, 27–30, 39, 109, 143, 264
Africa, exploration of, 92–95
Aha, 23–25, 27, 30
Ahmose, 139–145
Ahmose Pen Nekhber, 140, 145, 155
Ahmose, son of Ebana, 140–41, 145–46
Akhenaton, 210, 212–235, 239–248
Akhetaton, 217, 225, 235
Akhtoy, 104–05
Alexander, 159, 199, 319
Alphabet, 258–60
Amarna letters, 226–31, 255
Amarna period, 210, 217–247
Amélineau, 27–28
Amenemhab, 179, 187, 189–90, 193
Amenemhat I, 112–16
Amenemhat II, 116, 121
Amenemhat III, 124–27
Amenemopet, wisdom of, 316–18
Amenhotep I, 145
Amenhotep II, 202–05, 245, 295, 298
Amenhotep III, 198, 209–10, 215–16, 228, 229, 234, 246–47

Amenhotep IV, see Akhenaton
Amon, 106, 151, 156, 159, 169–71, 196–98, 215, 216–25, 236, 237–48, 286–87, 290, 301, 304
Amratian, 14
Ankhesenamon, 236–39, 246
Apophis, 136–39
Arkell, A. J., 95, 119–20
Army, 195, 265–66
Art, 73–76, 130, 143, 212–14, 219–22, 315
Asiatics, 134–36
Asshurbanipal, 308–09, 315
Assiut, 104, 109, 119
Assyria, 186, 228, 301, 307–10, 314–15, 318
Aswan, 90, 92
Aswan Dam, 14, 95, 274
Aton, 216–19, 222–25
Avaris, 138–41
Ay, 232, 238–39, 247, 260–16
Aziru, 229–30

Ba, 81, 86
Babylonia, 6, 226, 228, 318
Badarian, 14
Beer, 57

Biban el Moluk, *see* Valley of the Kings
Bocchoris, 306
Book of the Dead, The, 82, 83
Breasted, James Henry, 34–35, 176, 189, 214, 223
Brunton, Guy, 123
Byblos, 188, 230, 288–91
Brugsch, Emil, 297

Cairo, 29, 298–99
Cairo Museum, 59, 75, 109, 122, 142, 201, 212, 298–99
Calendar, 37–38
Cambyses, 318
Canopic jars, 86, 212
Carbon 14, 2, 10, 30–34
Carnarvon, Lord, 212
Carter, Howard, 212
Cartouche, 23–24
Caton-Thompson, Gertrude, 10
Champollion, Jean François, 206
Chariots, 135, 142
Cheops, *see Khufu*
Chephren, *see Khafre*
Chronology, 30–39
Civilization, Egyptian, origin of, 17–20; decline of, 310–14
Coffin Texts, 82–84
Coffins, 212, 236–40, 292
Colossi of Memnon, 215
Conspiracies, 113–14, 284
Contracts, mortuary, 76, 119
Coptic, 253–55
Cuneiform, 226, 255
Cush, 119, 138–39, 303–10
Cyprus, 291
Cyrus, 318

Danaoi, 283
Dahshur, 54, 62–64, 112, 121, 127
Darfur, 95
Deffufa, 118–19
Deir el Bahri, 107–08, 156–58, 161–65, 167–69, 295–98
de Morgan, Jacques, 121
Demotic, 253
Diffusion, cultural, 17
Diodorus, 85
Djer, 28
Djoser, 32, 46, 49

Dongola Reach, 118, 303
Door of the South, 90
Dwarf, 92–93

Edgerton, William F., 175–77
Edwin Smith Papyrus, 50–52
Elephantine, 90, 93–94
El Kab, 140
"Eloquent Peasant, The Tale of the," 130–31
Embalming, *see* Mummification
Erman, Adolf, 317–18
Esarhaddon, 308
Ethics, 79–80
Ethiopia, *see* Nubia
Etruscans, 277
Euphrates, 6, 146, 188–89
Exodus, 135, 274–81
Extradition, 272

Fayum, 103, 112, 124–25
Fayum A, 14, 15
Fields of Yaru, 81
Flints, 2–4, 16, 108
Forts, 117
Freud, Sigmund, 311–12

Gardiner, Sir Alan, 114, 251, 256, 258–60
Gerzean, 14, 15, 16
Giza, 53, 54, 56–58, 66, 69–72, 205
Graffiti, 62
Greece, 277
Greeks, 318, 319
Gunn, Battiscombe, 63

Habiru, 230–31
Habusoneb, 155, 170
Hapdjefa, 119–20
Harkhuf, 92–95
Harmhab, 232, 247, 261
Harpers' songs, 101
Harris, Papyrus, 285, 286
Hathor, 259
Hatshepsut, 148–77, 206–07
Hatti, *see* Hittites
Hawara, 112, 125–26
Heart, weighing of, 103, 218
Hebrews, 135–36, 230, 274–81
Hememieh, 10
Hemiun, 54–57, 72

Herakleopolis, 103–04, 105–07, 304
Hereditary succession to throne, 206–09
Herihor, 286–87, 288
Hermopolis, 303–05
Herodotus, 69, 85, 97, 125
Hetepheres, Queen, 54–61
Hetepheres II, Queen, 97–98; furniture of, 59–60
Hieratic, 252–53
Hieroglyphs, 249–59
Hittites, 227–29, 236–37, 265–73, 277–78, 283
Horses, 142, 165, 184–85, 305
Horus, 40–43, 196
Huni, 61–63
Hyksos, 133–42, 160

Imhotep, 46, 49, 52, 101
Ineni, 146–47, 155, 176–77
Inheritance, 205–08
Instruction literature, *see* Wisdom literature
Intef, 106
Inundation, 11–12, 37
Iron, 310
Irrigation, 12
Isis, 40–41, 196
Israel, 278–79, 307
It-tawi, 112, 124
Ivory Road, 95

Jerusalem, 231, 300
Jewelry, 28, 121–24, 212
Jews, *see* Hebrews
Joseph, 135–36
Josephus, 35, 133
Judgment of dead, 103, 105, 131–32, 218
Justice, 131, 192

Ka, 156
Kadesh, 184–85, 186–87, 192–95, 265–71
Kamose, 138–39
Karnak, 138, 146, 167, 169, 179, 262, 274
Kashta, 303
Kerma, 118–20
Khafre, 70
Khasekhem, 42–43
Khasekhemui, 43

Khnum, 156
Khufu, 54–57, 66, 68–72, 77–79
Labyrinth, 125–26
Lahun, 112
Language, Egyptian, 19–20, 250–59; Hittite, 227–28
Law, 192, 272
Lebanon, 63, 185
Libby, W. F., 31–32
Libyan Dynasty, 300
Libyans, 277–78, 283
Lisht, 112
Literature, 77–84, 99–102, 104–05, 113–16, 130–31, 223–24, 288–91, 315–18
Lower Egypt, 10–11
Luxor, 161, 274

Maadi, 14, 15
Maat, 151, 218–19
Magic, 51, 52, 77–79, 81–84, 284
Manetho, 35–36, 40, 133–34, 136–37, 306
Mariette, Auguste, 106
Maspero, Gaston, 4–5, 106, 296–97
Mastaba, 65, 66, 72
Mazghuna, 128
Medicine, 50–52
Medinet Habu, 282–83
Medum, 61–63
Megiddo, 179–85, 231
Memphis, 26, 29, 112, 308–09
Menes, 21–22, 23–26, 30, 105
Menkaure, 70
Mentuhotep, 107–08, 110–11
Merikare, 104–05, 107
Merimde, 14, 15
Meritaton, 232–35, 246
Merneptah, 276–81
Meroë, 146, 309
Meshwesh, 300
Mesopotamia, 17–18
Metropolitan Museum, 107, 109, 122–24, 167
Meyer, Eduard, 175
Mitanni, 188, 192, 227–29
Models, tomb, 109–10
Montet, Pierre, 292
Moses, 135, 224
Mummies, royal, 204–05, 295–300
Mummification, 84–87
Mycerinus, see Menkaure

Naharin, *see* Mitanni
Nakada, 15
Napata, 303, 307–09
Narmer, 22–25
Narmer Palette, 22
Naville, Edouard, 174–75
Nebtawi, 111–12
Nefertiti, 220, 233–34, 245, 246, 261
Neolithic, 2–3
Nesubanebded, see Smendes
Nile, 11–12
Nineveh, 309
Nitokris, 97–98
Nubia, 90, 95–96, 112, 116–20, 145–46, 195, 203, 206, 301–08

Obelisks, 158, 167, 195, 205
Oedipus, 312
Oriental Institute, Chicago, 34, 282
Orontes, 193, 229, 266
Osiris, 27, 40–41, 132, 196, 264
Osorkon, 304

Painting, 73
Paleolithic, 2–3
Palermo Stone, 39
Palestine, 140, 141, 228, 231, 283
Palette, Narmer, 22–23
Parker, Richard, 37–38
Peoples of the Sea, 277–78, 283
Pepi I, 88
Pepi II, 92–93, 96
Persia, 318–19
Petrie, Sir W. M. F., 4–10, 27–28, 67–68, 123, 126–27, 258
Pharaoh, 152
Philistines, 283
Phoenicia, 187
Physicians, 51–52
Piankhi, 303–06
Pottery, 2–4, 7–9
Proverbs, 317–18
Psamtik, 315
Psusennes I, 292
Ptah, 196, 300
Ptahhotep, Instruction of, 104–05, 316
Punt, 158–59, 190
Pyramid complex, 64–65
Pyramid mystics, 66–68
Pyramid Texts, 81–84

Pyramids, 29, 45–49, 52–54, 62–72, 81, 112–13, 121, 125–27, 301, 307, 309

Queen, position of, 206–09, 273

Radiocarbon, *see* Carbon 14
Ramses I, 262
Ramses II, 199, 264–76
Ramses III, 282–85
Ramses IV-XI, 285–87
Re, 77, 79, 103, 196–98, 205
Reisner, George, 57–61, 118–20, 203, 308
Rekhmire 190–92
Ribaddi, 230
Rosetta Stone, 206

Sacrifice, human, 28–29
Sais, 303, 315
Saite period, 315–18
Sakkara, 29, 39, 45, 61, 81
Sarcophagus, 53, 57–61, 110–12, 165, 168
Scarab, 18–19, 216
Sculpture, 73–76, 130, 214
Sea Peoples, *see* Peoples of the Sea
Sekhemib-Peribsen, 42
Sekenenre, 136–38, 139
Semainean, 14
Semites, 19–20, 135
Semna, 117, 120, 203
Senmut, 159–68
Sennacherib, 307, 308
Senusert I, 113–16
Senusert II, 116
Senusert III, 116, 117, 118, 120–21
Sequence dating, 6–10
Serapeum, 300
Serapis, 300
Serekh, 24
Sesostris, see Senusert
Set, 40–43, 134, 264
Sethe, Kurt, 174–75, 176
Seti I, 262–64
Shabaka, 306, 307
Shabatka, 307
Sharuhen, 141
Shepherd Kings, *see* Hyksos
Sheshonk I, 300
Shubilulliuma, 228–29, 236–37
Sinai, 63, 258–59, 285
Sinuhe, The Story of, 114–16

Smendes, 288, 292

Smenkhkare, 232, 233, 234–35, 239, 243, 244

Snefru, 32, 56, 61–64, 78, 80

Sobekneferu, Queen, 128

Soldiers, 107–09

Sothic cycle, 37–38

Sphinx, 70, 205

Statue, *see* Sculpture

Stimulus diffusion, 19

Strabo, 125

Sumer, 17–18

Syria, 120, 170–71, 181–94, 203, 228–30

Taharqa, 307–09

Tanis, 288, 291, 292, 300

Tanutamon, 309–10

Tasian, 14

Tell el Amarna, 217, 220, 245

Temples, *see* site names, such as Deir el Bahri

Teti, 88

Tetisheri, 143–45

Thebes, 106, 136–38, 142, 145, 190, 215, 217, 232, 233, 235, 292–98, 300, 304, 306, 309

Thoth, 196, 255

Thutmose I, 145–47, 189

Thutmose II, 147, 149–50, 154

Thutmose III, 151, 159, 160, 165–73, 178–201; Annals of, 179

Thutmose IV, 205, 208–09

Thutmosid succession, 173–77

Ti, Queen, 216, 232, 246

Tigris, 6

Titles, 152, 273, 306

Titulary, 23–24

Tomb robberies, 72–73, 204–05, 285, 293–98

Tombs, 27–30, 39–40, 70–72, 87, 88, 92, 107–08, 118, 146–47, 154, 162–63, 164–65, 167, 190–91, 199–201, 204–05, 212–14, 225–26, 239, 246–47, 262, 285, 292–98; *See also* Pyramids

Treaty, 272

Truth, *see* Maat

Turin Papyrus, 39

Tutankhamon, 196, 212–14, 234–37, 298

Uni, 92

Unis, 81

Upper Egypt, 10–11

Ur, 28

Valley of the Kings, 147, 154, 162–63, 200–01, 236, 239, 262

Vizier, 46, 154, 190–92

Wadi el Hammamat, 111

Wadi Halfa, 117

Weapons, 108, 135, 142

Wenamon, Tale of, 288–91

Winlock, H. E., 107–08, 175, 199

Wisdom literature, 80, 104–05, 316–18

Woolley, Sir L., 28

Xois, 136

Yam, 92, 93–96

Zawaiyet el Aryan, 53, 61

Ziggurats, 17–18

Zoser, *see* Djoser